CHINA'S
INTELLECTUALS

ADVISE
AND
DISSENT

MERLE GOLDMAN

HARVARD UNIVERSITY PRESS

CAMBRIDGE, MASSACHUSETTS
AND LONDON, ENGLAND

Library of Congress Cataloging in Publication Data

Goldman, Merle.
    China's intellectuals.

    Includes bibliographical references and index.
        1.   China—Intellectual life—1949   .   I.   Title.
DS777.6. G64   951.05   81-2945
ISBN 0-674-11970-3   (cloth)   AACR2
ISBN 0-674-11971-1   (paper)

CHINA'S
INTELLECTUALS
ADVISE
AND
DISSENT

To my mother
and in memory of my father

ACKNOWLEDGMENTS

This book has taken too many years to write. I could offer as an excuse that the period it covers, from the Great Leap Forward to the aftermath of the Cultural Revolution, was one of unfolding crisis that made it difficult for an historian to gain a perspective. Ideally, one should wait decades or even centuries before attempting an assessment. Nevertheless, the long period of composition had as much to do with personal factors as with changing political developments. In this period I have seen three of my children, Ethan, Avra, and Karla, go to college, two of them now embarked on their careers. My youngest, Seth, who is in high school, exclaimed when I finished, "You've been working on that book almost all my life!"

Over the years, so many colleagues in the field of Chinese studies have contributed to the book in one way or another that it is impossible to acknowledge them all. Nevertheless, I must thank my former teachers John K. Fairbank and Benjamin I. Schwartz, who always were interested; together with Thomas Bernstein, Timothy Cheek, Paul A. Cohen, Roderick MacFarquhar, Bonnie McDougall, Charles Neuhauser, James Polachek, and Ezra Vogel, who read the manuscript and gave me immeasurable advice; Anna Laura Rosow, who intelligently typed the book, complaining all the time; Nancy Hearst, the librarian at the John K. Fairbank Center Library at Harvard University, who assisted with the footnotes; and finally my editor, Virginia LaPlante, who helped give the book shape and focus.

The Fairbank Center for East Asian Research gave me material, moral, and intellectual support for many, many years. I am grateful to the Social Science Research Council for a grant to do the research and to the State Department for a grant to work on the post-Cultural Revolution campaigns. The Bunting Institute of Radcliffe College made possible the time free from teaching to write.

Finally, I must thank my in-laws, my children, and especially my parents for their love, encouragement, and faith; and my husband for his intellectual stimulation, forbearance, and impatience. Without Marshall's prodding, I would still be writing this book.

CONTENTS

MAJOR INTELLECTUAL GROUPS AND THEIR POLITICAL PATRONS

The distinction between intellectual groups and their political patrons is not clear-cut, for intellectuals were often officials, and officials were sometimes intellectuals. Individuals are classified here according to their main concerns in 1959–1976. Those who shifted groups appear in their original group. Other intellectuals belonged to no particular group and had no official patron.

Liberal Intellectuals

Ba Jin
  Writer; chairman of Shanghai branch, All-China Federation of Literature and Art

Deng Tuo
  Journalist; secretary of the Secretariat of Beijing Party Committee, 1959–1966

Feng Ding
  Ideological theorist, Beijing University

Feng Youlan
  Philosopher, Beijing University

Jian Bozan
  Historian; vice-president of Beijing University

Kang Zhuo
  Literary critic; deputy director of Hunan branch, Chinese Writers Union

Liao Mosha
  Writer; director of United Front Department, Beijing Party Committee

Liu Jie
  Philosopher, Zhongshan University

Mao Dun
  Writer; minister of culture, 1949–1965; chairman of Chinese Writers Union, 1963–1965

Meng Chao
  Writer; Executive Committee, Chinese Writers Union

Ouyang Shan
  Writer; chairman of Guangzhou branch, Chinese Writers Union

Sun Yefang
  Economist, Economic Institute, Chinese Academy of Sciences

Tian Han
  Playwright; chairman of All-China Union of Stage Artists

Wu Han
  Historian; vice-mayor of Beijing, 1949–1966

Xia Yan
  Scenarist; vice-chairman of All-China Federation of Literature and Art, 1960–1965; vice-minister of culture, 1954–1965

Yang Hansheng
  Playwright; vice-chairman of All-China Federation of Literature and Art

Zhao Shuli
  Writer; chairman of Chinese Ballet Artists

Zhou Gucheng
  Historian; Praesidium of Chinese Workers and Peasants Democratic Party

Zhou Peiyuan
  Physicist; vice-president of Beijing University

Liberals' Political Patrons

Chen Yi
  Minister of foreign affairs,
  1958–1972
Hu Qiaomu
  Ideological theorist; deputy
  director of Propaganda Depart-
  ment; alternate secretary of Sec-
  retariat; president of Chinese
  Academy of Social Sciences,
  1977–
Lu Dingyi
  Director of Propaganda Depart-
  ment, 1944–1966; alternate mem-
  ber of Politburo, 1956–1966
Peng Zhen
  Mayor of Beijing; member of
  Politburo and Secretariat to 1966
Shao Quanlin
  Deputy director of Propaganda
  Department to 1966

Tao Zhu
  First secretary of Central-South
  Region to 1966
Wu Lengxi
  Director of New China News
  Agency, 1952–1966; editor
  in chief *People's Daily*, 1957–
  1966
Xu Liqun
  Deputy editor of *Red Flag*,
  1958–1966; Deputy director of
  Propaganda Department,
  1961–1966
Zhou Enlai
  Prime Minister
Zhou Rongxin
  Minister of Education, 1974–
  1976
Zhou Yang
  Deputy director of Propaganda
  Department to 1966

Radical Intellectuals

Guan Feng
  Philosopher, Philosophy and So-
  cial Sciences Department, Chi-
  nese Academy of Sciences
Lin Jie
  Philosopher, Philosophy and So-
  cial Sciences Department, Chi-
  nese Academy of Sciences
Lin Youshi
  Philosophy and Social Sciences
  Department, Chinese Academy
  of Sciences
Mu Xin
  Journalist; editor of *Guangming
  Daily*
Nie Yuanzi
  Instructor of Philosophy, Beijing
  University

Qi Benyu
  Historian, Modern History Insti-
  tute, Chinese Academy of Sci-
  ences
Wang Jie
  Philosophy and Social Sciences
  Department, Chinese Academy
  of Sciences
Wang Li
  Ideological theorist; deputy edi-
  tor of *Red Flag*, 1964–1967
Yao Wenyuan
  Literary critic, Propaganda De-
  partment, Shanghai Party Com-
  mittee
Zhang Chunqiao
  Ideological theorist, Propaganda
  Department, Shanghai Party
  Committee

Writing groups of the Shanghai group: Chi Heng, Chu Lan, Liang Xiao, Luo
Siding, Zhou Si

Radicals' Political Patrons

Chen Boda
Editor of *Red Flag*, 1958–1967; alternate member of Politburo, 1956–1966

Jiang Qing
Wife of Mao Zendong

Kang Sheng
Supervisor of party's public security system; alternate member of Politburo, 1956–1966

Ke Qingshi
Mayor of Shanghai; member of Politburo, 1958–1965

Mao Yuanxin
Mao Zedong's nephew

Mao Zedong
Chairman of Chinese Communist Party

Wang Hongwen
Vice-chairman of Shanghai Revolutionary Committee, 1967–1973; second-ranking vice-chairman at Tenth Party Congress, 1973

1

DISSIDENT INTELLECTUALS AND THE REGIME

At moments of crisis in the People's Republic of China, intellectuals have questioned the prevailing system in order to sway policies in the direction of their own ideas and values. In the early 1960s, in the aftermath of the economic disaster of the Great Leap Forward, a group of senior, relatively liberal intellectuals challenged Maoist policies. This challenge was answered in the mid-decade by a group of young, radical intellectuals. Again in the early 1970s, in the wake of the political chaos of the Cultural Revolution, a similar liberal challenge and radical response occurred. The intellectual contenders ranged from reformers to revolutionaries, but they shared certain features. They were trained primarily in the humanities, history, literature, and philosophy. Their numbers were small, in the hundreds rather than in the thousands. They were a critical, politically aware segment of the intellectual class, in the tradition of the nineteenth century Russian intelligentsia and the dissident Confucian literati of the dynastic era. And they were interested more in transmitting a set of ideas than in practicing a profession.

What distinguished this tiny minority from the majority of China's intellectuals was a sense of responsibility to address issues of political policy in a public forum. Even those whose purpose was also to enhance their political position regarded themselves as the conscience of society. Although they held diverse views and spoke in many voices, their intellectual work had a similar purpose: to point out society's imperfections in order to rectify them. Their operating arenas—academia, journalism, and the creative arts—were at the periphery of power, but their impact on Chinese politics and power relationships was profound.

The political controversies that developed over the Great Leap Forward and the Cultural Revolution gave these intellectuals the opportunity to express their views. The political leadership broke up into factions over these issues, and the factions then enlisted intellectual groups in their conflict. However, the interests of the intellectual groups coincided only in part with the political factions with which they became associated. The political faction of the Chinese Communist Party bureaucracy, under the leadership of Liu Shaoqi, Deng Xiaoping, and Zhou Enlai, was dominated by officials committed to party control and a rationalized economy. The liberal intellectuals who were associated with this bureaucracy shared its commitments, but unlike their political patrons, they were also concerned with perpetuating both the Western values introduced into China in the early decades of the twentieth century and the humanistic values of the Chinese tradition. Thus, despite their allegiance to Marxism-Leninism, they were "liberal" in the Western sense in that they were concerned with intellectual and professional autonomy, and they were "liberal" in the traditional Chinese sense in that they sought to improve the prevailing system by expressing a variety of viewpoints within a broad ideological framework. Their pluralistic approach ran counter to their patrons' utilitarian emphasis on tight organization and orderly administration.

The radical intellectuals, who were allied with the political faction led by Mao Zedong, chairman of the Chinese Communist Party, shared his commitment to a Marxism-Leninism diffused with faith in the power of the will and the revolutionary consciousness to remold reality. They also shared Mao's populist belief that the masses, if mobilized, could overcome all obstacles, whether economic or bureaucratic, in achieving Communist ideals. But whereas the radicals maintained this voluntarist position steadfastly, their political benefactor straddled it and the pragmatic approach of the bureaucratic leaders and, even in his most radical periods, was prepared to compromise. Mao willingly sacrificed stability and even accepted a degree of chaos in order to realize his revolutionary vision, but not to the point of courting anarchy, a state that his intellectual allies at times advocated.

Both liberal and radical intellectuals used the opportunity of political factionalism not only to espouse their patrons' cause, but also to shape policy in ways that the leadership did not intend. For brief periods these intellectual groups were able to express their own views. However, they were stopped abruptly when their proposals diverged too far from the practices of their political patrons and galvanized the opposing faction into action.

Traditional Precedents for Intellectual Dissent

The intellectual dissidents related to the political leadership and articulated their views in a style consistent with their history and culture. The older intellectuals may have consciously followed the historical precedents, but for the younger intellectuals who had less knowledge of tradition, their behavior may have been an unconscious or preconscious use of these precedents. Historically in China, as in the West, the participation of intellectuals in the political system has ranged from total submission to total withdrawal.[1] Since most intellectuals until the twentieth century were Confucian literati who had access to official positions, the majority upheld the status quo. Nevertheless, in some cases, the literati were both participants in and critics of their government. Because the literati were members of the ruling elite, those who dissented were often close to the centers of power. Similarly, their intellectual descendants in the People's Republic held official positions at the same time that they criticized official policies.

Quasi-official dissent was integrated into the traditional system. Inherent in Confucianism was the obligation for any degree holder to speak out when the government deviated from Confucian ideals. Unlike the West, Confucianism did not legally guarantee a loyal opposition, but it justified one ideologically. To criticize government misdeeds was not the literati's right, as in the West, but their responsibility. Thus, there was a tension between the literati's loyalty to the prevailing political power and their loyalty to their beliefs. Because regimes often did not live up to Confucian teachings, the literati sometimes risked punishment or even death in order to lead the way to what ought to be instead of what was. Their approach was primarily ideological, based on the Confucian tenet that rectification of ideas would lead to rectification of policy. The literati's obligation to criticize deviations from the ideal and their belief that ideological change was a prerequisite for political change were also articles of faith for their modern descendants. Even the liberal intellectuals, who stressed economic change, believed that the expression of views in the ideological realm would lead to change in the political realm.

The literati were to act as individuals, not as part of a group. The formation of a group to fight for views was regarded as disruptive. Since the rights of groups were never institutionalized, the literati lacked a corporate entity or autonomous organization with sufficient power to exert influence. Yet in periods of economic and political crisis in Chinese history, groups of intellectuals have gathered together informally to express views that differed from their government. By the eleventh century in the Song dynasty, some Confucians favored the association of literati on the basis of common principles. Ouyang Xiu in his essay "On Factions" (Pengdang lun), demonstrated historically that the rulers who listened to criticism from groups of literati prospered, whereas those who suppressed the literati were destroyed.[2] In the seventeenth century during the Qing dynasty the scholar Huang Zongxi defended centers of learning that expounded different views, not because of the desire for a diversity of ideas, as in Western societies, but because "ultimately right and wrong are to be determined by scholar-philosophers in the schools, for they are the custodians of the Truth."[3] Similarly, the groups of dissident intellectuals that formed in the People's Republic saw their function as directing China along the correct path from which it had deviated.

Since dissenting literati groups had only ideological justification and no institutional standing, they were unable to gain a hearing unless they had allies in positions of authority. Such an alliance was most likely to occur in the context of factional rivalry, when the literati were drawn into the political struggle. Because the literati were looked to for leadership, the political factions used them to win support for their side. Similarly, factional struggles in the People's Republic provided intellectuals with the opportunity to be heard.

DISSIDENT INTELLECTUALS

When political leaders involved in factional struggles needed their talents to gain support, groups of intellectuals were allowed to express themselves publicly. Like their literati predecessors, the radical and liberal intellectuals, in the process of articulating their patrons' positions, inserted views that differed from the prevailing orthodoxy and sometimes even from their patrons.

Groups of literati working together for China's spiritual revival, called *qingyi* ("pure opinion"), usually emerged when China was beset by economic and political difficulties or a succession crisis. Such events provoked the literati to organize in an effort to address problems that they believed the bureaucracy or ruler had not handled adequately. They couched their political criticisms in ideological discourse and referred to past ideals in order to change present realities. The qingyi movements were prototypes for the informal organization of intellectuals in the People's Republic during periods of crisis.

One of these models for the liberal intellectuals was the Donglin movement of the early seventeenth century. During a time of troubles in the Ming dynasty a group of literati met together at the Donglin Academy in order to revitalize public morality, which they believed had been corrupted by the regime. They used letters, pamphlets, and forums to spread their ideas and gain adherents. Although they had a regional connection, their identification was more ideological than geographic. Well-known scholars brought with them circles of disciples and friends. The group's activities were philosophically dissident at first and became politically dissident only when a factional struggle broke out at court. One of the factions with ties to the Donglin group drew them into the political struggle as a source of support. The movement ended in 1620 when the Donglin and their backers were purged from government. Like their modern descendants, the Donglin failed because their approach, primarily ideological and philosophical, was no match for the political and military forces arrayed against them.[4]

Another qingyi movement, at the end of the Qing dynasty in the late nineteenth century, prefigured the intellectual critics in the People's Republic, particularly the radicals associated with Mao. Like the radicals, the late Qing group consisted of young scholar-bureaucrats who had been trained in the humanities and held low- and middle-level positions. They also were engaged in an intergenerational conflict to secure promotions from which they were blocked by older officials in the government bureaucracy. They, too, urged their ruler, the Guangxu emperor, to appoint new people to high positions. In words that could have been used by their radical descendants, they declared, "Now if we do not reform, we cannot strengthen ourselves, but if we do not use new people, we will not be able to reform."[5] And they, too, believed that China needed a revival of spirit to resolve its problems. These literati gained access to policy making when the emperor enlisted them as allies in his conflict with the empress dowager and senior officials. Likewise, the radical intellectuals gained access to policy making when Mao used them in his struggle with the party bureaucracy. Similarly, the qingyi literati, like their radical and liberal descendants, eventually found themselves in conflict with their political patrons. The pressures on rulers to compromise sooner or later created a rift between them and their idealistic intellectual allies.[6]

Even the strategies used by the literati to influence policy had counterparts in the People's Republic. Mao declared in 1962 that, "in order to overthrow any political power, one must first create public opinion and engage in ideological and philosophical work."[7] His traditional predecessors also believed that it was necessary to win the ideological support of the public in order to carry out policies. The literati used the tools of their trade—essays, philosophical debate, historical interpretation, literary criticism, poetry, and drama—to influence public opinion as well as the policy makers. In the late nineteenth century, as Westernized learning, newspapers, and journals developed, the public whom they sought to influence expanded from the scholar-bureaucrat elite to include students, professionals, managers, and skilled workers, including some stratum of the peasantry.[8] This wider definition of the public was similarly the focus of the liberal and radical intellectuals, and they used both traditional and modern channels of communication to influence their expanded audience.

Even the indirect language with which social and political issues were debated in the People's Republic resembled that used in traditional times. Because the appearance of consensus is necessary to preserve the legitimacy of a Chinese regime, controversial issues are discussed obliquely and debated subtly in order to mobilize support without overtly upsetting the consensus.[9] Moreover, because Mao, like the emperors of old, and the party, like the Confucian bureaucracy, had extraordinary political power and charismatic appeal, critics could not oppose them directly without great personal danger.

DISSIDENT INTELLECTUALS

Indirect methods reduced the risks of criticism. Hence there is a tradition of allegorical political criticism. This indirect method, called "pointing at the mulberry to revile the ash" or "killing the rooster to warn the monkey," obliquely chided the regime under the guise of discussing another historical period or an abstract philosophical concept. The population, particularly the literati, were attuned to reading the dissident political message between the lines. Political criticism was also invariably veiled in pedantic language and moralistic rhetoric which spoke not so much to specific issues as to broad ideological concerns.[10] The literati's modern descendants utilized these traditional methods deftly. Under even more pressure for conformity, they became practitioners of the nuance, the symbol, and the allusion. Their messages were more abstract than concrete, more general than specific. They, too, shrouded their ideas in erudite discussions of ideology, philosophy, literature, and history. They, too, picked and chose from a variety of Chinese sources in addition to Marxist-Leninist works to support their positions. Like their predecessors, through subtle reinterpretations of ideology they expressed unorthodox views. Their rhetoric was abstruse, indirect, at times obscure.

These modes of dissent are not unique to China. They are used elsewhere in authoritarian regimes. Intellectuals in czarist Russia and in the Soviet Union, like their Chinese counterparts, have used innuendo, Aesopian language, and historical analogy to express indignation at official injustices. What is distinctive to China is that these methods are used not only by dissident intellectuals to get around censorship but also by officials at the highest level. Even Mao himself, an advocate of open conflict, expressed himself with semiesoteric aphorisms. Political leaders as well as their intellectual allies feared that open confrontation would undermine the regime. With the notable exception of the Cultural Revolution, the Maoists and the party bureaucracy sought to maintain the appearance of consensus. As in the traditional system, these indirect methods were designed to prevent the disruption of factionalism and to offer an outlet for policy debate.[11]

Intellectuals in the People's Republic were also heirs to the May Fourth movement, named for a student demonstration on May 4, 1919, against imperialism and corrupt government. This movement, marked by an explosion of intellectual criticism against the traditional Confucian system and by the infusion of Western ideas into

China, lasted through the next two decades. May Fourth intellectuals, those who were involved in the movement, were the most articulate and sensitive spokesmen of their time, not only interpreting events but also preparing the way ideologically for the overthrow of the old system and the introduction in 1949 of revolutionary change. Similarly, the liberal and radical intellectuals regarded their written words as tools with which to fight social and political ills and to mold political consciousness.

In some respects, however, the liberals were more directly descended from the May Fourth intellectuals than were the radicals. Whereas the radicals, like their qingyi predecessors, sought to return to fundamental principles, the liberal intellectuals, like their May Fourth predecessors, sought fundamental change. The liberals regarded Mao's revolutionary principles as no longer appropriate in an increasingly complex society. They wanted to move China into a new stage of development in which the guiding principles would be pragmatic economic practices and technological, scientific, and administrative skills.

The liberals' demand for a degree of intellectual autonomy also owed much to the values introduced into China during the May Fourth movement. In the 1920s and 1930s, many nonbureaucratic intellectuals, unattached to any political group, had formed strong intellectual and cultural organizations and communities. Although they described their purpose as achieving China's political regeneration and unity, they conceived of their activities as free and independent of political control. Even those May Fourth intellectuals who were committed to the Communist movement, like China's preeminent writer Lu Xun, believed in intellectual autonomy. This emergence of independent intellectuals was owing not only to the breakdown of political authority but also to the impact of Western liberalism. However, unlike similar movements in the West, particularly in nineteenth century Russia, the May Fourth intellectuals were not alienated.[12] Though in despair over their situation and that of their country, they were not paralyzed by it. Indeed, they dedicated themselves to their society and its people, believing that they could revitalize and enrich China. Thus the May Fourth tradition of intellectual independence but political commitment served as a model for the liberal intellectuals, many of whom had been active participants in that movement.

In the near anarchy of the early decades of the twentieth century, intellectuals had been able to congregate in cafés, publishing houses, bookstores, and journal offices in Shanghai and Beijing to debate and publish their ideas relatively freely and openly. Beginning in the early 1940s and increasingly after the establishment of the People's Republic in 1949, the party mounted campaigns to indoctrinate the intellectuals in Marxism-Leninism and Mao's thought and to force them to follow the party's shifting political line. However, the party's policies toward the intellectuals were not ones of simple repression. Because the party was determined to build an industrialized society, it was anxious not to produce an atmosphere that would stifle the initiative and creativity needed to modernize China. Its approach toward intellectuals was therefore contradictory. On the one hand, it compelled them to strict orthodoxy; on the other, it tried to stimulate them to work productively in their disciplines.

These contradictory goals produced a cyclical policy toward the intellectuals, which oscillated between periods of repression and briefer periods of relative relaxation. Each cycle was different, and each shift was determined in part by internal political and economic factors and by international events. The oscillations were also governed by their own dialectic as the regime sought to establish a balance between the opposing forces of orthodoxy and creativity. Thus, during the 1950s the party carried out repeated thought reform campaigns against nonconforming intellectuals. In the early years of that decade, it forced Westernized intellectuals to turn toward the Soviet Union; in 1955 it treated the dissident left-wing writer Hu Feng and his coterie as negative examples; and in the antirightist campaign of the second half of 1957 it attacked the intellectuals who had criticized party policies as "rightists." But when the intellectuals grew reluctant to produce, the party terminated each campaign and introduced an interval of relative relaxation. The relaxation in 1956 and the first half of 1957 following the anti-Hu Feng campaign and called the Hundred Flowers, was the most far-reaching in any Communist country up to that time. In these intervals, the party extolled the role that intellectuals played in China's modernization and even encouraged criticism of officials, known as cadres, for their suppression, in the belief that a loosening of control would stimulate intellectual activity. However, when intellectuals challenged not only the cadres' but the party's overall control, the party quickly suppressed them by launching yet another thought reform campaign.[13]

This cyclical policy toward intellectuals continued in the 1960s and 1970s, but in those decades the dissident intellectuals exerted more direct political influence. In the earlier periods of relaxation the intellectuals had expressed criticism informally and fleetingly, in private statements to the party's decision-making body, the Politburo, as well as in wall posters, unofficial pamphlets, and spontaneous demonstrations. In the 1960s and 1970s, the liberal and radical intellectuals resorted to the traditional Chinese practice of allying themselves with political factions. Their alliances with political patrons gave them the opportunity to express their views publicly in the media, under official auspices, over a more sustained period of time, and to a much larger audience.

Again this pattern is not unique to China. For example, after Stalin's death, an informal alliance emerged between Khrushchev and Soviet dissident writers in the struggle against the Stalinists. Having been allowed officially to attack the evils of Stalinism, the Soviet writers also demanded the right to criticize publicly other political evils, a right that Khrushchev soon denied them. The Soviet official media continues to publish literature and produce plays subtly critical of the Soviet system. But unlike China, the major way to express dissent in the Soviet Union is to go outside the system, to the underground or the foreign press. In the People's Republic, although underground writings have become increasingly important, the major method to get a hearing for divergent ideas in the 1960s and 1970s was, as in traditional times, through alliances with factions in the establishment. As in the past, this procedure had the characteristics of a quasi-official form of dissent.

Conflict Between Liberal and Radical Intellectuals

The Great Leap Forward of the late 1950s was the impetus for cleavages in the party leadership and the coalescence of informal groups of intellectuals around political factions. The Leap was Mao's program to push China rapidly into a communist society by means of mass mobilization and aroused revolutionary consciousness. He sought to cover China with a vast network of self-sustaining communes as preparation for the transition to a classless society. He dispensed with his former policy of gradual economic development patterned after the Soviet model and disregarded the preconditions

DISSIDENT INTELLECTUALS

of economic abundance that Marx had declared necessary for the move to communism.

The consensus in the party and in intellectual circles broke down not only over Leap policies but also, more fundamentally, over visions of how China should develop. The coalitions of political factions and intellectual groups were formed on the basis of similar approaches to China's development. Mao and the radical intellectuals saw the party as a revolutionary, ideological force dedicated to unending struggle to achieve the utopian goal of a classless society. The party bureaucracy, under the leadership of Liu Shaoqi, president of the People's Republic, and the liberal intellectuals viewed the party as a rational organizing body, working in cooperation with a technological meritocracy gradually to modernize Chinese society.

Both groups agreed that the revolution required a change in basic values, but the party bureaucracy and liberal intellectuals, more in line with traditional Marxism, believed that such change would arise out of the economic and technological sphere, that is, in what Marxists call the infrastructure, whereas Mao and the radicals believed that change could not be sustained unless it was preceded by a transformation of ideology, that is, in the superstructure. The party bureaucracy and the liberal intellectuals rejected the methods of ideological struggle and mass mobilization used in the Leap and sought instead to employ more conventional economic practices. By contrast, Mao and his associates regarded the drastic decline in production in the Leap as due not so much to the methods as to the party's improper indoctrination of the population. However, the differences between the political factions were ones of emphasis, and at times their concerns coincided, whereas the differences between the intellectual groups associated with them were ones of substance.

In 1959, Mao suppressed criticism of his Great Leap policies in the inner party councils, making it impossible to resolve the differences behind closed doors. With official avenues for policy debate thus blocked, the party bureaucracy in the early 1960s moved the conflict into the public arena. Each side, first the bureaucracy and then Mao, enlisted intellectual followers to make known its views and disagreements and to win broader support for its positions. As a result, no longer was one authoritative opinion presented in the media, but several more or less authoritative and divergent positions. Informal networks of intellectuals not only articulated the respective differences of the political factions but also took advantage of the opportunity to express their own special concerns. These groups, not being autonomous, and allowed to criticize publicly only because their views overlapped those of the political leaders, could not depart too far from their political sponsors. But as they were not mere objects of manipulation, they transmitted ideas that were subtly different from those of their sponsors. Thus, in using intellectuals in their own political battles, the political leadership unleashed forces that they were unable fully to control. Moreover, the expression of divergent ideas inspired other intellectuals and other political factions to speak out. Consequently, the use of intellectual spokesmen stimulated the expression of a variety of viewpoints.

When intellectuals in the People's Republic had earlier been used by political leaders for political purposes, their response also went much further than the regime intended. In the Hundred Flowers, for example, Mao had set the intellectuals against the party officials in order to expose and rectify bureaucratism. On the mistaken assumption that the intellectuals had been ideologically reformed, he failed to anticipate that their criticism of bureaucratism would develop into criticism of the party's control of the universities, and certainly not into criticism of the party itself. Yet the Hundred Flowers differed from the post-Leap period in that it was a result not so much of the factionalization of the leadership as of the difficulties encountered in rapid economic development, Mao's own experiment with new approaches, and the need to reactivate the intellectuals after their demoralization in the Hu Feng campaign. Moreover, the intellectuals' response was spontaneous, as opposed to the more organized response of the 1960s and early 1970s.

In the post-Leap period, the divided leadership sought the assistance of intellectuals with politically relevant training and talent, whose arguments would convince others. Whereas scientists and engineers had little contact with the public, humanistic and literary intellectuals had the capability of reaching a relatively wide audience, because of their skill with words and their access to the media. They could influence the public consciousness by exposing misconceptions, ridiculing the sacrosanct, and inculcating values. As specialists in symbols and polemics, they could communicate, persuade, and perhaps convince. These qualifications gave them the opportunity to debate indirectly issues that in a democratic society would have been debated outrightly.

DISSIDENT INTELLECTUALS

Even while denouncing tradition, the dissident intellectuals used a style of political debate that was quintessentially traditional. In the guise of an historical or philosophical discussion or theatrical production, they challenged doctrines, criticized individuals, asked questions, and suggested alternatives in a way that their political patrons could not do publicly. Their works, though sometimes of academic value, were intrinsically related to the political and ideological conflict. Until the leadership conflict broke out into the open during the Cultural Revolution of 1966–1969 and again at the time of Mao's death in 1976, these subtle debates were surrogate weapons of political struggle, and the debaters were surrogates for the political leaders who did not want to confront each other directly on issues that might split the party. Debates within the elite, which in most authoritarian societies go on in private, in China were conducted in the open behind a veil of symbols, nuances, and analogies.[14] Issues were debated publicly within defined limits. Although there probably was no prearranged plan to the debates, a pattern of attack and response emerged, escalating until it erupted into open conflict.

The liberal and radical intellectuals shared much in common. Most of them came out of the Westernized urban culture but were also well versed in their own traditional culture. Both groups generally supported the socialist system and the leading role of the party. They operated within a Marxist-Leninist ideological framework and, like their traditional predecessors, criticized their opponents for advocating views contrary to doctrine.

Although members of both groups were officials of professional associations, research institutes, party municipal committees, and propaganda departments, they did not express their views through these formal organizations. For one reason, professional associations, such as the All-China Federation of Literature and Art or the All-China Journalists Association, with chapters in all provinces and numerous affiliated societies, were too large and unwieldy. Moreover, since both intellectual groups belonged to the same organizations, these organizations were so factionalized that they could not function as cohesive units in pursuit of common interests. Instead, the dissident intellectuals divided into informal, nonorganizational groups on the basis of similar views on political issues, particularly the Leap, and on the basis of personal and professional connections.

Despite the similarity of the two groups in background, tradition, and profession, they had sharp differences, extending beyond ideology to geography, generation, and rank. The leaders of the liberal intellectuals had been born around the first decade of the twentieth century. Most had spent their formative years in the cosmopolitan cultural circles of Shanghai, where they led various efforts to Westernize Chinese culture. When the Communist Party came to power in 1949, they moved into important positions in the cultural, academic, and journalistic hierarchy in Beijing, specifically in the Beijing Party Committee and the party's central Propaganda Department.

Although several of the radical intellectuals also came from Shanghai, they had grown up later, at a period less open to Western ideas and under the increasing domination of Marxism-Leninism. Most had been educated before 1949 but achieved prominence afterward. In relation to the liberal intellectuals, they belonged to a lower level of officials in the cultural and academic hierarchy, and most of them were based at two centers, the Shanghai Party Committee's Propaganda Department and the Philosophy and Social Sciences Department of the Chinese Academy of Sciences in Beijing. The struggle between these two groups of intellectuals was therefore not just a conflict over policy. As was the case in the traditional qingyi movements, political conflict was intertwined with personal rivalry and generational conflict. Though the two groups divided primarily along ideological lines, the liberals identified with the professionals and technocrats spawned by modernization, whereas the radicals identified with the younger elite trying to make their way up the political ladder.

There is no question that the liberal intellectuals' criticism of Mao and the Leap could not have been aired if it had not been tolerated and, most likely, countenanced by Liu Shaoqi, as well as by Deng Xiaoping, head of the Secretariat, the party's administrative organ. Yet the details of the connection are not known. The liberal intellectuals were closely connected to the party officials directly in charge of the cultural realm. Peng Zhen, head of the Beijing Party Committee and a member of the Politburo and Secretariat, where he had specific jurisdiction over cultural and intellectual matters, and Lu Dingyi and Zhou Yang, director and deputy director respectively of the central Propaganda Department, had direct and sustained contact with the liberal intellectuals. There is more evidence of the encouragement and assistance of Mao and his wife Jiang Qing to the radical intellectuals. Jiang Qing helped assemble this informal group of intellectuals, to whom Mao turned in the mid-1960s when disillusioned with the party bureaucracy. Although these two intellectual groups were instruments of their respective political mentors, their frames of reference and styles of presentation were for the most part their own. Their numerous articles and ready access to the major journals and newspapers gave these informal groups of intellectuals the potential for a political role.

When in 1966 Mao, with the support of his wife and the army under Lin Biao, moved the surrogate struggle from the defined limits of an intellectual debate into the open as a political struggle, the radical intellectuals were able to move from the periphery to the center of power. With their new political power, they ruthlessly purged the liberal intellectuals, along with their political backers in the Beijing Party Committee and the central Propaganda Department. Whether the radicals merely articulated the views of the Maoist faction or acted as a stimulus in launching the Cultural Revolution, or both, there is no question that their arguments, models, and intellectual predilections provided its ideological underpinnings. Mao indicated the general direction of the Cultural Revolution but gave little detailed guidance. His vagueness gave the radical intellectuals the opportunity to provide the substance. However, at the height of the Cultural Revolution the branch of the radicals associated with the Philosophy and Social Sciences Department of the Academy of Sciences were in turn purged by Mao, because they had moved politically as well as ideologically in a more radical direction than he. As in traditional times, practical considerations, including pressure from the military and the political establishments, forced the ruler to divest himself of allies demanding unrealistic ideological purity.

The other branch of the radical intellectuals, the Shanghai wing, under the patronage of Jiang Qing, at this time retreated temporarily from their radicalism, so that when the Cultural Revolution concluded in 1969, they were able to move into the highest levels of the party as members of the Politburo. With the fall of Lin Biao in 1971, the management of the government by Prime Minister Zhou Enlai in the early 1970s, and the rehabilitation in 1973 of Deng Xiaoping, who had been purged in the Cultural Revolution, the distribution of power once again became more favorable to the veteran party bureaucracy. As the Shanghai group of radicals became increasingly isolated from the centers of economic and political power, they took on a dual role: though still a political faction, they reassumed the characteristics of an intellectual group. Their ability to express themselves publicly, and even their very existence, now depended on Mao. Their bases of power were primarily in the universities, the arts, and journalism. Since their radical values and goals once more diverged from the mainstream, they again resorted to the traditional methods of camouflaged debate to influence public opinion and sway policy makers.

The Shanghai group sought to organize support for their policies in the trade unions and urban militias, but without much success. Their major weapon in the fight to regain authority was a series of ideological campaigns launched in 1973–1976. Although Mao may not have initiated these campaigns, they could not have been launched without his approval and sponsorship. Yet here again, the group moved in directions that Mao had not sanctioned. Just as in the early 1960s the liberal intellectuals presented views that diverged from their political sponsors, so in the mid-1970s the Shanghai group espoused more radical positions than Mao as well as the party establishment. Lacking the full support of their political patron, they were again pushed to the periphery of power and ultimately, in 1976, met their downfall upon Mao's death.

Ironically, whereas the era from the Leap to Mao's death was one of cruel intellectual suppression and increasing cultural impoverishment, it was also one of vigorous philosophical and ideological debate. This period was characterized by some of the worst features of a totalitarian society. Thousands of intellectuals were persecuted, killed, or driven to suicide. The damage done to China's educational institutions, libraries, and cultural life may take generations to repair. Yet the period was also characterized by a political factionalism and intellectual contention that made possible the emergence of more than one vision of reality, and indeed rival visions. The intellectuals who participated, unlike their counterparts in the West, risked their lives as well as their careers to express these different beliefs. This was a time of intermittent, yet genuine, public debate on the fundamental issues facing China, as well as all other modernizing societies—the role of the will, of economic limitations, of charismatic leadership, and of the new technocratic class.

The issues were modern, but the ways in which they were debated had deep-rooted continuity with the traditional Chinese patterns of political debate. Informal groups of like-minded intellectuals joined together to create a political consciousness that might

DISSIDENT INTELLECTUALS

influence policy; they took advantage of factional strife to gain a hearing for their ideas; and they used journalism, scholarship, literary criticism, ideological exegesis, and drama to state their differing political views. Although the overwhelming majority of intellectuals, as in the past, conformed to the prevailing political orthodoxy, a small number of prominent intellectuals, consciously or unconsciously, followed the precedents for political criticism that had been established by their literati ancestors over the course of Chinese history.

2

THE LIBERAL
INTELLECTUALS

The failure of the Great Leap Forward was propitious for the emergence of the liberal intellectuals. As food shortages and depressed peasant morale propelled China toward economic chaos, the party bureaucracy itself, as well as intellectuals and technocrats, became gradually disillusioned with Mao's policies. It is not known whether Mao was compelled to withdraw by colleagues who were enraged at the Leap policies or whether he withdrew willingly, but in April 1959 he stepped down from the presidency of the government, to be replaced by Liu Shaoqi. At the same time, Mao retained chairmanship of the party, at the center of power, and continued as the dominant ideological theoretician. Thus, he remained the chief policymaker, principally handling the Sino-Soviet dispute, and retained veto power over policy, but was cut off from the day-to-day functions of the party.

Although the Leap had been modified with Mao's endorsement, the head of the army, Peng Dehuai, implied in July 1959 at a party meeting in Lushan that the Leap was a tragic mistake, and he called for further modifications. Peng's criticism, like the traditional memorials to the emperor, sought to win the ruler over to his views rather than to attack him directly. But because of Mao's deep involvement in the Leap's conceptualization, he interpreted Peng's criticism as a personal challenge to his authority rather than as legitimate dissent within the party leadership. Mao demanded Peng's removal as head of the army, threatening to break ranks over the issue. Party officials, for the sake of party unity, reluctantly supported his demand.

But as the economy continued to worsen, party leaders, with a sense of urgency, sought to revive it by whatever means worked. In addition to reintroducing material incentives and private ownership of plots, which had been eliminated in the Leap, they sought to reenergize the intellectuals who had been demoralized by the Leap's rejection of their expertise in favor of the know-how of the masses. Thus, the party initiated a period of relaxation in order to gain the cooperation of the intellectuals to help solve the economic difficulties and to replace the Soviet experts who had been withdrawn following the break with the Soviet Union in 1960.

The intellectual relaxation as well as the economic readjustments were under the direction of the party bureaucracy, led by Liu. Whereas he and Peng Zhen had earlier gone along reluctantly with the relaxation of the Hundred Flowers, they now led the effort to rejuvenate the intellectual community. Concomitantly, Mao, who had pushed the earlier relaxation in the face of their resistance, now took a minor role. Neither Mao nor the party's bureaucratic leaders had an interest in liberalizing China's intellectual life or making it more pluralistic, but they were willing to encourage a degree of intellectual ferment and criticism if it created a more favorable atmosphere for scientific, technological, and economic development and did not endanger political control.

Several of Mao's close associates championed the need for some intellectual independence as a prerequisite for development. Vice-Premier Chen Yi, an old comrade with whom Mao exchanged verses, in a speech in August 1961 argued, as Mao had during the Hundred Flowers, that years of party indoctrination had rendered the intellectuals politically trustworthy. In fact, the transformation of the intellectuals was such, Chen believed, that they need no longer spend time in political sessions or manual labor to the neglect of their own work: "As long as experts show results in their profession and contribute to the construction of socialism, there should be no objection to their taking only a small part in political activity." Nor need they be thoroughly versed in Marxism-Leninism or completely committed to party ideology. He acknowledged that he himself and the majority of the Central Committee, the party's governing body, had come not from worker and peasant families but from landlord and middle-class backgrounds. He defined Communism in pragmatic terms. Intellectuals demonstrated their political spirit not by constantly professing devotion to the political regime but by contributing to the development of modern industry, agriculture, science, and culture. In Chen's view, such activity was "a manifestation of the politics of socialism." And unless the regime allowed intellectuals more leeway in this work, "Our country's science and culture will lag behind forever."[1]

Another close colleague, Prime Minister Zhou Enlai, also encouraged greater freedom of speech and even dissent in a talk on June 19, 1961, which was not published until 1979 but whose ideas must have been known to the intellectual community. He complained that people who dared to think new thoughts were afraid to act upon them: "What one man says goes." This statement could have been interpreted as directed against Mao's rule as well as against bureaucratic controls. Zhou sanctioned criticism of decisions that had already been accepted by the party: "Even things officially approved and passed by the working conference convened by the party's Central Committee can be discussed and can be revised."[2]

Although Zhou did not ask for any legal guarantees of the right to speak, he suggested an approach that was more in tune with Western treatment of intellectuals than with previous party practice, except perhaps for the Hundred Flowers. As long as one's work was not antiparty and antisocialist, it should be allowed. Literary and academic work should be relatively separate from political dictates: "The leadership has the right to state their views on political questions," but on intellectual and creative work, on which "we know very little, we have little right to speak. Therefore, we should not interfere unnecessarily." Intellectuals should be allowed free choice in subject matter and style because, "If politics were substituted for culture, then there would be no culture."[3] Zhou also called for greater separation between politics and the professions, asserting that anyone who did not spend time studying politics but did well in his work was much more valuable for socialism than one who con-

THE LIBERAL INTELLECTUALS

tinually talked politics but was unskilled in his work. Zhou's approach was summed up by Deng Xiaoping's remark, made in 1961 with reference to the peasants' private plots, that it did not matter whether a cat was black or white so long as it caught mice.

Mao also expressed the general feeling of the early 1960s that intellectuals should be allowed to work relatively unhindered by political considerations. At an enlarged party work conference on January 30, 1962, he commented that intellectuals need not be revolutionary: "As long as they are patriotic, we shall unite with them and let them get on with their work."[4] In apparent support of the relaxation, he urged that people speak out without fear of punishment, so long as they did not violate party discipline or engage in secret activities: "In the beginning, truth is not in the hands of the majority, but in those of the minority."[5] He admitted that the party had handled some dissidents incorrectly in the past, as in the case of the ideological theorist Wang Shiwei, who had been killed in 1947 for criticizing the party. Mao now insisted that Wang should rather have been put through labor reform. Mao, like his intellectual critics, also used historical analogies to make his point. He cited the ancient thinkers Confucius and Sun Zi who, despite persecution, had been courageous in expressing indignation at the injustices of the day. He also praised the founder of the Han Dynasty, Liu Bang, who, unlike his opponent Xiang Yu, had accepted ideas different from his own and been "generous and open-minded."[6] It was no accident, Mao concluded, that Liu had won and Xiang Yu had lost.

As in the Hundred Flowers, in 1961–1962 the party convened academic forums throughout the country where intellectuals could debate ideas relatively freely. Anyone taking a minority view in these forms could defend his opinions and offer countercriticism. This approach was justified in an editorial in the party's theoretical organ, *Red Flag (Hongqi)*: "The atmosphere becomes lively in any field so long as there are controversies, mutual exchanges of opinion, and mutual criticism. Such a lively atmosphere is extremely beneficial and very necessary for the development of science ... Questions of right and wrong in arts and sciences should be settled through free discussion."[7] Intellectuals were even urged to use the forums to criticize the cadres in charge of their disciplines, whom the regime blamed for its own repressive policies. It charged them with bureaucratic attitudes, ignorance of the work under their command, and disrespect for scholars. The party assumed that this relaxation and

protection of political patrons. Similarly in the early 1960s, the liberal intellectuals appear to have had protection at the highest level of the party.

There is little proof for the charges made later that Liu Shaoqi and Deng Xiaoping were the behind-the-scenes manipulators of the liberal intellectuals. Liu had in fact gone along with the Leap policy and had been in charge of implementing it. Yet in a speech of January 26–27, 1962, before the enlarged party work conference, he expressed disillusionment with the Leap. He described a visit to his native Hunan to investigate the conditions of the peasants, whom he found bitter, weary, and apathetic from the pressure put on them to produce. In contradiction to the official excuse that the Leap's difficulties were a result of natural disasters and Soviet perfidy, Liu quoted a Hunanese peasant's remark that the troubles were 30 percent natural disaster and 70 percent human error. Indirectly criticizing Mao, Liu warned, "Let us not be those 'leftists' who divorce themselves from reality and from the masses and who are adventuristic."[11] The Leap's method of revolutionary exhortation, mass mobilization, and episodic upheaval, which had been appropriate to the guerrilla days, he now condemned as detrimental to building an industrialized, modernized society. Liu favored balanced, steady economic growth and political institutionalization.

Although Mao had himself criticized some aspects of the Leap, he had rejected criticism by others and directed the party to stress its successes rather than its failures. Liu, however, felt that this sort of evasion did not display "the courage of a revolutionary, nor is it the attitude a Marxist-Leninist should take."[12] He urged his associates to criticize the Leap's methods forthrightly. He also criticized Mao's purge of Peng Dehuai for its irregularity and disregard of party norms, pointing out that a member of the Politburo had the right to dissent. Liu was expressing the views of a substantial body of party officials who believed that Peng had been treated unfairly and too harshly, especially as events had proven him right. Although Liu was not yet ready to pardon Peng for his reputed relations with the Soviet Union, he called for the rehabilitation of other critics, inferring that their criticism had been correct. Liu was not a manipulator of the liberal intellectuals, but this kind of position gave implicit sanction to their criticisms.

The liberal intellectuals were linked more directly to the head of the Beijing Party Committee Peng Zhen, director of propaganda Lu

THE LIBERAL INTELLECTUALS

Dingyi and deputy director of propaganda Zhou Yang. Although Peng had acquired extensive powers in the Secretariat and was ranked eighth in the Politburo, he was not a member of the Standing Committee, the inner circle of party leaders. It is unlikely that these savvy officials would have allowed the liberal intellectuals to attack Mao and his policies unless they had tacit support from the top leaders, who could not explicitly criticize Mao themselves without shattering the facade of a coherent, unified leadership. Thus the process of de-Maoization began in the early 1960s.

The criticisms of Mao, the Leap, and Peng's purge, which some party leaders expressed behind closed doors, the liberal intellectuals expressed publicly in the early 1960s. They demonstrated what Liu had called "the courage of a revolutionary" by pointing out the defects of the Leap. They also articulated the party bureaucracy's fear of another Leap as well as its desire for economic and institutional rationalization. At the same time, they inserted their own demands for a degree of pluralism in the political as well as the cultural arena and for a return to certain values of Confucianism, such as its emphasis on conciliation and compromise. Theirs was a plea not for a retreat into the past but for more moderate, flexible policies to counter the divisive and arbitrary reshaping of society carried out in the Leap. Members of the party bureaucracy, though willing to tolerate the introduction of scientific and professional criteria, were far less receptive to the assertion of humanistic and pluralistic values. More important, they were willing to allow a degree of intellectual diversity, but not of political diversity. Thus, there was an inherent tension in the relationship between the party bureaucracy and the liberal intellectuals.

The Beijing Party Committee Intellectuals

In November 1961, Peng Zhen, without authorization from the Politburo, instructed his closest deputies in the Beijing Party Committee to review the directives issued by the Central Committee during the Leap, explaining, "Let us trace the responsibility for the hunger we have suffered for these years."[13] Under the direction of Deng Tuo, head of the Beijing Party Committee Secretariat, about a dozen members of the committee gathered to study these documents. As a result of their deliberations, they not only presented Peng Zhen with

historical incidents to criticize contemporary people and events. On the surface his essays appeared to be mild historical commentaries, but in reality they were devastating criticisms of Mao's leadership and policies. Like Lu Xun's zawen, Deng's were written in an Aesopian language intended to be understood only by a limited circle.

Deng Tuo was relatively more forthright than his associates in his criticism of Mao. Several of his essays emphasized the need for the ruler to listen to others. In one essay he described an official during the Song dynasty who exhorted a prominent statesman, an allusion to Mao, "I hope that you will invite other people to make suggestions because it is not necessary for you to be the author of every scheme." The official stated that some persons "always want to assert their own ideas . . . and refuse to accept the good ideas of the masses under them. If persons with such shortcomings do not wake up and rectify their shortcomings themselves, they will pay dearly one day," a warning that was to hurt Deng as well as Mao.[17] Other zawen of Deng's pointed out that it was impossible for one person or even a small group to understand and command everything, a criticism that could have been directed at the party leadership as well as Mao. True wisdom, in Deng's view, came only from consulting widely and heeding the sentiments of the majority.

Like his Confucian predecessors, Deng Tuo's zawen were also concerned with the suffering of the peasants. Much earlier he had written a history of famine relief in China, published in 1937, which treated famine not as a question of natural disaster or class struggle but as a result of poor administration and official callousness.[18] Republication of the study in 1959 implied a similar explanation for the hunger in the Leap. Deng's zawen of the early 1960s urged China's leaders to go to the countryside and learn personally of the plight of the peasants so as to devise policies more in accord with their needs. He thus implied that Mao and the party were no longer in touch with the realities of peasant life.

Deng also advised that policies be studied carefully and their implications understood fully before they were enacted, which was an indictment of Mao's hasty, untried economic and social experiments in the Leap. As an apparent analogue to Mao, he cited the Song dynasty statesman Wang Anshi who initiated untested, unrealistic programs. Wang had new ideas, but lacked practical experience and concrete knowledge. He considered others inferior to him without any grounds: "His major shortcoming was his lack of humility." As

THE LIBERAL INTELLECTUALS

Deng advised, "From the experience of the ancients we need to understand one principle, that is, toward all things we need to study more, criticize less, and maintain a humble attitude."[19]

In "Notes from a Three-Family Village," Deng Tuo, Wu Han, and Liao Mosha even implied that Mao suffered from a form of mental disorder which led him to irrational behavior and decisions. They observed that the disorder "will not only bring forgetfulness, but gradually lead to abnormal pleasure or anger . . . easiness to lose one's temper and finally insanity." Their advice, apparently directed to Mao, was to take "a complete rest," or else "he will get into a lot of trouble."[20] In Deng's most daring criticism of Mao, he contrasted the ancient historian Liu Xiang's definition of the "royal way," which combined "human sentiments with law and morality," to the "tyrant's way," which "relied on authority and power, used violence and coercion, ordered others about, and robbed people by force or by tricks." In terms of the present, Deng continued, the "royal way" would be called "following the mass line," whereas the "tyrant's way," and implicitly Mao's would be called "arrogant, subjective, dogmatic, and arbitrary."[21]

As sharply as Deng Tuo questioned Mao's ability to rule, he also questioned his policies. Deng protested the use of forced peasant labor on large-scale construction projects, as had happened in the Leap. Once again he used the example of ancient times to criticize the present. Citing the *Book of Rites*, which stated that the labor power of people could be requisitioned no more than three days a year, he concluded that the people should not be asked to "do the impossible" and that more care should be taken "to treasure our labor power."[22] Elsewhere Deng directly referred to the food shortages caused by the Leap, pointing out that whereas ancient governments had guarded against such shortages by storing grain, the present government had not fulfilled its responsibilities to the people in this regard.

In another essay, Deng Tuo allegorically denounced the Leap as without basis in practical experience or economic principles by relating the tale of a merchant who dreamed he would make a fortune from a hen who laid an egg. Excitedly the merchant told his wife that, because the hen could lay fifteen eggs each month, after three years he would become rich. Deng ridiculed the merchant's lack of realism, for wealth could not be produced simply by whipping up enthusiasm, an allusion to the fervor of the Leap. The merchant's

CHINA'S INTELLECTUALS

Ancient cartoonists similarly used drawings "to expose evil persons and evil deeds and praise good persons and good deeds." Yet they had to use allegory and subtlety: "In the society of that time, if that artist had used the cartoon directly to satirize living men, he would have been asking for trouble, but if he satirized ghosts, he would be quite safe."[30] This was a graphic description of Deng's own methods.

Deng Tuo diverged from the party on foreign policy as well, criticizing the break with the Soviet Union in 1960. He urged that China re-establish contact with the Soviets and reemerge from isolation in order to acquire the expertise of a developed country. In an apparent reference to China's rejection of Soviet assistance, he warned that, "If a man with a swelled head thinks he can learn a subject easily and then kicks out his teacher, he will never learn anything." He advocated alliances with more advanced countries, quoting a statesman of the Ming who said, "Some like to ally with those who are as good as they are, but do not like to unite with those who are better than they are, because they lack a 'humble attitude.' " Yet, the statesman advised, it is important "to make friends with others, especially those in a competitive position," in order to learn from them.[31]

Deng Tuo even called for closer contact with the United States at a time when the United States was viewed as the main enemy. He insisted that the Chinese had first discovered the United States, by way of the Aleutian Islands in Alaska, in the sixth century, a thousand years before Columbus. It was even possible that the culture of the Aztecs of Mexico had come from ancient China. Thus there was a long and important tradition of Chinese-American friendship.[32] Deng, together with Wu Han and Liao Mosha, wrote an essay mocking Mao's rejection of both the Soviet Union and the West. They ridiculed Mao's teaching: "The East wind is our benefactor, the West wind our enemy." These words were eye-catching, but "their abusive use has made hackneyed tunes of them . . . the more is said, the greater the confusion."[33]

Although Deng Tuo's close associate, Wu Han, had written little since 1949 and in 1957 had attacked his colleagues in the China Democratic League in the antirightist campaign, in the early 1960s he suddenly burst forth with several pieces on Ming history. Whereas in the 1940s he had written on the Ming to criticize the Guomindang and Chiang Kai-shek, he now used the subject to criticize Mao. Wu Han specifically wrote about the Ming official Hai Rui, who in true Confucian fashion had been loyal to the emperor while at the same

THE LIBERAL INTELLECTUALS

time criticizing his shortcomings. Actually, Mao himself at the April-May 1959 party meeting had approved the use of Hai Rui to encourage criticism of the defects in Leap policies, although he still believed that the Leap on the whole was appropriate for China's needs.[34] However, Mao had underestimated the disenchantment of his fellow officials with the Leap program which they initially had supported. Thus, when Wu Han used the Hai Rui symbol, he used it not merely to point out a few defects but to express the widespread disillusionment with Mao's policies and to encourage the expression of a loyal opposition.

In a vernacular translation of Hai Rui's memorial to the Jiajing Emperor in 1566, entitled "Hai Rui Scolds the Emperor," which was published in the *People's Daily* on June 16, 1959, Wu Han presented a view of the emperor that bore an unmistakable resemblance to Mao during the Leap. Hai Rui praised the emperor for past deeds but criticized him for his recent waste of resources in useless public works while the population went hungry and rebelled. Hai Rui charged: "Your mind is deluded and you are dogmatic and biased. You think you are always right and refuse criticism."[35] He complained that honest officials who pointed out these facts were punished, and he warned that some ministers were so indignant that they would risk death in the hope that the emperor will listen. Thus, Hai Rui urged the emperor to heed the criticism. Through this translation Wu Han, in the style of his literati predecessors, was pleading with China's present ruler to forsake a mode of rule that had led to economic disaster.

After Peng Dehuai's dismissal in August 1959, Hu Qiaomu, an alternate secretary of the Secretariat, a close associate of Deng Xiaoping, and an ideological theorist, encouraged Wu Han to write more on Hai Rui, and Wu Han sent an essay on the subject to Hu for revision and approval. It was published in the *People's Daily* on September 17, 1959, at the height of the campaign against Peng Dehuai. Obviously, Wu could not have published such a piece at such a moment in the party newspaper unless he had the support and permission of members of the political hierarchy. The article urged Confucian-style criticism of the misdeeds of the ruler. It presented Hai Rui as "a man of courage for all times," an example for the present. "Unintimidated by threats of punishment," Hai Rui fearlessly rebuked the emperor for failings that resembled Mao's: "craving vainly for immortality, absenting himself from court audiences for

he tried to reconcile these conflicting approaches. He advised that historical characters "should not be expected to live up to present standards." Rather, one should draw on their "useful experience and fine qualities" to make "the ancients serve the moderns."[40]

Deng Tuo's and Wu Han's articles were not unique. Other intellectuals used historical figures not only to criticize the Leap and Mao but also to question ideological conformity. Some cited the agnostic thinker Wang Chong of the late Han dynasty, who rejected blind faith in any one doctrine and complained that scholars did not know how to raise doubts. He was also cited because he questioned great thinkers and did not treat their words as if they came from God. Other intellectuals cited Wei Zheng, a Tang dynasty statesman, because he welcomed differing viewpoints. According to one writer, when Emperor Taizong (Li Shimin) asked Wei Zheng, "Why is an emperor brilliant and why is he muddled?" Wei replied, "Listening to all sides makes him brilliant and listening to one side makes him muddled." To the objection that opposite views might provoke trouble, the writer retorted: "We need exactly this kind of 'trouble' ... If we do not have any trouble today, we are likely to have greater trouble in the future." The writer called for regularized procedures for expressing criticism because, "If we do not have the proper methods regarding divergent opinions, then certain people will hesitate to air their own views."[41]

Some intellectuals even advocated the establishment of different political parties so that critical views could be stated with a degree of impunity. One article in the *People's Daily* suggested such a system on a local level: "To be ready to listen to different opinions and even to set up opposite parties purposely to encourage people to express their different opinions and to enable them to speak their mind without fear should be the attitude and method to be adopted at meetings and in conducting surveys and research."[42] The writer stated that regularized procedures for criticism were necessary if the nation was to be intellectually alive and to develop economically. This proposal for opposition parties, though made in a primarily low-level academic context, implicitly challenged China's one-party system. Open criticism was also advocated as a stimulus to the revolution. Another writer declared that "Criticism from one's comrades, friends, superiors, and the masses serves as whipping or spurring ... a force that urges one forward, a companion whom a revolutionary

THE LIBERAL INTELLECTUALS

cannot do without even for a moment."[43] These writers urged a more open, more democratic system as a prerequisite for continuation of the revolution and China's modernization.

As the articles of Deng Tuo and his associates were reprinted around the country, newspapers in other areas started their own zawen columns, whose very titles, such as "Rambling Talks Beneath the Clouds of Yunnan" or "Amusing Chats" in the *Guangzhou Evening News,* indicated that they had been modeled on the ones in Beijing. Deng was later accused of directing newspapers and journals throughout the country to publish columns like his in order to spread similar ideas. There probably is some validity to these charges, since the central Propaganda Department with which he was also associated, controlled the provincial media. However, there appears to have been an element of spontaneity as well. Even Deng's radical adversary Yao Wenyuan later admitted that Deng's knowledge and style attracted admirers in journalism, education, the arts, and academia. In fact, Deng's zawen had become so popular that Yao himself wrote to the Shanghai Publishing House requesting publication of a collection of his own articles in the style of Deng Tuo, appropriately entitled "Random Thoughts of a Crab."

Liu Shaoqi and the party bureaucracy desired more intellectual ferment and a loosening of ideological restraints on scholarship and creative work to help resolve some of the problems brought on by the Leap. But even in the later charges hurled against the party leaders during the Cultural Revolution, no evidence was offered that the leaders were willing to give up political and ideological control over scholarship, particularly humanistic scholarship, as Deng Tuo, Wu Han, and their associates were asking. Furthermore, Liu and the party bureaucracy were as unwilling as Mao to allow intellectuals a voice in policy making or public criticism of their political decisions through regularized procedures or lower-level political parties. The fact that the leadership encouraged specific criticisms and a relative relaxation of control did not mean it would tolerate pluralism or a genuine diffusion of power.

Possibly aware of the increasing tension between his views and those of the party bureaucracy and perhaps informed by Peng Zhen of a forthcoming call by Mao for renewed ideological struggle, Deng Tuo on September 2, 1962, published the last article in his series of "Evening Talks at Yanshan." Entitled "Thirty-Six Strategies," it por-

It was later alleged that he was the first to use Hai Rui as a figure to protest the Leap, most likely at Mao's suggestion. Even before Wu Han's Hai Rui pieces appeared, Zhou had gone to Hainan Island, Hai Rui's home, to collect material on him. Subsequently he asked the opera singer Zhou Xinfang to perform the Beijing opera *Hai Rui Submits a Memorial to the Emperor*, which was presented in August 1959 just after Peng Dehuai's criticism of Mao. As in Wu Han's works, Hai Rui was depicted as upbraiding the emperor for his misdeeds.

Zhou Yang in the early 1960s opposed the very same anti-intellectual, antiprofessional programs that he had advocated during the Leap. The reason may be that, having purged his old rivals in the campaigns of the 1950s, he felt secure enough to expound views that he shared with them and which he had formulated in his early days. In the 1930s, at the same time that he was hounding deviationists from the party line, he read widely in Western literature, especially Russian, and translated Tolstoy and Chernyshevsky, two writers whom he greatly admired. He participated in the lively literary debates of the time sparked by differing interpretations of Western culture. Although a cultural bureaucrat par excellence, he was also an urbane intellectual steeped in nineteenth century Western culture. Thus, though a leader in the Leap's movement to promote collectivized, amateur writing inspired by native folk tales, he retained a conventional Western view of literature. Not only did some of his close associates, like the poet He Qifang, director of the Literary Research Institute of the Chinese Academy of Sciences, and the novelist Mao Dun, Minister of Culture, find it difficult to accept folk and group literature as the main trend of writing, but Zhou too found it difficult to accept a culture that completely eliminated Western literature and replaced individual writers with amateur writing groups directed by party cadres. Throughout his career Zhou juggled his commitment to the party organization with a taste for Western culture that often conflicted with his official duties. His contradictory words and actions often reflected these divided loyalties.

Thus, as a result of his own beliefs as well as a shift in the party line, Zhou Yang and his colleagues sought in the early 1960s to lessen the effects of the Leap on culture and to reinvigorate China's creative life. This approach was expressed in the major literary journal, the *Literary Gazette* (*Wenyi Bao*), run by Zhou's colleagues in the cultural bureaucracy. In the early 1960s, the journal called for a diversification of styles and subject matter: "Definite regulations on subject matter have not only limited the development of many kinds of literary styles and spirit, but have had an unfavorable influence on the brilliance and development of literary work." Writers no longer had to conform to Mao's formula of revolutionary realism and revolutionary romanticism, a formula that Zhou himself had helped make dogma in the late 1950s: "A writer, according to his different circumstances, should clearly select and arrange the material with which he is most familiar and which he most enjoys." Writers need not depict politically oriented subjects, such as class struggle and construction projects, but could now describe family life, love affairs, nature, friendship, and everyday happenings.[46] At a literary forum in 1961 Zhou himself recommended a deliberate depoliticization of culture as a way to reduce the strains caused by the Leap: "Now that life has become tense enough, the atmosphere must not be made so tense when we watch a play . . . We must produce things in a lighter vein, and more comic films may be produced."[47] To advocate apolitical creativity in such a highly politicized society was a significant political act, but one in conformity with the party's efforts to moderate the political zeal of the previous period.

Zhou also downplayed class orientation as a criterion for judging literature. Literature should appeal not just to workers and peasants but to all classes, with the exception of the reactionaries. A *People's Daily* editorial of May 13, 1962, explained that since the times had changed in the twenty years since Mao's Yanan directives to writers and artists, it was necessary to serve a more sophisticated, diverse audience by giving writers and artists a degree of autonomy: "We must not hamper and interfere with them by means of administrative orders."[48]

As with the scientists, the party was willing to give the artists more authority over their creative activities. In talks during this period, Zhou called for a joint leadership of artists and the party in creative enterprises, but with the artists controlling their own work. At the Changchun Film Studio in 1961 he said: "Party leadership is leadership in a general sense, but specific departments should be subject to joint leadership—with experts exercising leadership over concrete problems . . . If anyone seeks to dominate and oversimplify academic work, or exercise leadership by administrative orders, we should rise to oppose and rectify this tendency." He even suggested

The play was well received, and its performance led to general praise for ghost plays. Liao Mosha, writing under the pseudonym Fan Xing, explained that ghosts were harmless because they did not spread superstition but represented oppressed people: "If the ghost is a good one, it can inspire one with a fighting will."[55] Wu Han pointed out that writers in ancient times who had been forbidden to write about popular uprisings against the emperor did so by means of ghost plays, in order to resist oppression in real life. He concluded: "Since fairy tales reflect the sufferings, hopes, and wishes of the people and encourage them to struggle and change existing practices with their own strength, they have practical significance today," for there "still exist in certain quarters, states of affairs which are not completely reasonable."[56]

Given the purges since the 1940s of a number of May Fourth writers, older writers, perhaps reluctant to venture forth with new work, mostly revived plays they had written in the relatively freer atmosphere of Shanghai in the 1920s and 1930s and made film adaptations of works of those decades. May Fourth literature, which had been denounced as elitist in the Leap, was now described by Zhou Yang as a great literary movement without parallel in Chinese history, paving the way for China's revolution. The implication was that May Fourth literature was superior to the literature written after Mao had formulated the correct line on literature at Yanan in 1942.

One play that was revived was *The Death of Li Xiucheng*. It had first been performed in 1937 as an example of literature that promoted the United Front, in accordance with the party's official cultural policy at that time. The play was revived in 1956 and was restaged in February 1963 at the China Youth Art Theater. Its author, Yang Hansheng, was vice-chairman and party secretary of the All-China Federation of Literature and Art as well as a close associate of Zhou Yang. The play advocated class collaboration against the common enemy, but in the context of the early 1960s it appeared to allude to the conflict between Peng Dehuai and Mao. Li Xiucheng, a general of the Taipings, was depicted as a courageous figure who had dared to risk his life to challenge the leader of the Taipings, Hong Xiuquan, who was portrayed as unwilling to listen to advice and as adhering stubbornly to a policy that would lead to defeat.

The protagonists of the May Fourth novels and stories recreated on the screen were agonized, ambivalent individuals, caught in the midst of revolution and uncertain which way to turn. They were

very different from the idealized heroes and villains of the Leap literature who, as in traditional Chinese literature, were meant to teach
idealized values and norms. By contrast, May Fourth writers, influenced by nineteenth and early twentieth century Western literature, presented more complex characters who, like themselves, were
torn between the traditional society and revolutionary changes. The
1960s films of their work appealed to a broader audience than their
books or plays and had a particular appeal to urban audiences.

The major figure in the film world was the screen writer Xia Yan.
Like his colleagues, he had been born in the early twentieth century,
studied in Japan, and returned to Shanghai in the 1930s, where he
became a close associate of Zhou Yang. In the early 1950s he became
director of the Film Bureau of the Ministry of Culture, vice-minister
of culture, and secretary of the party group of the Chinese Film Artists Union. In the early 1960s, he encouraged innovative films, more
in tune with Western than with traditional or Communist culture.
He believed that literature and other art "must express thoughts
through images, episodes, and characters and must not proceed from
concepts." Authors must create "credible characters of flesh and
blood to influence their readers" and should "not regard characters
as mere trumpets." Endorsing Engels' statement that "writers need
not impose on readers the future historical solution of social conflicts," he urged that writers, directors, and actors be given more
freedom to choose their own materials and present them in their
own styles.[57]

Xia Yan did just that in his film scenario, shown in 1959, of a story
written in the 1930s by Mao Dun called "The Lin Family Shop." The
story concerned a small-town shopkeeper who, because he sold Japanese wares during the boycott of Japanese goods in 1931, was
forced into bankruptcy. The shopkeeper was a good man who did
not exploit his shop assistants and who cut his prices for the poor,
but he was forced by adversity to extract payment from his debtors.
He was the antithesis of the Leap heroes and villains because he was
exploited by the warlords and bureaucrats at the same time that he
exploited others. His relations with his workers did not reflect class
conflict and at times even exhibited class cooperation. He ate with
them and took care of them in time of need. He was a not unattrac-
tive capitalist whose plight evoked sympathy.[58]

Another controversial film produced under Xia Yan's auspices
was based on the story "Early Spring in February," by the May

long and complicated process of transformation from the old to the new society. If writers wanted to show "the real face of social change and feel its love, hatred, anger, and joy," they should not pursue epic subjects of glory and grandeur but should depict actual people in their familiar surroundings. Works that extolled "brightness" and ignored "darkness" were artistically dishonest, because "in reality both brightness and darkness are intertwined."[62]

After Mao's "Talks," these views remained dormant for twenty years, only to come to life again in the relaxation of the 1960s. Shao Quanlin perhaps revived them then rather than in the earlier, more far-reaching relaxation of the Hundred Flowers because the Hundred Flowers had been directed against bureaucrats like himself, whereas the early 1960s relaxation was against the excesses of the Leap. Or perhaps the deification of peasant and worker heroes in the Leap had touched a core of his thinking which, despite several decades of ideological remolding, had remained unchanged. Moreover, he probably thought he had reached a high enough position to state unorthodox views with impunity.

Whatever the reason, in 1961 and 1962, Shao Quanlin repeated his divergent views frequently, especially at staff meetings of the *Literary Gazette*. At the Dalian conference he rejected the party's literary formulas which he himself had had a large part in prescribing, because they produced one-dimensional fictional characters who "all have red faces." Though he had earlier indicted Hu Feng for this criticism, he now implored writers to "smash oversimplification, doctrinairism, and mechanical theory."[63] He feared that unless China's problems were approached with tough-minded realism rather than ideological stereotypes, the party's efforts to mold reality in accordance with the revolutionary will would fail.

Shao Quanlin felt that the main conflict in society no longer was between classes but was within the individual self. In Shao's view, most people, particularly the peasants, were not the heroes the party prescribed but were people in an intermediate stage between "backward" and "advanced" thinking. Most people had both positive and negative elements within themselves. Instead of depicting heroic and villainous extremes, writers should portray this vast majority of people whom Shao termed "the people in the middle," as yet uncommitted to the revolution. This view of the peasant as nonrevolutionary was shared even by some political leaders. For example, Tao Zhu, first secretary of the Central-South Region, expressed the view

THE LIBERAL INTELLECTUALS

that, "In a production team, only a small number of people would resolutely follow the socialist road . . . The majority, who belong to an intermediate state, would watch and wait . . . The peasants must first fill their stomachs, otherwise all talk is useless."[64]

Although the workers were also affected by the Leap, its critics, despite their Marxist ideology, gave the workers little attention. In addition to the peasants, the other major concern of the liberal intellectuals was the intellectuals themselves. This focus may have been a legacy of the Confucian solicitude for the peasants and literati as well as an expression of their own self-interest. Shao Quanlin described vividly the intellectuals' agonizing struggle to remold themselves: "For the intellectual, the change from the old to the new is a painful process. He has to be immersed in clear water three times, bathed in bloody water three times, and cooked in salt water three times."[65] A similarly painful process went on within the peasant as he moved from a system of individual land ownership to a collective economy.

Like the political leadership, Shao Quanlin believed that literature was a form of propaganda, but in his view it would be far more effective as such if it presented characters with whom the reader could identify rather than standard heroes and villains whom no one could believe. Furthermore, literature would affect the reader more profoundly if reality were depicted accurately and artistically without idealized images and ideological exhortations. The writer should raise problems without solving them: "Let the reader draw his own conclusions . . . Let people see the cause and effect themselves." Not only should the work speak for itself, but the author should speak for himself: "Let each develop his own style; let him see the greatness in common events; let him look at life with a smile or a knitted brow." Shao urged writers to emulate Chekhov and Lu Xun, who viewed "a kaleidoscopic world from a grain of rice."[66]

Shao Quanlin's approach, in addition to diverging from Mao's literary dicta, struck directly at the party's basic political and ideological teachings. Couched in a literary discussion, Shao exposed the differences between the official view of reality and what actually existed. He maintained that the millions of Chinese peasants, who were supposedly the bulwark of the revolution, were not the exemplary revolutionaries as officially pictured. In reality, those who wavered between the "advanced" and "backward" paths were not just a small number of bourgeoisie and intellectuals, as the party

Benjamin Schwartz has pointed out, the Manichean passion in Western thought and Marxism to see history as a constant struggle between opposites is alien to Chinese culture. By looking for the middle ground in their respective fields, the academics implicitly subverted Mao's call for an ideological class struggle.

Mao's call for both ideological struggle and tighter control over the intellectual community was also undermined by the party organizations responsible for these areas, the Propaganda Department and the Beijing Party Committee, the very organizations which had presided over the relaxation of 1961–1962. Verbally their officials went along with Mao's demands, but actually they held back from launching a new campaign, for fear it would lead to disruptions like those produced by the Leap. Disenchantment with Mao's previous policies made these organizations less responsive to his new demands. Furthermore, since their bailiwicks were the centers of dissidence, they were not anxious to pursue a campaign that would ultimately backfire on them.

As Mao later charged in the Cultural Revolution, a growing process of bureaucratization had also occurred in the party's cultural establishment, as is inevitable in any revolutionary organization once it comes to power. Moreover, exhausted and embittered by previous campaigns, the cultural officials were reluctant to carry out the kind of nationwide, intensive remolding drives they had engineered in the past. Hence, though their rhetoric called for class struggle, their tone was moderate. And though they may not have agreed with the dissenting academics, whose views were as opposed to theirs and Liu Shaoqi's as to Mao's, they permitted genuine ideological debates to take place. In the aftermath of the Great Leap Forward, cultural officials as well as intellectuals desired unity rather than conflict.

In contrast to their half-hearted implementation of Mao's policies toward the intellectuals, the cultural officials played an active role in changing the revolutionary educational practices of the Leap to more conventional ones. The Secretariat put Zhou Yang in charge of the liberal arts courses in the universities. Zhou sought to deemphasize the Leap's stress on politics, Mao's thought, and mass research and to reemphasize professional and academically oriented education in order to help China's modernization. He pointed out: "If we train all students to be political activists, then we will have too many political activists. These will become empty-headed politicians without professional knowledge. National construction chiefly depends on the production of large numbers engaged in economic and cultural construction." He also believed that China's development was dependent on maintaining contact with Western as well as with traditional Chinese culture, because "without such knowledge, there would be nothing to compare with and it would be impossible to carry out research in a proper way."[70] This attitude was reflected in a considerable increase in the salaries of the older, Western-trained professors above those of the younger teachers spawned in the Leap.

In order to raise academic standards, Zhou Yang appointed outstanding, Western-trained scholars to head the committees selecting liberal arts texts to replace the mass-oriented materials prepared by the younger teachers and students in the Leap. These outstanding scholars also dominated the major academic journals, as the May Fourth writers dominated the literary journals. For example, Li Shu, an historian as well as a bureaucrat, who had been deputy director of the Modern History Institute of the Chinese Academy of Sciences, became editor of *Historical Research* (*Lishi yanjiu*). He filled the editorial board with such noted historians as Deng Tuo, Wu Han, Jian Bozan, and Hou Wailu. Through the pages of the academic journals raged intellectual debates that ultimately touched on the fundamental ideological questions facing China's leadership.

One question was the reevaluation of Confucianism. The renewed interest in Confucianism in the early 1960s was more than a reflection of the nationalist resurgence that had occurred as a result of the Sino-Soviet rift in 1960. A number of scholars treated Confucianism positively because it was seen as embodying universal and enduring moral values that would help to unify Chinese society after the disruptions of the Leap. This effort to reassess Confucianism in universal terms had begun during the Hundred Flowers. Resurrected after the Leap, the reassessment gained momentum by 1963.

Scholars clothed their reevaluation of Confucianism in Marxist terminology, much as the nineteenth century Chinese reformers had clothed their introduction of Western thought in Confucian doctrine. Like the late nineteenth century reformer Kang Youwei, who cited an obscure Confucian commentary as the basis for his Westernized view of history, the philosopher Feng Youlan cited an early work of Marx, *The German Ideology*, as the basis for his view of the universality of Confucianism. In both cases, the original sources were misinterpreted in order to provide support for their authors' arguments.

The German Ideology maintained that in a transition period the new ruling class must give its ideas the form of universality in order to gain power from the old ruling class. At this stage its interests were more closely connected with the common interests of the nonruling class. Thus, Feng Youlan depicted Confucius as representing the emerging landlord class in China's move in the first millennium BC. from a slave-holding to a feudal society. The ideology Confucius enunciated therefore had meaning for the nonruling classes—peasants, artisans, and merchants—as well as for landlords. The landlords recognized that, "from a certain angle and to a certain degree, there was a certain relationship of equality between one man and another. This was merely an abstract recognition, but even then it had a certain positive value."[71]

Feng Youlan maintained that the newly emerging landlord class, in attempting to replace the old ruling class, appeared in the beginning not as a single class but as a representative of most of society. In the struggle with the slave masters and the nobility, it was necessary to endow the landlords' ideology with a "universal pattern."[72] According to Feng, the Confucian concept of *ren*, or benevolence and human kindness, not only had a class character but also embodied a universal ethic for all classes because the landlords used it to gain broad support. Moreover, Confucius and Mencius encouraged people of ability in order to undermine the hereditary system of the slave owners and the nobility. The philosopher Mo Zi represented the small handicrafts producer, but he also fostered men of eminent ability. The shared views of these thinkers demonstrated that classes do join together at times against a common enemy. These Confucian values, as well as the bourgeois values of a later historical period, took on a universal quality, Feng explained, that had meaning for most of society.

Thus, in a revolutionary era there was a uniformity of interest among different classes. They still worked for their own class interests, but their commonality formed the general interest of the times. In explanation, Feng Youlan cited the Buddhist parable in which four lamps placed in four corners of a room lit their own space, yet it seemed as if there was only one light. Likewise, the interests of different classes were separate and often contradictory, but under special circumstances the struggle for a class's own interest could be a struggle for the common interest.

Another impetus to a more positive evaluation of Confucianism

THE LIBERAL INTELLECTUALS

came from a conference of historians held under the supervision of Zhou Yang in November 1962, just a month after Mao's Tenth Plenum speech. The conference became a platform for a variety of non-Marxist interpretations of Chinese history. One of the most controversial was the view of the philosopher Liu Jie from Zhongshan University in Guangzhou that China's history had a different pattern from that of the West. Whereas class struggle may have governed Western historical development, Liu explained, it had not governed China's development. Because the theory of class struggle was formulated by Marx and Engels in modern times, the thinkers of ancient times could not have understood this concept: "We must not improperly impose on the ancients the problems of our times."[73] Liu Jie and others at the conference contended that the Confucian concept of ren transcended the feudal society from which it came. The concept, having induced cooperation among classes in the past, could serve a similar function in the present. Still others suggested that Confucianism had helped to pave the way for Marxism-Leninism. For example, Confucius' view that practice generated knowledge and knowledge enhanced practice agreed essentially with the Marxist-Leninist view of acquiring knowledge. There was an apparently deliberate effort at the conference to entangle Confucianism with Marxism-Leninism, contradicting Mao's effort to polarize ideologies.

Following the conference, Liu Jie and others continued to argue in newspapers and journals that the Confucian ren, as well as other traditional concepts, such as Mo Zi's "love without distinction," had produced in China an evolutionary rather than a revolutionary historical process. According to Liu, since Chinese civilization was in part the implementation of ren, groups and classes worked together rather than in opposition to one another: "It is not in conformity with historical fact to say that the opposing sides were sharply defined and divided . . . without mixing with each other."[74] This picture of history in terms of class cooperation rather than class struggle was meant not only to explain the past but also to guide the present.

Debates on history similarly challenged the Maoist as well as the Marxist view of history. Several of China's most prominent historians protested, as had their colleague Wu Han, against the straitjacket into which history had been forced, particularly since the Leap. They specifically resented having to explain Chinese history on the basis of class struggle and peasant wars. Their demands for the removal of ideological shackles and for greater attention to historical facts was called "historicism" (lishi zhuyi). The veteran historian and party member Jian Bozan, chairman of the History Department and vice-president of Beijing University, contended that a theory of history should be produced from historical facts, not substituted for the facts: "The starting point of research is not principle but particular concrete facts." Even Marxism could become dogmatic, if its theories replaced rather than illuminated historical data and cultural patterns. Then, "rich, colorful, concrete, and lively history has been turned into a monotonous, lifeless, and insipid dogma and into a desert."[75] Moreover, scholars were reluctant to undertake serious historical research for fear of committing an error.

Several historians challenged the Maoist orthodoxy that the peasant uprisings in Chinese history were revolutionary movements. Although these historians employed Maoist phraseology, they too, like the literary critics who called for the portrayal of middle men, challenged Mao's glorification of the peasant revolutionary and indirectly criticized the use of mass movements. Contending that political elites as well as peasants made history, they warned against exaggerating the role of peasant rebellion. The historian Zhou Liangxia charged, "Some comrades attributed greater awareness to the peasants than is warranted."[76] These historians presented the traditional Marxist view that the peasants lacked revolutionary potential because, like the upper classes, they sought not a new order but their own enrichment. In the Western academic tradition of letting historical facts determine analysis, they also pointed out that peasant rebellions against the ruling class had been spontaneous, improvised actions against repression, not organized revolutionary movements. The peasants rose up against the exploitation of particular landlords, not against the landlord class; they opposed certain emperors, not the dynastic system itself.

For a number of years, Jian Bozan espoused a concept that came to be called the "concession theory," which implicitly questioned revolution as the impetus for improving the lot of the Chinese peasant. After a dynasty had been overthrown, the new unifying dynasty temporarily relaxed its suppression of the peasants. It offered concessions to them, such as reducing taxes, parceling out small plots of land, and opening up new land. These actions were not revolutionary; on the contrary, they prevented revolution by contributing gradually to the improvement of the peasants' welfare. Therefore, it was class reconciliation rather than class struggle which improved the peasants' livelihood. Feng Youlan, in line with his view of the common interests among classes, also pointed out that members of the ruling class, "for the sake of the long-range interest of their own class, often advocated that some concessions be made to the interest of the ruled classes in order to diminish the latter's opposition."[77] The threat of peasant insurrection gave the opposing classes an impulse to work together, which in turn advanced society. Unlike Mao, these scholars argued that the amelioration, not the intensification, of class struggle was the motive force of history and the impetus to the peasants' betterment. Thus, into their contradictory blend of traditional Marxism and Western academic methodology they mixed another contradictory ingredient, the Confucian concern for the welfare of the peasants.

The kind of debate these views evoked was typified by the reaction to a series of articles by Wu Han demonstrating that the values as well as the interests of the ruling class and the peasants had at times coincided. Using as his authority Mao's directive of the early 1950s "to assimilate critically the past," Wu Han also asserted just before the Tenth Plenum that certain traditional values should be revived. In addition to ren, other values of Confucian society, such as loyalty, filial piety, honesty, diligence, and courage, should be incorporated into present-day China, as should particular values of bourgeois society, such as democracy and the profit motive.

There was little response to these views for almost a year, until on August 15, 1963, an article in the *Guangming Daily* charged that Wu Han treated the morality of the ruling class as the morality of all the people, when in reality it conflicted with the morality of the masses. Four days later, again in the *Guangming Daily*, Wu Han rebutted these criticisms, explaining that "Under certain conditions and certain limitations, individuals of the ruling class undertook actions compatible with the interests of the people." Whereas the masses absorbed moral principles of the ruling class, values of the ruled class were also adopted by the ruling class. It was therefore wrong "to present without exception any individual of the two classes of any period as against each other and not to search for the interaction between them. It is because of this interaction of classes that it is possible to inherit the morality of the past."[78] Like the "concession theory," Wu Han's belief that the morals of the ruling and ruled classes were mutually compatible implicitly sabotaged Mao's directive for ideological class struggle. Moreover, Wu subtly attacked the intensifying cult of Mao. Despite his advocacy of traditional values, Wu remarked that some of the values handed down by previous generations had to change with the times, such as the concept of loyalty, which should now mean loyalty to the party, not to a ruler.

Following Wu Han's rebuttal, a number of academics joined the discussion carried in scholarly journals. Although the majority disagreed with Wu, a minority upheld his view of the mutuality of class interests and values. Several mentioned that when in the past China had been faced with an alien invasion, some members of the ruling class had displayed a spirit of patriotism which was more helpful to the masses than to the landlord class. The historian Wang Xuhua argued that opposing classes shared the desire to maintain stability and economic activity. For example, since the landlord class exploited the peasants, it had "to safeguard the interests of the peasants and see to it that they were not killed at will . . . If the landlord class did not safeguard their interests, it would have no people to exploit and the peasants would rise up in revolution."[79]

Whereas historians and philosophers talked of a mutuality between the ruling and ruled classes in a political and moral sense, the historian-aesthetician Zhou Gucheng talked of mutuality in an aesthetic sense. Zhou, a member of the Presidium of the Chinese Workers and Peasants Democratic Party, one of the supposedly "democratic" parties, and a professor at Fudan University in Shanghai, had risen to political prominence as a result of his denunciation of rightists in the antirightist campaign in 1957. Mao referred to him as one of his "right-wing" friends. But Zhou's view of consciousness, which he elaborated after the Tenth Plenum, directly opposed Mao's view of ideology as a reflection of class struggle. Zhou wrote: "The age of feudalism had various ideologies and ideological consciousnesses which merged to become the spirit of the age; the age of capitalism also had a variety of consciousnesses which merged to become the spirit of the age. The spirit of the age of each era, while it is a unified, integral whole, is nevertheless reflected through different individuals and classes, all of which are distinct."[80] This view, which saw consciousness as the unified expression of various ideologies representing different groups coexisting in society, conflicted with the Maoist vision, which regarded consciousness as the expression of one class in conflict with or transforming another. Similarly, Zhou regarded art as transcending class divisions and as reflecting various

social classes in a particular era. These aesthetic concepts undermined Mao's effort to intensify class struggle ideologically and culturally.

Likewise, Mao's stress on political criteria in economic matters
was questioned by a number of economists. A prominent academic,
Ma Yinchu, who had been educated at Yale and Columbia, argued in
November 1959 that the population expansion promoted in the Leap
was economically irrational. Modernization, he insisted, would be
achieved not by increasing but by limiting the population. For his
advice, he was dismissed as president of Beijing University.

However, after the Leap, several economists in the Economic Institute of the Chinese Academy of Sciences, emboldened by the general relaxation and by the expressed desire of party leaders to prevent another economic crisis and improve economic performance,
obliquely questioned the economic policies. They offered suggestions paralleling ones being made by reformist economists in the
Soviet Union in the early 1960s. They advised that profitability and
efficiency instead of politics and ideology be made the basis for in-
vestments, and that the marketplace instead of administrative decisions determine some prices. In addition, they recommended the use
of mathematical methods, differentiated rent, economic accounting,
and interest on capital as means for promoting China's modernization.

The most prominent of these economists was Sun Yefang, director of the Economic Institute. A party member since the 1920s, he
had studied in the Soviet Union and had visited Moscow in the 1950s
and again in the early 1960s when economic reforms, particularly
those of Evsey Liberman, were being discussed. Upon Sun's return,
he suggested similar reforms, such as giving more autonomy to the
operation of an enterprise and allowing a portion of the profit to remain with the enterprise to be used as a bonus to stimulate increased
production and better management. As scientific know-how was to
replace mass movements, profits rather than political criteria were to
determine investment and development. Sun saw profit as the most
sensitive indicator of technological feasibility and managerial competence. He also proposed that prices be guided more by production
costs than by political norms.

More directly critical of Mao's approach was Sun Yefang's characterization in 1962 of the commune as a "mistake of rash and reck-
less advance." Echoing traditional Marxism, he complained: "We

want to reach heaven in one step and so think the bigger [the project] the better, and as a result we have encouraged blind direction . . . We have forgotten productivity and overexaggerated man's subjective initiative."[81] Although Liu Shaoqi was accused in the Cultural Revolution of parroting Sun's emphasis on "profits in command" and substantial material incentives, Liu had not stressed profits and his material incentives policies in the early 1960s were relatively narrow, less than those of the First Five Year Plan. Sun's economic recommendations, like the recommendations of intellectuals in other fields, did not stay within the bounds of official policy.

Thus, like their traditional predecessors, groups of relatively liberal intellectuals—writers, historians, philosophers, and economists—in the first half of the 1960s engaged in intellectual discussions that in actuality were political debates. As in traditional times, they were able to question prevailing doctrine because of their links to political patrons. Their criticisms and proposals helped to create a climate of opinion favorable to the party's shift away from the revolutionary practices of the Great Leap Forward and back to more conventional economic, educational, and cultural policies. Yet their criticisms and proposals were more far-reaching than their patrons had sanctioned. They marked the emergence of a body of public dissent which diverged not only from Mao, but from their political patrons as well. However, the liberal intellectuals were more directly a threat to Mao than to their patrons. Thus in 1963–1964, Mao and his allies enlisted a group of radical intellectuals to refute the criticisms and offer counterproposals.

3

RESPONSE
OF THE RADICAL
INTELLECTUALS

The radical intellectuals enlisted by Mao and his allies in the mid-1960s were ready to be recruited to his cause. They comprised two overlapping groups. The one from the Philosophy and Social Sciences Department of the Chinese Academy of Sciences was oriented more toward academic pursuits; the other from the Shanghai Party Committee's Propaganda Department was oriented more toward the creative arts and journalism. They, like the liberal intellectuals, were skilled in intellectual debate, but they differed from the liberal intellectuals in that they had a more Marxist-oriented education and were lower in the intellectual hierarchy. They also had less experience in organization and administration. They resembled their late nineteenth century qingyi ancestors in that they opposed the older intellectual establishment. Likewise, their opposition was generational, personal, and opportunistic as well as ideological. In the manner of their predecessors, they sought to arouse public opinion against their rivals by charging them with deviating from the true ideology. Also like their predecessors, they based their arguments on the same doctrines as their rivals, but their different emphases produced opposing interpretations.

Zhang Chunqiao was the elder of this group. He had been born in 1917 into an intellectual family. Like his intellectual rivals, he was active in left-wing literary circles in Shanghai in the 1930s and did propaganda work in the Border Areas in the 1940s. It was not until after 1949, however, that he began to achieve important positions. In 1955 he became a vice-chairman of the All-China Journalists Association, of which Deng Tuo was chairman, and acting secretary of the Literary and Art Work Committee of the Shanghai Party Committee. In the Great Leap Forward, his articulation of Mao's policies in the media caught Mao's attention. One of Zhang's articles published in the *People's Daily* was accompanied by an editorial note supposedly written by Mao which did not fully endorse its ideas but urged readers to use it as a starting point for discussion.[1] Shortly afterward, Zhang was made a member of the Shanghai Party Committee and of its standing committee. More direct contact with Mao and his wife Jiang Qing began in 1963–1964 when Ke Qingshi, a Politburo member, first secretary of the Shanghai Party Committee, and confidant of Mao, helped Jiang Qing reform the Beijing Opera. As opposed to the central Propaganda Committee and the Beijing Party Committee, which had blocked her reforms of the Beijing Opera, the Shanghai Propaganda Department, particularly Zhang and his younger colleague Yao Wenyuan, provided ready assistance.

Yao Wenyuan, born of a father active in left-wing literary circles in the 1930s, had first made a name for himself in the 1950s by allying with the literary bureaucrats around Zhou Yang in the central Propaganda Department in opposition to the writers once associated with Lu Xun, a few of whom had been friends of his father. He was active in the campaigns against Hu Feng, Ai Qing, Ding Ling, and Feng Xuefeng. He was conspicuous in the late 1950s for his denunciation of "rightists," especially the literary theorist Ba Ren, who stressed that elements of human nature were common to all classes. Yao also criticized May Fourth writers like He Qifang and Mao Dun for questioning the mass literary movement of the Leap, and he labeled another May Fourth writer, Ba Jin, a "reactionary." Yao came to be known as "the stick" for suppressing writers by calling them names.[2]

Though in 1961–1962 Yao Wenyuan conformed, as he had in the

THE RADICAL INTELLECTUALS

Hundred Flowers, to the relative relaxation and even indirectly criticized the Leap, his earlier criticisms so infuriated older May Fourth writers that Zhou Yang and his colleague Lin Mohan personally intervened against Yao. Lin branded him "oversimple" and "rude" and urged the Shanghai Party Committee to criticize him.[3] Ba Jin, who as a well-known writer was superior to Yao in the Shanghai cultural scene, indirectly blamed literary officials like Yao for preventing him from carrying out his duty as a writer by dictating what he could write. Ba Jin described these bureaucrats as "people with a hoop in one hand and a stick in the other who go everywhere looking for persons who have gone astray . . . They enjoy making simple hoops . . . and wish to make everyone jump through them . . . If there are people who do not wish to go through their hoops and if there are some who have several kinds of flowers blooming in their gardens . . . these people become angry, raise up their sticks and strike out." These bureaucrats also held writers responsible for the actions of their readers, "as if a novelist could thoroughly transform the spirit of man."[4] This was an indirect criticism of Mao, who believed writers could transform men, whether for good or evil.

In Ba Jin's view, these bureaucrats did not understand literature, nor did they represent public opinion. They were interested merely in achieving power and elevating themselves above others. Consequently, writers had become frightened and did only what they were ordered, so that they would be left alone. Now was the time, according to Ba Jin, for writers to become literary warriors and do battle against such people by diligently upholding their own vision of reality in creative work: "I only know that the more the truth is discussed, the clearer it will become."[5] In this way, writers will fulfill the responsibility of their profession and demonstrate the bravery of their calling. Ba Jin did not draw the obvious conclusion that the existence of bureaucrats with hoops and clubs was due, not merely to the crude practices of individual officials, but to the policies of the party itself.

Zhang Chunqiao, Yao Wenyuan, and Jiang Qing joined together as natural allies in their common animus against this cultural establishment, which had criticized and blocked their efforts to achieve prominence in the cultural realm. Yao and Zhang's assistance to Jiang Qing in her reform of the Beijing Opera helped solidify their alliance. Their link-up with a group of young philosophers and historians associated with the Philosophy and Social Sciences Department of the Chinese Academy of Sciences—Guan Feng, Qi Benyu, Lin Youshi, and Lin Jie—added intellectual substance to their challenge to the views of the older intellectuals. Zhang had been associated with a few of these scholars at least as early as the Leap, when he, Guan Feng, and another colleague, Wu Quanqi, wrote articles echoing Mao's call for restrictions on material incentives, as in the guerrilla days, and for establishment of a supply system based on the goal of "to each according to his need."

A common denominator in the articles and speeches of the radical intellectuals in the early 1960s was their emphasis more on the voluntarist aspects of Mao's thought than on traditional Marxism. They continued to expound Mao's beliefs articulated in the Leap, except that because of the economic disaster of that period, they now expressed these beliefs in ideological and political, rather than economic, terms. Like their mentor, they insisted that socialist transformation of the economy did not automatically transform bourgeois ideology. It was therefore necessary to wage ideological class struggle against bourgeois ideas and values, the superstructure, which continued to exert influence even though its means of production had been eliminated. The subjective will that had been aroused to overcome the forces of nature and economic limitations in the Leap was now to be aroused against bourgeois ideological forces. Equating the subjective will with revolutionary zeal, the radical intellectuals sought to mobilize the revolutionary zeal of the masses against the prevailing bourgeois superstructure.

The arguments, rhetoric, and symbols used by the radical intellectuals in rebutting the liberal intellectuals in 1963–1964 provided the ideological foundation for the Cultural Revolution. The radical intellectuals also initiated the process that undermined the intellectual and bureaucratic establishment. They became China's new left. Their arguments not only expressed their own ideological disagreements and personal rivalries but also reflected the genuine socioeconomic grievances of a segment of the population, particularly among the educated youth, against the lack of mobility in the hierarchy and the inequalities between the older, better trained intellectuals and the younger, less well-trained ones. The radicals' verbal attacks on well-known intellectuals and bureaucrats gained them a prominence and notoriety that could be used by Mao against the party bureaucracy.

Whether the radical intellectuals knew that by attacking the liberal intellectuals, whom they called the spokesmen of the bourgeoisie, they would make vulnerable the party leadership is unclear. Nevertheless, in 1963 Guan Feng and Lin Youshi prophesied the overthrow of the leadership: "The historical facts show that the relations between the economic foundation and the superstructure are not mechanical. Under given conditions the status of the two can be transformed. The state power is the primary thing in the superstructure, and the struggle for the change of the economic system must be expressed in concentrated manner as the struggle for the capture of state power."[6]

To what extent Mao instigated this group and to what extent they instigated him is not clear. In the pre-Cultural Revolution period, Mao and his confidants Jiang Qing, Ke Qingshi, and Chen Boda, his secretary-ghost writer since the Yanan days, often suggested the general targets and lines of argument against the liberal intellectuals, but they did not directly supervise the writing of the radicals until the start of the Cultural Revolution. For example, in August 1964 Kang Sheng, another Mao ally and key man in public security matters, complained about centers of the liberal intellectuals: "The Institute of Literature pays no attention to Zhou Gucheng and the Economics Institutes pay no attention to Sun Yefang and to his going in for Libermanism, going in for capitalism."[7] The radicals attacked these particular intellectuals and the issues they represented, but the articles they wrote, the language they used, and the symbols they projected were their own.

The intellectual and ideological disagreements between the radical and liberal intellectuals were not as polarized in 1963–1964 as they would become in the Cultural Revolution. Positions had not hardened into an irrevocable split between Mao and the party bureaucracy or between the two intellectual groups. Although the radical intellectuals echoed Mao's call for renewed ideological struggle, their arguments were not yet simplified clichés. They used a wide range of references and acknowledged the complexities of a question. They engaged in lively exchanges and debated on an academic level and, for the most part, in a nonbelligerent, balanced manner. At this point, they were not in opposition to the central Propaganda Department but merely constituted one group within the propaganda organization.

Among the younger intellectuals in the Philosophy and Social Sciences Department, Guan Feng was the best known. Since the early

1950s he had written erudite articles on ancient Chinese philosophy, several of them in collaboration with two other colleagues, Lin Youshi and Lin Jie. He became prominent in the late 1950s for his criticism of Feng Youlan's view that the relationship between materialism and idealism was one of mutual influence as well as contradiction. Guan contended that materialism and idealism must be in sharp and constant conflict: "These two philosophies cannot ... coexist in peace."[8] He charged that Feng disregarded class characteristics and promoted supraclass interpretations of philosophical concepts, particularly in his view of ren.

Although Guan Feng's attack on so prominent a philosopher may have been motivated partly by a desire for fame, it was also consistent with his previous stress on the class character of philosophical concepts and social theory. On the whole, however, Guan's writings conformed to the party's shifting line. In accord with the Leap, he emphasized the need to develop the "subjective initiative" in order to move from socialism to communism at the earliest possible time. Then in 1961–1962, in line with the regime's retreat, he downplayed subjective initiative and urged investigating "objective," that is, economic limitations before taking action.

In contrast to the liberal intellectuals who resisted Mao's call of September 1962 for ideological struggle, Guan Feng and his cohorts responded with alacrity and resumed their criticism of senior scholars with renewed vigor. They charged the older scholars with spreading the illusion of common interests between classes when in reality there was only class struggle. Like their qingyi predecessors, they saw the fields of history, philosophy, and aesthetics as arenas in which to conduct great moral struggles between the forces of good and evil, namely between the heroic masses and the villainous elite. Their arenas had no place for those who espoused complementary ideas and talked of common denominators.

One of the radical intellectuals' major targets was again Feng Youlan, whom they criticized in *Philosophical Research* (*Zhexue Yanjiu*), the very same journal in which Feng had presented his ideas. Although the liberal intellectuals dominated the editorial boards of scholarly journals, the radicals were able to publish in them. Guan Feng, with his collaborator Lin Youshi, insisted that Feng's belief in both the Confucian concept of ren and the bourgeois values of liberty and equality as being "ideas of universal pattern" was based on a misunderstanding of *The German Ideology*. True, *The German Ideology*

THE RADICAL INTELLECTUALS

mentioned interests that the new exploiting class held in common with other nonruling classes, but it described such links as an "illusion," not an "actuality." Moreover, because this early Marxist work had been written at a time when Marx and Engels had just changed from idealism to materialism and from democracy to communism, some of its basic concepts were "expressed in not too authentic terms."[9] The talk of universality in Marxism was a "false image."[10] Contrary to Feng's interpretation of Marx, Guan and Lin argued that the mature Marx proved that the ideology of the exploiting class was concerned only with the interests of its own class and was unable to represent the interests of other classes, certainly not of the ruled class.

Guan Feng and Lin Youshi used the concept of "historicism," or the emphasis on historical fact, against the liberal intellectuals just as the latter had used it against them. They accused Feng Youlan of violating historicism because he treated ancient philosophy as bourgeois philosophy. Although Feng claimed that Confucius represented the interests of the landlord class, he actually presented Confucius as espousing the bourgeois philosophy that "there is a certain relationship of equality between one man and another."[11] In line with historical materialism, Guan and Lin granted that feudal exploitation was more progressive than slavery, but the fact that the landlord did not, like the slave master, kill a peasant at will did not make for an equitable relationship. Finding universal values and patterns in history was not historicism but ahistoricism or "bourgeois objectivism." They viewed history as a combination of both class analysis and historicism: "The history of objective civilized society is a history of class struggle." China could develop only through class struggle because "the process of development and class struggle are inseparable."[12]

Yet the radicals themselves presented an ahistorical interpretation of China's past. In response to their senior colleagues, they argued that peasant uprisings were not spontaneous acts against oppressors but concerted actions to overthrow the feudal system of relations. Qi Benyu, a member of the Modern History Institute of the Chinese Academy of Sciences, and Lin Jie asserted in a later article that those who denied that rebellions against landlords were rebellions against feudalism denied the revolutionary character of the peasants. Furthermore, it was not the concessions to the peasants but the peasants' "revolutionary struggles against the landlord class" that had "impelled historical development." Consequently, it was necessary "to adhere firmly to the theory of class struggle and to wage a tit-for-tat struggle against the class enemy."[13] Qi and Lin charged, however, that scholars like Jian Bozan not only opposed using class struggle to interpret history but disapproved of using historical research to serve present-day politics. This rebuttal presaged the Cultural Revolution and, more specifically, the attack on intellectuals who refused to obey Mao's summons to struggle, whether it be in research or against colleagues.

Like their liberal adversaries, the radical intellectuals used historical figures to symbolize current leaders. Both groups often used the same historical figures for different ends. Whereas Yang Hansheng had depicted the Taiping general Li Xiucheng as a courageous figure challenging an arbitrary leader, the radical historian Qi Benyu depicted Li as one who had abandoned the revolutionary struggle and betrayed its leader. In the context of the efforts in the early 1960s to rehabilitate Peng Dehuai and denounce the Leap, Qi's portrayal of Li alluded to Peng Dehuai's criticism of Mao and perhaps to the subsequent rejection of Maoist policies by Liu Shaoqi and the party leaders. Whereas the view expressed by Yang and a number of historians that Li's contributions outweighed his shortcomings could be interpreted as supportive of Peng, Qi's negative portrayal could be interpreted as a denunciation of Peng and perhaps of Liu and his associates. Qi did not deny that Li had taken part in a revolutionary struggle, "but his participation and his position as a commander could not negate the facts about his surrender and desertion at the last minute." Qi rejected the argument that Li's surrender to the regime was not a betrayal but an effort to buy time for the Taipings, for desertion under any circumstances was counterrevolutionary. Li, therefore, could not be pardoned because "the foremost question about revolution is to distinguish between friend and foe."[14] Through his repudiation of Li, Qi argued against any tolerance toward critics of revolutionary policies.

The controversy over Li Xiucheng reflected a factional dispute at the highest political level. Qi Benyu's article was published in *Historical Research* in August 1963 and was reprinted a year later in the *People's Daily* and *Guangming Daily*. This belatedly prominent coverage given to an article by a relative unknown suggests that Qi had acquired top-level patronage. Jiang Qing brought Qi's article to the attention of Mao, who observed, "That [Li] could not maintain his loy-

THE RADICAL INTELLECTUALS

alty in his late years is a lesson for us."[15] Apparently Mao personally identified with Qi's attack on a subordinate who dared to defy the leader.

The liberal intellectuals responded to the reprinting of Qi Benyu's article by convening a symposium of the Modern History Institute, organized by Zhou Yang and attended by such prominent historians as Jian Bozan, Wu Han, Deng Tuo, Liu Danian, and Hou Wailu, who refuted Qi's interpretation and defended Li Xiucheng as a national hero. The *People's Daily* published several articles that rebuked Qi for his harsh tone and for selecting facts to fit his conclusion. Yet the criticism of Qi was not pressed home, evidently because Mao intervened to stop it. When the controversy reached a climax in the summer of 1964, neither view prevailed, but rather a composite of the two. Li was criticized for capitulating to the enemy, but he was also praised for his contribution to the Taipings. It was not clear whether his achievements outweighed his shortcomings. The debate ended in a standoff.

Just as the radical intellectuals in the Philosophy and Social Sciences Department upheld the Maoist position on questions of philosophy and history, so Yao Wenyuan argued the radical position on the aesthetic issues raised by Zhou Gucheng. Although Yao had incurred the wrath of cultural officials for his attacks on May Fourth writers in the late 1950s, when in 1963 Ke Qingshi appointed Zhang Chunqiao director of the Shanghai Propaganda Department, Yao was made his assistant. From this improved position, Yao in 1963–1965 fired off articles on literary and ideological questions. Intellectually, these articles were not as "oversimple" as Lin Mohan had earlier charged. They demonstrated a modicum of scholarship and made plentiful use of non-Marxist references. They also expressed some appreciation for aesthetic values. Although Yao insisted that art was subordinate to ideology, he acknowledged that literary skill might enhance receptivity to party propaganda. Even in his criticism of Zhou's ideas, he articulated relatively complicated views, for he was willing to accept some aspects of Zhou's arguments while rejecting others.

Yao Wenyuan's discussions with Zhou Gucheng in the pages of *Guangming Daily* emerged as a genuine debate. He agreed with Zhou that society was composed of a variety of complex, contradictory class views, but he disagreed with the corollary that the combination of these various views encapsulated the spirit of an age, for mutually antagonistic class consciousnesses could never form an integrated spirit. In the present age, Yao insisted, the prevailing spirit was rather represented by the revolutionary consciousness of the proletariat. He warned that, "If one completely separated oneself from all moorings with present reality, one will ultimately move into absurdity."[16]

Yet "unrealistic" was exactly the way that Zhou Gucheng and his colleagues described Yao Wenyuan's—and Mao's—contention that the spirit of the present age was one of revolutionary consciousness. In rebuttal, Zhou wrote that, "Besides a revolutionary spirit, there is some nonrevolutionary and even antirevolutionary spirit." He saw the conflicting forces ultimately converging to form a unified whole, just as the People's Republic of China, despite incorporating different classes, nationalities, languages, and religions, was a unified whole: "If it is held that different parts cannot form a whole, then a unified China, Chinese history, and Chinese cultural legacy would not exist." Zhou charged that Yao was "fond of making abstract generalizations, but does not like to analyze facts."[17]

Yao Wenyuan's response was surprisingly mild considering that Zhou Gucheng had implicitly challenged his and Mao's scholarship and their assumption that China was a revolutionary society. In fact, Yao did not even confront the issue, asserting instead that Zhou himself was not revolutionary because he denied that different kinds of consciousness were being transformed into proletarian consciousness. As if seeking to divert the debate to a less controversial issue, Yao devoted himself to a critique of Zhou's aesthetic theory that creativity was the merging of subjective and objective feelings, which he charged was based on the "bourgeois idealistic thinking of Western philosophy," as in Schopenhauer and Bergson.[18]

Despite the aggressive role of the radical intellectuals in these debates, their general tone was moderate, not strident as it was to become in the Cultural Revolution. Their restraint was probably due to the domination of the cultural establishment by the liberal intellectuals and their political patrons. The only way that the radical intellectuals could publish rebuttals was to shroud them in historical, philosophical, or literary language and to attack politely and indirectly. Indeed, none of their targets was labeled "antiparty," as Hu Feng had been in 1955, or "rightist," as Ding Ling and Ai Qing had been in 1957. Nor were they called "reactionary," as they were to be in the Cultural Revolution. The debaters referred to one another as "comrade" or "mister." The only negative examples used as symbols of unorthodoxy were dead ones, like Li Xiucheng. The most extreme epithet applied to a living person was "bourgeois humanitarian" or, less frequently, "revisionist." There was scarcely any raking up of past "evil deeds," as was customary when criticizing an individual for "incorrect" views.

Moreover, a number of relevant articles took an in-between position, or presented views that diverged from both intellectual groups. The effect was to diffuse the debate, to blur the lines of battle. For example, one article chastized the philosopher Liu Jie for treating Confucianism as "the fountainhead of all civilization, culture, and morality," but also praised him for helping to redress the May Fourth tendency to dispense with China's cultural heritage.[19] Even the article that opened the attack on Wu Han for suggesting that various classes shared a moral inheritance admitted that "the moral legacies of the ruling class did have a dual character . . . in which some elements of the people's character and democracy and sciences were apparent."[20] Although it did not point to the same moral qualities as Wu, it asserted that certain values of the traditional ruling class could be accepted in the present.

Although the radical intellectuals criticized prominent scholars like Feng Youlan, Zhou Gucheng, and Jian Bozan, they did not publicly attack those highly connected to the Beijing Party Committee or the central Propaganda Department. Some of Wu Han's ideas on classless morality were refuted, but no public mention was made of his zawen or his use of the Hai Rui figure. His critics debated his ostensibly less political articles on morality, confining their discussions to narrow philosophical or historical implications and ignoring his subtle criticisms of Mao during the early 1960s. In 1964, Qi Benyu, Guan Feng, and Lin Jie wrote direct criticisms of Wu, but they alleged in 1966 that their articles were blocked from publication by the Beijing Party Committee and the Propaganda Department. It was only in April 1966, when the Beijing intellectuals and their political backers were about to be overthrown, that these criticisms were finally published. There was a deliberate effort by both groups of political patrons at this time to keep the debates within a strictly historical and philosophical context in order to prevent attacks on specific individuals and specific policies. Consequently, the debates had the appearance of academic discussions rather than of surrogate political and ideological struggles, which they in fact were. Both sides, even the radicals, cited a range of Western as well as Chinese historical sources and acknowledged complexities and qualifications. Although the radicals' arguments were to become popular slogans in the Cultural Revolution, in this period they seemed very scholarly.

Whereas the attacks on Wu Han and Feng Youlan were relatively mild, those against the philosopher Liu Jie were more severe, probably because Liu, as a lesser known professor at Zhongshan University, did not have the high-powered official protection of Peng Zhen, Zhou Yang, and Lu Dingyi. The historical societies in Beijing and Guangzhou held special meetings on Liu. Yet even in Liu's case, the criticisms were more of his historical method than of his political views. The forum convened in Beijing, under the leadership of Wu Han and his associates, in fact endorsed some of Liu's views. These attacks subsided by the end of 1963, though they reverberated into 1964.

Unlike the intellectuals criticized in other periods, the liberal intellectuals involved in the academic debates of 1963 for the most part continued to hold their positions. The first of five volumes of a new history of ancient China compiled under Wu Han's direction appeared in October 1963. The reprinting of the first volume and publication of the second volume of Feng Youlan's *New Compendium of the History of Chinese Philosophy*, in which he described the universality of some aspects of Confucianism, appeared in 1964. These works had to be approved by the central Propaganda Department. There were newspaper accounts and pictures in January 1964 of Liu Shaoqi and Zhou Enlai holding receptions for philosophers and historians, among them Wu Han and Feng Youlan. Despite the attacks of the radical intellectuals, the party bureaucracy continued to support, or at least tolerate, the liberal intellectuals and their ideas.

Thus, following Mao's Tenth Plenum call for ideological class struggle, there was debate and controversy, but not the kind of thought reform campaign that customarily accompanied a shift toward ideological regimentation. Nor was one definitive line imposed. This hesitancy to move in the ideological realm was reflected in the thinking and actions of Zhou Yang, the official in charge of the cultural realm. Little he said or did showed a responsiveness to Mao's criticism or a demand for renewed ideological struggle. True, he admitted in a self-criticism that he had not been alert to subversive tendencies in literary works, but he also insisted that the cultural sphere was on the whole ideologically correct.

THE RADICAL INTELLECTUALS

It was not until over a year later, on October 16, 1963, that Zhou Yang, in a speech before the Philosophy and Social Sciences Department of the Academy of Sciences, gave strong backing to Mao's Tenth Plenum line. As if in anticipation of greater pressure from Mao, Zhou decried the current reluctance in intellectual circles to apply class struggle to research and cultural activity. He used a phrase that was to gain wide currency, even after he himself had been condemned: "Everything tends to divide itself in two." In contrast to the liberal intellectuals under his patronage, Zhou signified in this phrase that contradictions in society were irreconcilable and must be resolved through struggle. Contradiction and struggle, not unity, were the forces that pushed society forward. He labeled theories on the merging of contradictions as "revisionism" and claimed that they provided a philosophical basis for the concept of "a state of the whole people."[21]

Although this aspect of Zhou Yang's talk conformed to Mao's line at the Tenth Plenum, other aspects deviated from it. Zhou spoke primarily in terms of Soviet rather than of Chinese revisionism. His accusations were general rather than specific. He touched upon a topic seldom discussed in the People's Republic of China, the Marxist theory of alienation. Though he ultimately rejected the validity of this concept in present-day China, the fact that he alluded to alienation at all suggests that the feeling was palpable in intellectual circles. He referred to the belief of some people that a socialist society under the dictatorship of the proletariat was not free politically, economically, or ideologically, and that "any restraint imposed on the individual by society represents the 'alienation of man.' Therefore, the only way to make man return to himself is to get rid of all kinds of social restraint."[22] Zhou finally condemned this feeling of alienation as typically bourgeois and revisionist.

Despite Zhou Yang's renewed stress on class struggle, his speech, in direct contrast to the radical intellectuals and their patron Mao, recommended a less doctrinal approach to intellectual questions. He declared that, "In studying a problem, it is necessary to do systematic and thorough investigation and derive its inherent laws and not imaginary ones . . . To use the simple methods of sticking this or that label on something may seem to conform with historical materialism and the class viewpoint, but in fact it is subjectivism." These last words could have applied to himself at an earlier stage as well as to the radical intellectuals. He pleaded for academic procedures akin to those used in Western academic communities: "If . . . free exploration and debate and independent thinking are discouraged, and if the method of simply issuing administrative decrees to solve complicated questions in the intellectual field is employed instead, then the result will be ossification of thought in the academic world." Whereas Mao and the radical intellectuals espoused ideological struggle and mass creativity, Zhou and his liberal associates looked forward to a society which would glow with "a galaxy of brilliant scholars."[23]

Jiang Qing and Opera Reform

While the radical intellectuals undermined the establishment in academia and sought power by criticizing prominent scholars, Mao's wife, Jiang Qing, undermined the establishment in the performing arts and sought power by reforming the Beijing Opera. Not only was the opera the most potent medium used by the liberal intellectuals to criticize her husband's policies, but it also was under the direction of her old Shanghai enemies of the 1930s. Her authority derived from being in daily touch with Mao, whose views she supposedly represented. As Mao in his later years became increasingly suspicious of the party bureaucracy and old comrades, he turned to a handful of trusted intimates, particularly his wife and Chen Boda, who in turn developed close contacts with the radical intellectuals.

It was not surprising that Jiang Qing should try to inject herself into the performing arts, because that was the area of her own experience.[24] Although she regarded herself as an intellectual, her formal education was limited. She had graduated from junior high school and studied at the Shandong Experimental Drama Academy. In the early 1930s she went to Shanghai, where she found jobs in the theater and in second-rate films. At that time the May Fourth writers Tian Han, Xia Yan, and Yang Hansheng, who would later become the leaders of theater and screen in the People's Republic, were among the major screen writers, playwrights, and film directors in left-wing circles. They were closely associated with Zhou Yang, who orchestrated the party's cultural activities in Shanghai. Unappreciative of Jiang Qing's dramatic talents, they refused to give her important parts, apparently instilling in her a deep hostility toward them, which she was later to avenge in the Cultural Revolution. She

THE RADICAL INTELLECTUALS

claimed to have joined the party in 1932 but to have lost contact with it while working sporadically in Shanghai.

When the Japanese bombed Shanghai in 1937, Jiang Qing, along with a large number of Shanghai intellectuals and students, made their way to Yanan. There she was befriended by Kang Sheng, who came from her county of Zhuzheng in Shandong. He helped her get a position in the Lu Xun Academy of Arts, and she resumed her affiliation with the party. In 1938 she married Mao, after his divorce from his third wife. Because of the protests from some members of the party hierarchy, she was made to promise that she would not engage in political affairs. In the early years of the People's Republic, her old "enemies" from Shanghai moved into powerful positions in the cultural establishment, while her own role was limited to membership in the Film Guidance Committee of the Ministry of Culture, which censored films. Nevertheless, she was involved in a few confrontations with the cultural officials, which were not brought to light at the time but which she publicized in the Cultural Revolution.

One of the controversies was over the film *Inside Story of the Qing Court*. Made in Hong Kong and shown in China in 1950, the film was about the Empress Dowager Cixi's manipulations of the succession to the throne at the end of the nineteenth century. It played to enthusiastic audiences and was even praised by Liu Shaoqi as "patriotic." Jiang Qing's ire was aroused toward the film, perhaps by the negative portrayal of the female ruler Cixi, and in the early 1950s she demanded that the film be criticized as well as banned, but Lu Dingyi and Zhou Yang refused. It was not until the Cultural Revolution that the film was denounced, primarily for its depiction of the Boxers as a reactionary movement.

Another dispute arose over the film *The Story of Wu Xun*. This film also opened to praise, but in 1951 Mao ordered it criticized for emphasizing reform instead of revolution. The central Propaganda Department launched a large-scale attack on the film led by Zhou Yang. In 1972, Jiang Qing claimed that it was she who had brought the film's weakness to Mao's attention and that Mao had empowered her to lead a delegation to the home province of the film's hero, Wu Xun, the educational reformer, in order to investigate his background.[25] However, when Zhou Yang found out, he sent along his cronies to ensure his control over the cultural realm. Moreover, Zhou's associate Yuan Shuibo, a deputy director of the Propaganda Department, rather than Jiang Qing led the delegation. No mention was made of Jiang Qing's role in the Wu Xun campaign in the press at the time. Reorganization of the Film Guidance Committee in 1954 dispensed with her position altogether. Illness from cancer in 1956 necessitated her going to the Soviet Union for treatment.

Thus, for reasons of personal antagonism and physical health, Jiang Qing was relatively inactive until the early 1960s, when the indirect criticisms of Mao and the Leap sparked her into action. She claimed that she had brought these criticisms to Mao's attention: "In the field of education and culture, I was a roving sentinel . . . My job was to go over some periodicals and newspapers and present to the Chairman . . . things . . . which are worthy of attention."[26] She reviewed over one hundred plays and had Kang Sheng transmit to her old adversary Xia Yan, the head of the theater, her views that the majority of recently performed plays were bad and that Wu Han's *The Dismissal of Hai Rui* should be withdrawn. Xia appears to have paid little heed. Though Wu Han's play was banned, traditional, historical, and ghost plays continued to be performed. Again in December 1962, Jiang Qing criticized the theatrical repertoire and this time called for the banning of ghost plays. Subsequently ghost plays were banned, but most of the traditional repertoire remained. Another of Mao and Jiang Qing's close associates, Ke Qingshi, early in 1963 proposed that literature depict the Communist era. But in April 1963 Zhou Yang at a meeting of the All-China Federation of Literature and Art encouraged the participants to write on any period as long as it reflected the spirit of the times.

With such resistance from the cultural establishment, Jiang Qing focused her attack on the traditional Beijing Opera. This dominant form of the traditional Chinese theater is called "opera" in the West because it combines singing, acting, mime, recitation, and acrobatics. Under the Qing dynasty it became the most prominent of the scores of local operas that had developed in different regions over the centuries. Its stereotyped characters and plots, which dramatized the confrontation between good and evil, were an effective medium for communicating ideological teachings and moral values to the illiterate masses as well as to the cultural elite.

Jiang Qing had Mao's support in this effort. Since Yanan, he had been concerned with transforming the traditional opera. In 1944, he wrote a letter to the Yanan Beijing Opera theater complaining that, "History is made by the people, yet the old opera (and all the old literature and art which are divorced from the people) presents the people as though they were dirt, and the stage is dominated by lords and ladies and their pampered sons and daughters."[27] Party theatrical troupes in the army and villages presented political and revolutionary plays, but traditional opera continued to be performed unchanged despite Mao's complaint. While fiction and theater were being transformed in the 1950s, the Beijing Opera was only slightly affected. Even in the Leap, when most literature depicted contemporary class struggle, the Beijing Opera continued to perform the traditional repertoire. In the early 1960s the Beijing Opera as well as regional opera flourished.

In November 1963, with more vehemence than in Yanan, Mao lashed out again at traditional opera, not only because it was resistant to change but also because, as Wu Han and Tian Han's plays demonstrated, it was now being used to criticize his policies. Mao also attacked the cultural officials who were responsible for staging the operas: "Operas abound in feudal emperors, kings, generals, ministers, scholars, and beautiful women, but the Ministry of Culture doesn't care a bit." He called on the Ministry of Culture to reform itself and "conduct investigations, and put things right in real earnest."[28] Mao's words presaged the rhetoric of the Cultural Revolution, except that they gave the party's cultural officials a chance to correct their ways.

With Mao's imprimatur, Jiang Qing embarked on her own program to produce model revolutionary operas. Its purposes were stated by Ke Qingshi at the East China Drama Festival, held from December 25, 1963, through January 26, 1964, under the auspices of the Shanghai Propaganda Department. Ke deplored the influence of "the unhealthy bourgeois atmosphere and reactionary, erratic, superstitious plays" on the masses. By contrast, socialist literature and art, which included the new model revolutionary operas, was "an ideological weapon to educate and rally the people and criticize and destroy the enemy."[29]

Like the radical intellectuals in the realm of scholarship, Jiang Qing sought to transform the moral struggle between good and bad in traditional opera into class conflict between worker, peasant, and soldier heroes and landlord and bourgeois villains. The operas produced under her auspices used the traditional method of highlighting the triumph of absolute good over absolute evil with bright lighting and prominent placement for the heroes and dim lighting and secondary placement for the villains. She also inserted some Western devices. The traditional melodies, percussion rhythms, and formalized techniques were combined not only with Chinese folk dances and revolutionary songs but also with Western ballet and military music. Western instruments such as winds, kettle drum, piano, and harp were added to the traditional musical instruments. Her operas were cultural hybrids.

Jiang Qing also sought to transform the ballet so as to convey a revolutionary message. In place of the traditional ballets *Swan Lake* and *Giselle* that the Soviets had introduced to China in the early 1950s, she imposed revolutionary ballets, such as *The Red Detachment of Women* and *White-Haired Girl*. Ironically, these ballets also drew on Soviet inspiration by way of the socialist realist ballets of the 1930s. They combined military drill, folk steps, clenched fists, and clutched weapons with classical Western motions of pirouettes and leaps. They were dances of the liberation of peasant slave girls rather than of black swans.

In contrast to the middle men and May Fourth protagonists, the heroes and heroines of Jiang Qing's operas and ballets suffered no doubts, weaknesses, sorrows, or disorders, were thoroughly infused with ideological goals, and carried out superhuman feats for the revolution. Her effort to reform China's traditional opera dispensed with its content but retained its formulas, techniques, and styles. She repudiated Western culture, but injected the most banal and conventional Soviet dance, music, and song. These devices, along with the content of class struggle, military conflict, and heroic models, presaged the official culture that would emerge in the Cultural Revolution.

While Jiang Qing was launching her opera reforms, the cultural officials were not unresponsive to Mao's demands. Even before the East China Festival and as if in anticipation of Mao's criticism, the Ministry of Culture, the Union of Chinese Stage Artists, and the Cultural Bureau in Beijing held a drama forum on September 21, 1963, where they recommended that fewer historical and traditional plays be performed and encouraged more plays on contemporary themes. Subsequently modern drama festivals were held all over the country. Historical plays by such May Fourth writers as Guo Moruo, Tian Han, and Cao Yu were gradually discontinued. Symposia were held to criticize traditional operas. Major figures in the cultural hierarchy, such as Zhou Yang, Yang Hansheng, and Yuan Shuibo, and major articles in the cultural journals now called for a theater that reflected present-day life and praised heroes of the new era. Even the Beijing Party Committee responded positively. A series of articles in the *Beijing Daily* called for the presentation on stage of "living people of the socialist era" in place of the traditional elite.[30] Beijing cultural officials also stressed the need for works of high artistic quality. But Ke Qingshi also cautioned that emphasis on political standards did not mean ignoring artistic standards: "Works of a low artistic level are always ineffective."[31]

Nevertheless, the cultural officials differed from Ke Qingshi in that they emphasized the need for more than one flower to bloom in the cultural realm. While calling for opera reform, they warned against total rejection of China's cultural heritage. As one official said about art, "It won't do to have flowers, birds, fish, and insects alone, but it also won't do to have class struggle alone."[32] A *Literary Gazette* editorial of February 1964 suggested that promoting revolutionary operas "did not mean that plays on other subjects could not be written. Good traditional plays, historical plays from a proletarian historical viewpoint, and other plays in the interest of the people should also be staged."[33] What the cultural officials resisted was a rigid formula for revolutionary opera and large-scale curtailment of traditional opera. In 1963 and early 1964 there was a genuine debate on opera reform. The *Guangming Daily* on September 9, 1963, opened a forum in its pages on the subject, proposing that there be competition among various artistic themes and experiments and that the correct approach be proven by free discussion and artistic practice, not by compulsory directives.

Admittedly the cultural establishment qualified its demand for opera reform, but to depict the controversy over this issue as an outright ideological confrontation between the establishment and Jiang Qing and her associates, as would later be maintained in the Cultural Revolution, was not exactly accurate. The cultural establishment, like Jiang Qing's group, advocated opera reform, while at the same time it tried to reconcile the reform with its own bureaucratic interests. Still, there was some conflict between the two groups. The fact that Jiang Qing was listed as a speaker in the discussions of opera reform but that her speeches were not recorded in the public media suggests that, as she later charged, the party bureaucracy refused to give her media coverage. Although some cultural officials were reluctant to reform the Beijing Opera, conflict between them and Jiang

Qing was not so much over the need to reform as over who was to do the reforming. It was more a factional than an ideological struggle. The rebuffs by the cultural officials were not so much because they were unwilling to go along with opera reform as because they resented her interference in their domain.[34]

It would have been easier for Jiang Qing to implement her reforms in Shanghai, where she had facilities and close allies. But as if to challenge the highest cultural authorities—namely Peng Zhen, the central Propaganda Department, and the Ministry of Culture—she sought to carry out her reforms in their bailiwicks in Beijing. In 1963 she gave the script of one of her model works, *The Red Lantern*, to the Beijing Opera Institute, which was attached to the Ministry of Culture, to be adapted into an opera. She also gave the script of a Shanghai drama, *Spark amid the Reeds*, to the First Beijing Opera Troupe attached to the Beijing Party Committee and invited the Shanghai Opera Troupe to Beijing to promote this production. Both of these actions were carried out without the permission of the cultural bureaucracy. With the backing of her prestigious patron, she obviously felt she could interfere at will and flout the regular bureaucratic procedures. Nevertheless, Peng Zhen banned the staging of *Spark amid the Reeds* with the excuse that it was written "crudely," although his objections had more to do with jurisdiction than with artistic quality. As a *People's Daily* editorial of April 1, 1964, declared, "The success of modern drama at the present stage is inseparably linked with the leadership and support of party organizations and the appropriate departments in various localities."[35]

The cultural officials' opposition to Jiang Qing was indirect. Verbally they went along with her reforms, but in actuality they sabotaged them. They did not provide her with a theater in Beijing. They diverted performers to other productions and denied her access to funds. They did not communicate her directives to the relevant organizations. They assigned people to the writing groups adapting her plays who made the heroes less than glorious. She later charged in the Cultural Revolution that the First Beijing Opera Troupe changed her theme and weakened the hero in *Spark amid the Reeds*. Frustrated in Beijing, she returned to Shanghai, where Zhang Chunqiao helped her revise the opera ten times and turn it into a model revolutionary work. Mao's support was signified by the fact that he attended its performance and changed its name to *Shajiabang*. Jiang Qing, who admitted that she could not read music, took part in every stage of

THE RADICAL INTELLECTUALS

the opera's production, direction, performance, dialogue, and music.

Jiang Qing also sought to reform the Central Philharmonic Orchestra. Again without going through the appropriate bureaucratic procedures, in January 1965 she brought the orchestra the score of *Shajiabang* and, invoking Mao's authority, requested that it be turned into a symphony for the masses. She suggested ways to bring out the main themes and orchestrate it with native instruments so that it would be appreciated by the masses. Though publicly Zhou Yang and Lin Mohan supported her suggestions, they ignored them in their plans for the orchestra. They informed her that the orchestra did not have time to work on the opera. Similarly, when she came to rehearsals to offer suggestions for the ballet *The Red Detachment of Women*, Lin Mohan usually countered with opposite suggestions.

The cultural officials' resistance to Jiang Qing's interference reached a climax at the Beijing Opera Festival on Contemporary Themes during June 5–July 31, 1964. This festival, where thirty-seven new operas were performed, may have been convened under Jiang Qing's pressure, and it gave her an opportunity to present a number of her model works. Mao showed his approval by his attendance. Yet from the very first the cultural officials dominated the proceedings. Lu Dingyi's opening remarks and Zhou Yang's usual summation, along with the speeches of Deng Tuo, Lin Mohan, and Mao Dun, were reprinted, while those of Jiang Qing and Zhang Chunqiao were not. The charge was made in the Cultural Revolution that, because the propaganda apparatus dominated the media, it again blocked the publication of her talk. Yet even if it had not, her views would have differed little from those expressed by the cultural establishment.

Peng Zhen's major address at the festival, reprinted in all the major media, enhanced further his stature as a cultural leader, whereas Jiang Qing's role, except for brief mention, went unnoticed. Ironically, Peng's remarks on opera reform in large part coincided with Jiang Qing's. Like Mao, he too objected to traditional Beijing Opera because it extolled feudal society and embellished emperors, ministers, and scholars. Though historical plays that extolled "the people's will" could still be staged, Peng felt that the major focus should be on contemporary revolutionary plays which promoted socialism and struggle. In order to develop such plays, every other kind of drama activity should be put aside. Like Jiang Qing, he urged that greater attention be given to script, directing, acting, singing, scenery, character, and even to every sentence sung or spoken. Writers, directors, and actors should live among the masses in order to reform their ideology and ultimately the opera. Like the radical intellectuals, Peng too criticized people who were still motivated by nonrevolutionary ideas: "Physically speaking, they have already entered socialist society, yet their heads are still in feudal and capitalist society." Whereas the verbal disagreements over opera reform may have been slight, there were indications in Peng's speech that clandestine divisive activities had already led to infighting. He urged that disputes be handled in "a comradely way" and that accusations "be made face to face and not behind someone's back."[36]

Some speakers at the Beijing Opera Festival continued to endorse traditional operas and historical plays as long as they fostered socialism and revolution, and they asked that the traditional techniques used in the contemporary operas retain their original features. But this line also was espoused at the festival by Jiang Qing in her speech, which was finally published during the Cultural Revolution. After proclaiming that the foremost task was to create contemporary revolutionary heroes, she declared, "Historical operas portraying the life and struggle of the people before our party came into being are also needed." Nor did she oppose all traditional operas: "Except for plays about ghosts and those extolling capitulation and betrayal, all good traditional operas can be staged." They must be re-edited and revised, she added, but the cultural officials had put in that proviso as well. They, like she, denounced feudal and ghost plays in their original form. She too wanted to retain the distinctive features of the Beijing Opera, insisting that "the adaptations must be in keeping with the characteristics of the Beijing Opera." Seemingly, the only major difference between her and the cultural officials at the festival was that they saw the theater moving in a positive direction, whereas she saw it stagnating: "In the last few years, the writing of new plays has lagged far behind real life . . . So it is only natural that no good plays are being created."[37]

Some political leaders actively resisted opera reform. In 1963 Chen Yi, for example, had selected Tian Han's subtly critical *Xie Yaohuan* for presentation in Kunming, and until the start of opera reform, he insisted that operas must entertain as well as educate, for "performance designed to serve purely political aims will soon find no audience." In fact, he did not want to revise the old operas at all but wanted to preserve them intact as part of China's heritage. Unlike Mao, his view, shared by other leaders, was that a film, opera, or literary work could not change the course of the revolution: "My bourgeois thoughts cannot be changed by a motion picture, nor can the revolution to which I have devoted myself for so many years be thrown away by a drama."[38] Although Liu Shaoqi did not openly resist opera reform, he felt that the lack of contemporary operas was because "Novels and plays written these days are often not comparable to those of the feudal days. That is why plays portraying emperors, prime ministers and generals . . . still predominate on the stage."[39] These sentiments of China's top leaders, however, were made privately before small groups. They were not part of the public debate.

The public disagreement in 1964 focused on the role of the party organization in opera reform. Before and following the Beijing Opera Festival, the national and Beijing press stressed official as opposed to ad hoc leadership of opera reform. The *Beijing Daily* on May 8 and 11, 1964, attributed the success of the revolutionary opera *Spark amid the Reeds* to party leadership. No mention was made of Jiang Qing's sponsorship. A *Guangming Daily* editorial of June 6, 1964, pointed out that the production of operas on contemporary life was due, "not to the subjective wish of any individual," but to the needs of the times and the party organization.[40]

While the concern of the cultural officials was primarily with intrusion on their turf, that of the writers and artists was more with the rejection of traditional opera. Although several Beijing Opera stars had declared at the festival that they would portray contemporary life, they resisted passively, by agreeing to perform in revised traditional operas or even in new historical plays, but by objecting to perform in new plays on contemporary themes. They were unprepared to exchange the skills of traditional opera for new skills.

Their sentiments were expressed in part by the writer Mao Dun at the festival. Unlike his fellow officials, Mao Dun was concerned not so much with revising traditional operas as with retaining their original form. What Chen Yi said privately, Mao Dun said publicly, though indirectly. He hoped that on the stage of the Beijing Opera, "plays on contemporary themes, traditional items, and new historical plays will coexist."[41] This view was reiterated in the *Guangming Daily* on June 2, 1964: "We should continue to preserve the favorable aspects of traditional art and culture. Those efforts to discard traditional culture or cast away through reform the essence or special quality of traditional drama are harmful to the development of culture and art and not welcomed by the people."[42] Contrary to Jiang Qing's assertion that the masses rejected the old operas, the newspaper insisted that they enjoyed them tremendously.

Despite the obstacles put in Jiang Qing's way, her persistent, active role in opera reform was nevertheless to project her from relative obscurity to prominence in the cultural realm. Her husband's backing was the source of her authority, but her opposition to the cultural establishment and her acquisition of a coterie of followers helped her to build a power base of her own to which those dissatisfied with the existing establishment could look for alternative leadership.

Tao Zhu and Opera Reform

Jiang Qing was not the only one who sought to use opera reform as a means to greater political power. Tao Zhu, first secretary of the Central-South Region, also sought to assert authority in the cultural realm in order to expand his political influence. He had risen from the head of Guangdong Province and a low-ranking member of the Central Committee in 1956 to become a powerful regional leader. Thus, while Jiang Qing in the mid-1960s was struggling to reform the Beijing Opera in the north, Tao Zhu led opera reform in the south, apparently in the expectation that an active role in a movement so dear to Mao might give him the opportunity to advance to the center of power.

Whereas Jiang Qing appears to have been motivated by a mixture of conviction, revenge, and desire for power, Tao Zhu was moved more by power than by ideological considerations. His career demonstrated the limitations of interpreting political behavior in terms of ideological views.[43] Until the 1964 opera reform, he agreed with the approach and priorities of the party bureaucracy, Peng Zhen, and the cultural establishment. In a number of articles in the national media, he more publicly than other regional officials expressed concern with agricultural development, recognized the country's economic limitations, and called for intellectual diversity. In some areas, his ideas even overlapped those of the liberal intellectuals. He articulated an extreme leftist line at the beginning of the Leap, but as that program ran into difficulties, he quickly drew back. Whereas Mao treated the negative aspects of the Leap lightly, Tao Zhu focused attention on them. Mao, for example, said that the mistakes of the Leap, compared to its achievements, were only one finger out of ten.[44] Tao Zhu pointed out in the *People's Daily* on June 3, 1959: "To use nine fingers and one finger to describe the major nature of the success of our work and the secondary nature of our defects and mistakes is no doubt very proper . . . But this is not the same as to talk about nine fingers and not to talk about one; even less does it mean one finger no longer exists (one finger hurts and is of secondary importance, but one finger can make one miserable)." In a phrase that would become a metaphor for the criticism of Mao and the Leap, Tao acknowledged the brilliance of the sun, an allusion to Mao, then added, "But the sun also has black spots."[45]

Not only did Tao Zhu criticize the Leap openly while the party bureaucracy criticized it behind closed doors, but he publicly stated views on intellectual life similar to those of the liberal intellectuals. In a speech before intellectuals on September 28, 1961, he indirectly criticized Mao, observing that the success of socialism was "not the work of one man" but was also dependent on the help of intellectuals who should no longer be treated with insult and disrespect. Like the liberal intellectuals and their literati predecessors, Tao pointed out that the periods when intellectuals were given opportunities to express a variety of viewpoints were the highest points in Chinese history. The Warring States was one such golden age because "learned men aired their views freely and contended with one another." However, the first emperor of the Qin, Shi Huang, eliminated the Hundred Schools of thought, thereby producing stagnation. Tao stressed the need to learn from "this lesson from history."[46] In another speech before intellectuals in the Central-South Region in October 1961, he directly related historical figures to the present: "Even such a feudal character as Prince Mengchang knew that it was necessary to pay great attention to the intellectuals. Without uniting all people with skills, how can we Communists build socialism with success?"[47]

To win the cooperation of the intellectuals, Tao Zhu proposed relaxing oppressive controls. Ideological problems were to be distinguished from political ones and then resolved in a friendly rather than hostile manner. People who were wrongfully accused in the past should be rehabilitated and offered apologies. Because the responsibility did not rest at the lower levels but at the upper levels,

Tao personally apologized, on behalf of the Central-South Region and his Provincial Party Committee, to those who had been wronged. Henceforth the term "bourgeois" intellectual should not be used and ideological criticism should be banned. He agreed with Chen Yi that many Communists were not pure Communists: "I cannot say that I am thoroughly red or even an outstanding Marxist."[48] Therefore, one should not expect such purity of intellectuals. As long as an intellectual supported the party and socialism, Tao believed, then the more expert that person was, the better.

Even Tao Zhu's views on the arts in the early 1960s were directly opposite to those he would enunciate in the 1964 opera reform. In March 1962, he warned against linking creative work too tightly to political policy and argued for giving writers a degree of autonomy: "We must respect the freedom of writers. The pens and ideas of writers are their own and we should allow them to write independently. We must not act like those leaders in some literary and art departments who order other people to write what they think. Let us give less misdirection in creative work, hold writers in respect, and give them full freedom of action." He divided literary works into three kinds: useful, harmful, and harmless. Useful works should be staged, harmful ones should not, and harmless works should be permitted "because they meet the needs of the people to a certain extent."[49] Thus, like the cultural establishment and the liberal intellectuals, Tao felt that it would be beneficial to perform nonpolitical works as a diversion from the traumas of the Leap.

Suddenly in 1963, as Jiang Qing began to take an active role in opera reform, so did Tao Zhu. In March 1963, he advised theatrical companies performing in rural areas to emphasize class character and militancy in their works, although he acknowledged that traditional art, such as the Beijing Opera, should still be allowed. Early in May 1963, Tao ordered the Guangzhou Opera to stage more modern plays. Then, in line with Mao's November 1963 criticism of the performing arts for glorifying the elite, Tao directed writers to present the proletariat instead of the bourgeoisie and to concentrate on class struggle. He also encouraged amateur writers and cadres as well as professional writers to engage in creative work, a move away from his earlier stress on professionalism and toward Jiang Qing's emphasis on a three-way combination of masses, cadres, and writers creating together.

In fact, Tao Zhu in his public statements went even further than

Jiang Qing. While she sanctioned good traditional plays and revolutionary historical plays, he believed that, "For the time being, production of traditional plays will be disallowed; only revolutionary modern plays will now be allowed to be written and produced." He even advocated strong-arm tactics to gain compliance, a threat Jiang Qing had not yet made: "A little bit of coercion will do some good. It may push everyone to do things better and faster."[50] He compared such actions to Qin Shi Huang's burning of books and burying scholars alive, explaining that, although he did not approve of such drastic measures, the ruling class in every dynasty had used firm tactics to impose its will. In addition to the opera, he advocated revolution in all other art forms. His overall attitude was to let bloom only one flower, in contrast to the rich variety of flowers he had recommended in 1961–1962.

On the model of the East China and Beijing festivals, Tao Zhu convened his own drama and opera festival on contemporary opera of the Central-South Region in the summer of 1965. He was as personally involved in this festival as Jiang Qing had been in previous festivals. At the festival, Tao declared that when contemporary revolutionary plays and operas had completely taken over the stage, revised traditional plays could be presented, but only as a sideline. Like Jiang Qing, he stressed that the new type of hero must be an exemplary person. Yet he again wavered in his commitment by asserting, as he had in the early 1960s, that faults as well as achievements should be presented: "It is not only permitted to write about people's shortcomings and criticize them, but it is also the obligation of socialist drama." He even warned against doing away with the distinctive qualities of the opera forms in the process of revolutionizing them: "If their own special characteristics are done away with, the audience will surely disapprove of them."[51]

Despite these reservations, Tao Zhu's assertive role in demanding more radical opera reform than either the cultural officials or even Jiang Qing had demanded succeeded in projecting him prominently onto the national political scene. Mao chose him as the director of the central Propaganda Department in mid-1966 when the old cultural bureaucracy was purged. Like Jiang Qing, Tao's vigorous efforts in opera reform in the preceding period had enhanced his ability to move to the center of power in the Cultural Revolution.

That Tao Zhu, a strong regional official, and Jiang Qing, the party chairman's wife, were able to gain power because of their advocacy

CHINA'S INTELLECTUALS

of an issue dear to the chairman's heart is not unusual in a Communist system. What is unusual is that a group of lower-level, politically inexperienced intellectuals were able to move close to the center of power on the basis of their ideological pronouncements woven into discourses on history, philosophy, and literature. Yet this is a recurring phenomenon in Chinese history. Like their traditional predecessors, the radical intellectuals were able to gain a hearing for their ideas because their views coincided with one of the political factions, specifically the ruler and his confidants, who were involved in an internal power struggle. Even their purposes resonated with those of their qingyi forebears. They sought through their writings to produce an ideological regeneration and to reverse the drift toward what they regarded as bureaucratism and ideological laxity. As their predecessors spewed forth memorials and communications, they spewed forth articles in newspapers and journals to arouse public opinion and alert the leadership to these dangers. Thus, this group of radicals emerged in the period just prior to the Cultural Revolution as a body to be reckoned with.

4

THE PARTY RECTIFICATION OF 1964-1965

Although Mao had withdrawn from day-to-day political activity because of the Great Leap debacle, this did not diminish his ability to intervene on important questions. As the economy gradually improved owing to the party's use of such pragmatic practices as material incentives, return of small plots to peasants, and reliance on technical expertise, Mao reasserted himself in the areas of his major concern. In agriculture, he sought to halt the trend toward "capitalism" the term used to describe the increasing inequalities that had resulted from the party's use of material incentives in order to rejuvenate the countryside. In culture, he sought to reverse the trend toward "revisionism" or ideological erosion and the reemergence of an intellectual elite that had resulted from the party's effort to win the cooperation of the intellectuals. In 1963 the Socialist Education Movement was launched to curb these by-products of the party's rehabilitation of the economy.

Mao specifically blamed the development of revi-

CHINA'S INTELLECTUALS

sionism on the cultural establishment. Although he did not openly accuse it of allowing criticism of his policies, he publicly charged it with succumbing to bureaucratism, which he believed was undermining the revolutionary character of the party. On December 12, 1963, he declared, "In many departments [of art] very little has been achieved so far in socialist transformation. The 'dead' still dominate . . . The social and economic base has changed, but the arts as part of the superstructure which serves this base still remain a serious problem. Hence we should proceed with the investigation and study and attend to this matter in earnest. Isn't it absurd that many Communists are enthusiastic about promoting feudal and capitalistic art, but not socialist art?"[1] The following day he called some party leaders "conservative, arrogant, and complacent."[2] They talked only of their achievements and either failed to admit their shortcomings or dealt with them superficially. Like Zhou Yang, Mao used the phrase "one divides into two," but applied it to the need to distinguish among achievements and shortcomings. What disturbed him was that the leaders had not acknowledged or remedied the bureaucratism he had pointed out.

Most revealing of Mao's feelings at this time were his poems, illusive, figurative phrases of which often expressed political sentiments. Ten poems, written over a period of fourteen years, were published on January 4, 1964, with great fanfare in all the major newspapers and journals. Mao, like his critics, probably chose this traditional, indirect method of criticism because he was not yet ready to seek an open confrontation with the intellectuals or their political protectors. The allusions in his poems most likely were understood by only a small group. At the time of publication, most of them were interpreted both by party officials and by scholars as implicit attacks on Soviet revisionism. From hindsight, it seems probable that they were also implicit attacks on China's cultural officials. But since the principal interpreters of the poems came from Zhou Yang's domain of the central Propaganda Department and the Ministry of Culture, they naturally deflected criticism from themselves and aimed it at the Soviets. Given the poems' subtlety and abstruseness, they were open to a wide range of interpretation, so that within certain limits the commentator could mold his interpretation to his needs.

The poem that appears directed more at Mao's internal than his external enemies is "Reply to Comrade Guo Moruo," written in January 1963:

> In this small globe, there are several flies crashing against the wall.
> They hum in a bitter tune and sob once and again.
> The ants taking their abode inside the ash tree claim their place is a large kingdom.
> It is not easy for the ants to take a tree.
> The direct Westerly winds tear down the leaves and pass Changan.
> Howling like whizzing arrows,
> So many things happen; they happen always fast.
> The earth is revolving; the time is too short.
> Ten thousand years is too long; we only seize the morning and the evening.
> The four seas are in a fury and the clouds and water in a rage.
> The five continents are in eruption under strong gales and loud thunder.
> It is necessary to wipe out all harmful insects to become invincible.[3]

The description of the "flies" was apparently a variation on the Tang writer Han Yu's poem that sarcastically compared officials over-reaching themselves to "mayflies who attempt to shake the giant tree." The "flies" could just as well refer to those who disagreed with Mao in his own party as to the revisionists in the Soviet Union. Flies, ants, and insects were terms used in traditional China to chide scholar-bureaucrats. Even more relevant, Lu Xun had used "flies" in the 1930s to refer specifically to Zhou Yang, Yang Hansheng, Tian Han, and Xia Yan when they were in conflict with him over his refusal to endorse wholeheartedly the party's United Front cultural policy. Since the party had posthumously made Lu Xun a hero, it is likely that Mao used the term to refer to those very same officials with whom he himself was now in conflict. "The flies crashing against the wall" could refer to those who vainly hit at Mao's thought. "They hum in a bitter tune and sob once and again" may allude to the complaints of the liberal intellectuals and party bureaucracy over the Leap. "The ants claim . . . a large kingdom" may signify the "independent kingdom" that Mao later charged Peng Zhen, head of the Beijing Party Committee, had set up in his domain, "the ash tree." Yet Mao warned that "Flies cannot shake a tree," a phrase later used repeatedly to describe the attempts of Lu Dingyi, Peng Zhen, Zhou Yang, and others to subvert Mao's policies.

"The direct Westerly winds tear down the leaves" may mean that Western influence, Soviet revisionism, or anti-Maoist ideas would destroy the fruits of revolution, and "pass Changan" may refer to the decline of the capital city of the Tang dynasty, a fate that awaited Beijing, the capital of the Chinese revolution. In the last five lines Mao expressed his sense of urgency that the revolution be continued and that internal as well as external subversion be stopped. If the revolution, which he equated with himself, was to succeed, then "all insects" must be squashed.

In addition to his poetry, Mao's formal speeches of early 1964 indicated an imminent shakeup in the cultural realm. On February 13, 1964, he belittled educational achievements: "Throughout history, very few of those who came in first in the imperial examinations have achieved great fame." He pointed out that the only two Ming emperors who had governed well were barely literate. He disparaged the role of intellectuals in Chinese history, saying of the sixteenth century reign of Jiajing, the same emperor to whom Hai Rui addressed his most critical memorials, that "when the intellectuals had power, things were in a bad state, the country was in disorder . . . It is evident that to read too many books is harmful."[4] Mao ordered that "actors, poets, dramatists, and writers" be "driven out of the cities" and government offices and periodically sent in groups to work in villages and factories. He even threatened harsh sanctions: "Only when they go down will they be fed."[5]

Although Mao's words called for a major rectification of the cultural realm, either the cultural officials did not understand, misinterpreted, or chose to ignore his wishes, for they responded only superficially in the early months of 1964. Although they did send groups of intellectuals, cultural cadres, and students to the countryside and factories to do manual labor, they disregarded Mao's instructions to implement an ideological struggle in their domain and investigate their own departments. Implicitly rejecting Mao's main criticism of them for obstructing the revolution, they accepted his lesser charge of not carrying out his cultural policies energetically enough.

THE PARTY RECTIFICATION

Zhou Yang in Janauary 1964 conceded the failure of cultural offi-cials "on some occasions to exercise a tight enough grip on work" and "to make enough effort in cultivating . . . the new things of so-cialism."[6] But his criticism of his department and his colleagues was half-hearted. While criticizing the ghost opera *Li Huiniang* as "anti-socialist in feeling," he declared that its author, Meng Chao, was not antisocialist. Moreover, he defended Tian Han's controversial play *Xie Yaohuan* on the ground that it was not reactionary but rather re-vealed "dissatisfaction with reality."[7] The mistakes of the Ministry of Culture were not necessarily mistakes of policy, as Mao had charged, but merely "of understanding."[8] Zhou's resistance to Mao's demand for ideological struggle in the cultural realm, the super-structure, may have been bolstered by the knowledge that Liu Shaoqi in 1963 had enunciated a view of the superstructure diametri-cally opposed to Mao's. Whereas Mao believed that the superstruc-ture lagged behind changes in the economic base, Liu believed that "the superstucture corresponds to the economic base these days."[9] Hence, Zhou had official support for his weak response to Mao's summons to rectify the cultural arena.

With the cultural officials sidestepping his orders, Mao on June 27, 1964, issued a more emphatic and accusatory directive. Again his anger was directed not so much at the liberal intellectuals as at the cultural bureaucracy which allowed them to express dissident views. He said of the party's cultural organs, "In the last fifteen years, these associations, most of their publications (it is said a few are good), and by and large the people in them (that is not everybody) have not carried out the policies of the party." Mao charged the cultural offi-cials with acting like "high and mighty" bureaucrats who did not re-spond to the needs of the masses, a charge that the liberal intellec-tuals had directed at him. They had "slid right down to the brink of revisionism" and needed to "remold themselves in real earnest."[10] Mao expressed similar sentiments on July 5, 1964, to his nephew, Mao Yuanxin, complaining that in China, as in the Soviet Union, there were cases "in which political power is in the grip of the bour-geoisie . . . Who is leading the Ministry of Culture? The cinema and theater are entirely in their service and not in the service of the ma-jority of the people."[11] In no way could the cultural officials continue to misinterpret Mao's wishes to carry out ideological struggle in their domain.

Finally in the summer of 1964, a rectification was launched in the cultural realm by the cultural officials. They were responding to Mao's pressure, but they also were concerned with the deterioration of ideological discipline. While some of the liberal intellectuals continued to press for a relaxation as in 1961–1962, the party bureaucracy sought to tighten controls. They had allowed the intellectuals to criticize the Leap only for practical reasons, not because they themselves advocated intellectual freedom. Now that economic recovery was underway, too much criticism, they feared, might be just as disruptive to orderly development as had been Jiang Qing's efforts to circumvent regular party procedures. The cultural officials diverged from Mao not so much on the need to reimpose tighter controls as on how to do it. Whereas Mao had called for a rectification that would reach the top levels of the party cultural establishment, the officials carried out a rectification that touched superficially only a very small number of the "high and mighty" cultural officials whom Mao had denounced.

The rectification, carried out from June 1964 to the spring of 1965 was implemented by the usual managers of such ideological remolding campaigns—officials in the central Propaganda Department, the Ministry of Culture, and the Beijing Party Committee. In the spring of 1964 the party Secretariat had already set up a high-level task force, known as the Group of Five, to coordinate the cultural reform. It was headed by Peng Zhen, with the help of Lu Dingyi; Kang Sheng; Yang Shangkun, director of the Secretariat office; and Wu Lengxi, editor-in-chief of the *People's Daily* and director of the New China News Agency. The only one of the group close to Jiang Qing and her radical associates was Kang Sheng. The rest were identified with the cultural establishment. Kang Sheng helped to orchestrate the rectification, and the radical intellectuals wrote numerous articles, but as in past rectifications, this one was directed by the cultural bureaucrats.

Ever since Lin Biao replaced Peng Dehuai as head of the army in 1959, the army had been increasingly conspicuous in cultural activities. In contrast to the party's cultural organs, the army carried out in its sphere the ideological revitalizaton that Mao called for. In the early 1960s, it established musical, literary, and art groups that stressed class struggle. Its cultural activities resembled Jiang Qing's efforts to transform opera, music, and dance. Lin Biao and Jiang Qing probably collaborated on these early efforts to revolutionize Chinese culture. Still, these army groups were only a sideshow to the party's cultural activities. To reinfuse the bureaucracy with Mao's thought, the army's political officers also maneuvered into the cultural, propaganda, and educational bureaus, as well as into the economic and administrative bureaus. However, since here they were under the control not of the General Political Department of the army but of the party's Central Committee, their effect was limited. The party leadership was very much in charge of the rectification, which it was determined to keep from exploding into a mass movement that could be turned against itself. Actually, the party's rectification was not one hard-hitting campaign but a series of diffuse minicampaigns against a number of intellectuals and officials just below the top echelon of the cultural hierarchy.

The Yang Xianzhen Campaign

In an apparent effort to divert attention from themselves, the cultural officials chose as their foremost target an intellectual outside their inner circle. He was Yang Xianzhen, a Central Committee member and leading Marxist theoretician. Unlike the officials in the Propaganda Department, Yang had spent twenty years in the Soviet Union, where in the 1920s he studied at the University of Toilers in Moscow and in the 1930s was head of the Chinese Department of the Soviet Foreign Languages Institute. Given the Chinese regime's increasingly anti-Soviet invective since its break with the Soviet Union in 1960, Yang was a convenient target. More important, he presented concepts that were in opposition to Mao's stress on class struggle.

On May 29, 1964, in the *Guangming Daily*, two of Yang Xianzhen's students, interpreted the phrase "one divides into two" differently from Mao or even from Zhou Yang.[12] Although they too held that everything was composed of opposites, they also stressed, much more emphatically than Mao, that these opposites were united by dependence as well as by conflict. Thus, the corollary "two unites into one" was also valid, which undermined the notion of struggle. To a certain extent, the concept of the unity of opposites was a theoretical restatement of Zhou Gucheng's "spirit of the age" and Wu Han's "universal ethics." When Yang's students applied their theory in a political context, their rejection of revolutionary struggle for present-day China was even clearer. The method of "one divides into two" should be used in achieving power, but once power had

CHINA'S INTELLECTUALS

been attained and the next move was to socialist construction, then the "two unites into one" approach should come into play. The students thus urged a period of moderation and reconciliation, rather than the continued struggle and polarization that Mao now advocated.

Despite the fact that Yang Xianzhen's students recommended an opposite approach to Mao's, their article did not at first cause a stir outside of the Higher Party School where they were studying. A rejoinder, published on June 5 in the *Guangming Daily* and charging that the two students had repudiated class struggle, drew little support. In fact, its author, Xiong Qing, was chastised a week later in the *Guangming Daily* for finding any difference between "one into two" and "two into one." This corollary meant the same as the proposition. The debate was essentially philosophical, similar to the academic debates of 1963.

However, with the launching of the party's rectification in early July, two other students at the Higher Party School charged in the party's paper *People's Daily* on July 17 that the two student writers were merely front men for their teacher Yang Xianzhen, who was the real author.[13] Their attack initiated a campaign against Yang that was carried on in the major media, the party's political schools, universities, and research institutes. It had overtones of the 1954 criticism of the respected scholar Yu Pingbo for his study of *The Dream of the Red Chamber*. As then, the initial attack was carried out by two unknowns using a myriad of quotes from Marxism-Leninism to denigrate the work of a well-known intellectual. Whereas Yang's students were not politically or academically influential enough to serve as a negative example to others, Yang was a prominent Marxist theorist.

Yang Xianzhen was apparently chosen for factional reasons as well. He had had conflicts with Chen Boda in the 1950s when Chen was vice-president of the Higher Party School, then known as the Marxist-Leninist Institute. However, Yang's main public critic in 1964 was another noted ideological theorist and a member of the cultural establishment, Ai Siqi, with whom he also had conflicts. Ai had taken over Yang's position as president of the Higher Party School in early 1961, after Yang had been labeled a "rightist" and demoted to director of the school's Philosophical Educational Research Bureau. With the removal of the "rightest" label in 1962, Yang once more became president of the school, but in 1963 he again stepped down, this time to the vice-presidency. Yang's ups and downs in the school's hierarchy signified not only the ideological disagreements but also the personal conflicts among China's major theorists.

Although Yang Xianzhen's Soviet background must also have played a role in his selection, the campaign against him was concerned more with countering the desire for compromise expressed in the "two into one" slogan than with exposing his Soviet connections. He was attacked primarily on the basis of his lecture notes of the early 1960s in which, in an example of the historical-mindedness of even China's Soviet-trained intellectuals, he traced the concept of "one into two/two into one" to Chinese tradition. He pointed to the Ming scholar Fang Yizhi's description of the underlying principle of the cosmos as one of opposites—*yin* and *yang*, day and night, sadness and happiness—which did not work in opposition to each other, but in harmony. He cited such words in the Chinese language as "thing" (*dongxi*), made up of the complementary words "east" and "west," or the word for "breathing" (*huxi*), made up of the complementary words "inhale" and "exhale." He also found the harmony of opposites in Chinese philosophical concepts, like Lao Zi's definition of origin, which was composed of the words "existence" and "nonexistence." Hence, Yang concluded, "two into one," or complementary opposites, were an integral part of China's cultural heritage.

Although Mao had acknowledged the temporary union of opposites, he emphasized that the transformation of one force by another in an endless struggle was more fundamental than was their union. Yang Xianzhen emphasized that union did not dissolve the opposites and that each remained separate, held together by mutual need. Consequently, in contrast to Mao, Yang advocated seeking a common ground between opposing ideologies while allowing differences to remain. Again he found the basis for his view in Chinese tradition, where the contrasting philosophies of Confucianism and Daoism coexisted without transforming each other. They lived together in a spirit of syncretism. Though considered a traditional Marxist, Yang, through this concept, "Sinocized" the Marxist dialectic. Instead of thesis and antithesis producing a synthesis, he saw thesis and antithesis producing a syncretism.

Yang Xiazhen's view of Chinese civilization implied a toleration of diversity of viewpoints and classes. In practice, this view led him to oppose full-scale collectivization. In a series of unpublished articles written in 1955 during the collectivization drive, he proposed a composite economy where collective ownership would exist together with individual peasant ownership. He called for a balanced, interrelated development of the economy based on five kinds of structures, ranging from collective to private ownership, which were complementary rather than antagonistic to one another.

Although there was little mention of the Soviet Union in Yang Xianzhen's works, his ideas were attributed in 1964 to Soviet revisionist influence. His critics called him a disciple of such unorthodox Marxists as Eduard Bernstein, Georgi Plekhanov, and Nikolai Bukharin. Yang's theory of "two into one" was traced directly to the Deborin school of philosophy which had developed in the Soviet Union in the late 1920s. Its founder, Abram Deborin, was a Menshevik before the Russian Revolution, a party member after. His view that thesis and antithesis "are not mutually exclusive opposites but are mutually conciliatory opposites" was imputed to Yang.[14] Stalin considered Deborin's theory an effort to conciliate the rich peasants and the bourgeoisie in the late 1920s and 1930s. Whether or not Yang was directly influenced by Deborin, it is likely that the Chinese regime shared a concern similar to Stalin's about Yang's ideas.

Another aim of the campaign against Yang Xianzhen was to stifle criticism of the Leap, still echoing in 1964. During the Leap, Yang had argued that no one, no matter how omniscient, could afford to disregard the inexorable laws of history or oppose his will to the built-in limitations of the economic realities. Implicit in Yang's argument was the Marxist orthodoxy that a society must go through economic stages of development and could not "leap" into communism as Mao tried to do in the Leap. Since China was an economically backward country, radical policies were counterproductive because they were not in accord with China's reality. In 1958 after a visit to the countryside, Yang questioned the revolutionary nature of Chinese society, particularly of the Chinese peasants. He warned that "abandonment of objective laws and one-sided discussion of subjective function means metaphysics, and this can only be changed into the theory of sole obedience to the will."[15] Although initially he was stopped from publishing this article, a revised version eventually came out. Yang was not a member of the liberal intellectuals' cotery, but his protest similarly pointed out the discrepancy between Mao's revolutionary ideals and the reality of nonrevolutionary peasants.

Yang Xianzhen's view of the economy was quite different from Mao's, which gave validity to the party's charge that Yang's objections to Mao's policies resembled Bukharin's objections to Stalin's Five-Year Plan. Both Yang and Bukharin favored an economy in which socialism and capitalism were developed side-by-side for a period of time. In an unpublished article, written in the midst of collectivization in 1955, Yang argued that China still had a "semisocialist system of ownership which allows some ownership to individual peasants." Those who did not understand this reality did not know "where the food they eat comes from."[16] Nor did they understand the role of the individual peasant in providing certain needs in a socialist society. Yang believed that the ideology which derived from this composite economic base should serve not one single economic group but a variety of groups. Otherwise its programs would not be in accord with the people for whom they were created. Like Bukharin, Yang believed that a single economic system would evolve gradually as the socialist economy expanded and the capitalist economy contracted. But at present, the population was not ready for a sudden transformation. To Yang, ideology and its accompanying programs must respond to existing needs, not to future visions.

Yang Xianzhen's major critic, Ai Siqi, did not specifically criticize his economic views but rather chastised him for preaching moderation of revolutionary struggle. Hinting at an imminent attack on party colleagues who sought moderation, Ai pointed out that the line dividing "one into two" is "not only between friend and foe but also among friends—distinguishing the closest friends from the vacillating ones."[17] He warned that if the party tolerated those who vacillated, socialism would never be achieved. Whereas Yang regarded Mao's approach as illusory, Ai regarded Yang's search for stability and harmony as illusory: "In reality, the identity between opposites is only a conditional identity of opposites that ceaselessly struggle against each other."[18] Yang's approach, Ai charged, undermined the need for ideological remolding and impeded the struggle necessary to move toward communism.

Concomitantly, the rectification attacked Yang Xianzhen's traditional Marxist view that policy must conform to the unfolding stages of history in order to create the conditions for socialism. Guan Feng and his radical colleagues had sporadically criticized this view during the Leap and did so again in 1964.[19] Using a number of pseudonyms, they participated prominently in attacking Yang on this question as well as on "two into one," but their arguments did not differ from the standard party line as represented by Ai Siqi. The discussion resonated with earlier ideological debates in the West between those who believed in the existence of immutable laws of history and those who believed in man's ability to shape his own history. At the beginning of the twentieth century the Russian theorist Plekhanov and other orthodox Marxists argued the doctrine of technological–economic causation, in opposition to Lenin who did not share their faith that impersonal historical forces would produce communism. Plekhanov asserted that the Promethean will could not change the course of history or the limits imposed by material existence, to which Lenin replied that man's function was not only to understand the objective world but more important to change it. In 1964, Yang was associated with Plekhanov's position, and Mao with Lenin's. In May 1963, for example, Mao had stated that once ideas "are grasped by the masses, these ideas turn into a material force which changes society and changes the world." The question of whether one correctly discerns the laws of the objective world is not known until "they are applied in practice."[20] Thus, Mao insisted, one must act in order to know if one's views accurately reflect the objective world.

In contrast to this belief that ideas depended on action, Yang Xianzhen was charged with believing that ideas were only a passive reflection of material progress. He was attacked for rejecting subjective initiative and revolutionary spirit. But this was an unfair polarization of his views, for as late as January 1964 he had said, "The revolutionary spirit alone without proper understanding of the necessary nature of objective things will not help us to develop subjective initiative."[21] Hence, he did not reject the revolutionary spirit but maintained that it had to be combined with a sober respect for objective limitations. Undoubtedly, Yang and members of the party hierarchy who shared his views felt they were acting in good Leninist, as well as Marxist, fashion. After all, Lenin's emphasis on the subjective factor and revolutionary will was accompanied by a genuine effort to comprehend "objective reality" accurately.

Most criticisms of Yang Xianzhen steered a middle course. A number denounced Yang's obsession with economic limitations and objective laws, but they did not wholeheartedly endorse the transformation of existence by revolutionary consciousness and practice. However, the criticisms in the media dominated respectively by the liberal and radical intellectuals emphasized the more polarized positions. The Beijing Party Committee's journal *Front Line*, edited by Deng Tuo, stressed the technological–economic causation view, contending that objective laws unfolded irrespective of man's subjective will. As one piece pointed out, "The objective truth, that capitalism will of necessity die, does not change with the will of any particular class or individual."[22] By contrast, the Shanghai newspaper *Wenhui Bao*, under the jurisdiction of the Shanghai Propaganda Department, emphasized the view that consciousness was the main revolutionary force. It decried Yang Xianzhen's downgrading of man's subjective will: "He says something about the leap from matter to spirit and nothing about the leap from spirit to matter. He explains that one's consciousness can reflect the objective being, but avoids explaining that one's consciousness may in turn transform the objective being."[23] Yang's approach maintained the status quo, for in asking people "to cast away so-called 'illusions' and adapt themselves to 'nature,' " Yang was asking people "to come to terms with the present."[24] Yang was charged with saying, "It is 'leftist' deviation to act before you acquire the necessary conditions."[25] This position, *Wenhui Bao* countered, detracted from man's role in revolution, for at some times objective conditions played a major role, but at other times conscious actions were decisive.

Although the use of specific journals to state opposing views implied a factional struggle, the debate at this time was primarily an ideological one between the orthodox Marxist belief in sequential stages in the development to communism and the voluntarist belief in the power of the will to leap into communism. For the most part, the party bureaucracy combined both approaches. As a result, Yang was removed once again from his positon as vice-president of the Higher Party School in 1964, to be replaced by his old rival Ai Siqi, but Yang was not denounced with the fervor and epithets that had been meted out to intellectual targets in previous campaigns. Most of the criticism was more academic than political, more balanced than polemical.

The Middle Man Campaign

As Yang Xianzhen's ideological views had criticized Mao for projecting future utopias rather than dealing with present realities, so Shao Quanlin's literary theory of the peasant as a middle man wavering between the old and new societies implied that Mao's revolutionary policies were contrary to the peasants' real needs. Shao's concern with the peasants was not just an isolated, temporary response to the Leap but an ongoing concern of certain intellectuals. In June 1964, for example, a number of articles in the *People's Daily* contended that the peasant's goal was not to establish a new egalitarian society but to improve his own livelihood.[26]

The fact that the Socialist Education Movement was directed against vacillating, capitalist-oriented peasants suggests that Shao and others were sketching a realistic picture. However, the stated purpose of the campaign launched against Shao and the fictional portrayals of the middle man in the summer of 1964 was to deny the accuracy of this picture. Instead of confronting the issue, the regime charged that those who depicted the middle man were out of touch with the peasantry. Thus Zhao Shuli, Zhou Libo, Ma Feng, and other fiction writers were criticized for portraying vacillating, ambivalent peasant characters, but Shao was the main target. The choice of someone like Shao, high in the cultural hierarchy, appears to have been made by the hierarchy itself in order to hold onto its power. Narrowing the attack to one important official protected his colleagues, particularly Zhou Yang. Thus Shao became the scapegoat for the "failings" of the cultural establishment.

Zhou Yang personally supervised the campaign against Shao. Zhou also revised a number of the criticisms to limit the discussion to literary matters and keep it away from political matters. The campaign quickly moved from the negative stage of denouncing Shao and the middle man to the positive stage of defining new behavior patterns, values, and beliefs for a new socialist man. In contrast to Shao's image of the peasant as suspicious of the revolution, riddled with conflicts, and desirous of material benefits, the regime depicted the peasant as a hero of unstinting self-sacrifice and abiding faith in the revolution.

Despite Zhou Yang's efforts to control the campaign, the radical intellectuals, most prominently Yao Wenyuan, injected themselves into the discussion. Their public views at this time did not differ markedly from those of the cultural establishment. Yao, for example, followed the standard Maoist line that the peasants were conscious revolutionaries, although he admitted that the old ways of life were still pervasive. Yet to write about the majority of peasants, he argued, would require "a fundamental exclusion and suppression of new things which are germinating or developing, and an extension of protection to old things which superficially still exist extensively."[27]

He therefore advised writers not to depict the majority but to portray the few "heroic" peasants, thereby "enlightening and encouraging the people."[28]

Several heroic figures were introduced in the period of rectification to contrast with the middle man. The shift from the nonheroic characters of the late 1950s and early 1960s to the heroic figures of the mid-1960s reflected a shift from the recognition of human and economic limitations to the belief that self-sacrificing people could overcome all obstacles. Literary protagonists changed from ordinary peasants and workers who were ambiguous about the revolution to "ordinary" heroes, usually from the army, who were unequivocally committed to Maoist principles. There was a corresponding move away from the conventional literary forms of the novel and short story, written by individual writers, to the more controllable semi-fictional diary, presented almost as myth and written by committees. Less and less was published by older established writers and more and more by anonymous groups, attached primarily to the army, an indication of the increasing intrusion of the army into the cultural realm.

The most prominent of this genre was *The Diary of Lei Feng*, which appeared early in 1963 and immediately became the source of a "Learn from Lei Feng Movement" to indoctrinate the nation in Maoist values. By late 1964 and early 1965 Lei Feng's diary had taken on the dimensions of a religious parable. Yet Lei was not a conventional religious or mythical figure. He had no extraordinary talents, nor did he perform any extraordinary feats. He led an obscure, unpretentious life and died, not in a struggle for his convictions, but by accident when a pole fell on his head. Though he was ordinary, he was indispensable to the revolution because he was unswerving in his commitment.

As opposed to the middle man, Lei Feng was a reliable figure of emulation. His early life consisted of one tragedy after another. Members of his family had been hounded to death by the Japanese, Guomindang, landlords, poverty, disease and suicide. When the army liberated his province and he discovered Mao, Lei's life, unlike that of the middle man, completely changed. He no longer suffered but devoted himself to building a new society. Most important, he embodied the qualities that Mao considered essential for the continuation of the revolution: selflessness, persistence, courage, frugality, discipline, and altruism. His activities were motivated not by the desire to make money or to rise in the official hierarchy but by a devotion to the revolution and other people. This ordinary yet extraordinary man was the model by which the entire nation was to measure itself.

Although Lei Feng was the embodiment of Mao's thought, he also had the qualities that the party bureaucracy considered important. As compared with later politicized models, Lei represented a compromise between the views of Liu Shaoqi and Mao. He embodied technical proficiency as well as political consciousness, whereas later models possessed only the second quality. When Lei drove a truck, he wanted to learn how it ran. At one point, he explained, "How fine it will be when the whole vastness of China's countryside is mechanized!"[29] He also represented the Liuist emphasis on discipline in his description of himself as "a screw in the machine."

With a few exceptions, the works of this mythical diary genre had neither characterization nor plot. Though Mao believed in struggle, there was none in these stories. The heroes had no external enemies to fight and few emotions to overcome. Such "bourgeois" sentiments as subjectivism, egoism, selfishness, competition, and individualism, which Shao Quanlin talked about, were suppressed. Unlike the Western hero, or even the earlier Chinese Communist hero, the protagonist did not face any great trials or overwhelming challenges. Nor did he win any decisive victories over himself, as the fictional middle man nonhero finally did. His actions were ordinary, almost pedestrian. These works could not even be called morality plays because there were no negative forces or emotions to act as a foil for the heroes. Whereas the middle man character was in the tradition of May Fourth literature, these "revolutionary heroes," obsessed with disinterested, virtuous conduct, were more like the Confucian literati. Effective propaganda was the regime's criterion for evaluating work, but literature could not move the reader if the world it depicted did not correspond in some way to the reader's perception of reality. Although Lei Feng was supposedly ordinary, his unflaggingly virtuous conduct could not strike a responsive chord in an ordinary reader. Even more important, the ordinary Chinese peasant could identify more readily with the ambivalent peasants in Zhao Shuli's stories than with the paragon soldier-peasant Lei Feng.

The campaign against the middle man carried over into the cinema. Not only had the cinema portrayed nonheroic protagonists, particularly in films based on the literary works of the May Fourth

THE PARTY RECTIFICATION

writers, but it was directed by the playwright-officials Xia Yan and Yang Hansheng, who had antagonized Jiang Qing in the 1930s. In 1964 she tried to insert herself into films as into the opera by pointing out to Lu Dingyi and Zhou Yang a number of films, several of them associated with her old enemies, which she claimed Mao wanted repudiated.

Generally, however, the rectification of the cinema was conducted under the supervision of the central Propaganda Department and was restrained and limited. The film that received the most attention was *The Lin Family Shop*, based on the Mao Dun story and adapted for the screen by Xia Yan. Though well received when it had first been shown in 1959, it was criticized in 1964 because the principal antagonist's relationships were not based on sharp class conflict. And although the story had originally been commended for showing the difficulties of the petty bourgeoisie and gaining their support for the revolution, it was now regarded as inappropriate because of its portrayal of cooperation between workers and bourgeoisie.

Besides *The Lin Family Shop*, only a few other films were criticized, such as *Early Spring in February* and *Jiangnan in the North*, based on a screenplay by Yang Hansheng. In contrast to the large-scale campaign against the film *The Story of Wu Xun* in the early 1950s, there were no mass campaigns or large-scale meetings to repudiate the films. Instead, there were bland critiques by colleagues closely connected with the people who had written and produced the films. A few criticisms, however, hinted at the kinds of attack that would later pour down on the May Fourth writers. One, for example, asserted that Xia Yan represented the type of intellectuals who, though party members, still had "a bourgeois realm hidden deep in their hearts."[30] Moreover, it was charged that their bourgeois ideas acted as a corrosive influence on the young.

A writer whose works were regarded as particularly harmful to the young was Ouyang Shan. One of the few May Fourth writers to publish novels after 1949, he wrote two historical novels on the revolution—*Three-Family Lane* in 1959, and *Bitter Struggle* in 1962—which were serialized in the Guangzhou newspaper *Yangcheng Evening News* (*Yangcheng Wan Bao*). He also had a long association with the cultural establishment dating from the 1930s. He was deputy director of the Guangdong Propaganda Department and chairman of the Guangdong Federation of Literature and Art and the Guangzhou branch of the Chinese Writers Union. Although his novels were at first praised, they too came to be criticized for fostering indeterminate views on the class struggle. Mao's criticism of novels at the Tenth Plenum for inciting antirevolutionary sentiments may have been directed at Ouyang's works, whose popularity was indicated by their sale of over a million copies, especially to the young.

Ouyang Shan's critics were especially concerned that his descriptions of romantic love diverted the youth from a revolutionary commitment. There were tortuous discussions in 1964 about the treatment of love in literary works. Yao Wenyuan denigrated the literature of romantic love because it distracted youth from their revolutionary tasks. Yet most of the criticism of Ouyang's "naturalistic" depiction of romantic feelings took a middle position, acknowledging that a man and a woman engaged in the revolution might fall in love as he described, but concerned that his depiction of passion in such detail overshadowed the revolutionary struggle. According to one critic, when revolution and love conflicted, it was "inadmissible" for a revolutionary to assume "a 'love first' attitude at the expense of the revolutionary interests."[31] As a result, Ouyang was sent to the countryside in September 1964 to reform himself through labor, although he spent most of the time in his room writing.

The rectification also renewed the criticism of ghost plays. When ghost plays had been banned in 1963, owing to pressure from Jiang Qing, cultural officials had tried to protect themselves from having permitted the performances. Li Xifan, for example, a member of Zhou Yang's cohort, reiterated Mao's dictum that selective traditions could be inherited and explained that certain traditional ghost plays had instilled a legitimate hatred of oppression.[32] Another literary critic pointed out that the ruled classes could use ghost plays "to expose the crimes of their oppressors and encourage the determination of the people to struggle against the ruling class."[33]

Despite such official support, Jiang Qing initiated criticism of the essay by Liao Mosha, written in 1961 to defend ghost plays, specifically Li Huiniang, the ghost play by his fellow May Fourth writer, Meng Chao. However it was not until the 1964 rectification that Liao repudiated his prior belief that ghost plays inspired resistance to oppression and agreed that the superstitions they spread were "a deceptive means used by the exploiting class to benumb the people."[34] Nevertheless, Liao continued to defend Meng's play for airing dissatisfaction with present-day reality. Because of Liao's partial self-criticism, the attacks on him were restricted to his views on ghost plays and he was not attacked personally. No mention was made of his participation in the Three-Family Village.

The Feng Ding Campaign

Concern about the ideological corruption of youth, touched upon in most of the criticisms, became the central focus of an attack on Feng Ding. Like Yang Xianzhen, Feng Ding was a Soviet-trained Marxist theorist. He was a professor of philosophy at Beijing University and chairman of the Beijing Philosophical Society. In 1963, he had been put in charge of compiling materials on Communist theory for university texts. Since Feng's work had a special appeal to educated youth, his choice as a target reflected the leadership's concern with the ideological commitment of the next generation of leaders. Mao in particular had expressed anxiety about the waning revolutionary spirit among youth and had resolved to prevent the next generation from following the "revisionist" road of the Soviet Union. Alarmed lest "imperialist prophets" were pinning their hopes on a less revolutionary third or fourth generation of the Chinese Communist leaders, Mao turned his attention to "the training and upbringing of successors to the revolutionary cause."[35] Criticism of Feng Ding was used to infuse the succeeding generation with revolutionary commitment.

As in the campaign against Yang Xianzhen, the one against Feng Ding followed the familiar pattern of a young activist student attacking a highly placed member of the intellectual establishment for ideological unorthodoxy. Also as in former attacks, the criticism of Feng was initially rejected by the press, but was subsequently published throughout the country. Again this movement was under the control of the central Propaganda Department.

Also as in the attack on Shao Quanlin, Feng Ding's values were contrasted with the new socialist values that the regime sought to instill. In particular, his view of happiness was presented as diametrically opposed to the "happiness" qua self-sacrifice that the regime promulgated. In 1955 Feng wrote, "If happiness means a normal life, then we can have it only when we have peace and no war, when we have good food to eat, fine clothes to wear, and a large and clean house in which to live, and when love and harmony prevail among husband and wife, parents and child."[36] He considered happiness a personal matter, which should be determined by the individual not the state. In the 1961 edition of "The Historical Task of the Working Class," he wrote, "One may like to eat this or that kind of food, to wear this or that kind of clothing, and to take part in this or that kind of cultural and recreational activity. This is private life in which nobody may interfere . . . In practical life, there are really quite a number of activities which have nothing to do with the class struggle."[37] Furthermore, he did not believe it was necessary to deny personal happiness in order to work for the revolution. Of all Feng's remarks, one published in 1956 was the most antithetical to the way of life represented by Lei Feng: "The idea of each man sacrificing himself for the good of the masses, even to the point of giving up his own life, is after all not usually necessary—first of all, if an individual cannot live himself, how can be possibly serve the masses?"[38]

That Feng Ding's view of happiness expressed the feelings of more than an elite group of intellectuals was evident from the responses of readers of provincial newspapers to an invitation to present their personal views of happiness. Readers from a wide range of backgrounds sent in responses that virtually paraphrased Feng Ding. One worker wrote, "If the purpose of our revolution is not for happiness, but for a lifetime of eating coarse rice and wearing rags, then there is no significance in its further advance."[39] Another worker noted that a person "will naturally pursue a life to satisfy his own desires and also naturally will not be willing to turn himself into a mere tool of laboring for the happiness of other people. This would be against the laws of nature."[40] Yet another reader observed: "If a man expends arduous labor to make others enjoy the fruits of his own labor, he of course will feel happy although in an abstract sense. This is similar to the case of a man who sacrifices his own life in order to save the life of a child from being drowned. Of course other people will praise this man for his act of valor and greatness, but will praise be of any use to him? He will be dead."[41] These comments reflected a desire to improve living standards rather than to sacrifice oneself for the revolution, and a desire to achieve a fuller personal life rather than to continue the revolution. As one writer stated, "I think that happiness means leading a peaceful, pleasant life, not a life of struggle amid hardship . . . It is strange logic to equate hardship with happiness and enjoyment of creature comforts with bourgeois thought."[42] Feng Ding, as the most articulate spokesman of these sentiments, was a fitting target for the regime's efforts in 1964 to counteract them and to superimpose its own values.

In this campaign Feng Ding's views were contrasted with those ascribed to the army-peasant heroes, such as Lei Feng and Ouyang Hai, whose story was published in 1965. Feng Ding's concern with personal happiness and material goals was repudiated in favor of the pursuit of revolution and service to the people exemplified by Lei Feng. In opposition to Feng Ding's affirmation of the simple pleasures of normal life, Lei Feng was hailed for giving up his small portion of food and only coat to help others. Feng Ding's rejection of the sacrifice of one's life for the people was juxtaposed with Ouyang Hai's act of pushing an ammunition-laden wagon and horse out of the way of an oncoming train at the sacrifice of his own life. It was pointed out that death had a different significance in the thought of Mao than in other ideologies, for the lost life served "the eternal preservation of the masses."[43]

The Feng Ding campaign was also used to combat what the regime called "social Darwinism," a Western concept that had been used to justify reforms in late Qing dynasty and the May Fourth movement. Social Darwinism was defined in 1964 as a view of man based on his biological development rather than his class relationship. Criticism of this concept was used to denigrate the views of the early 1960s that the main contradiction in society was no longer between classes but between man and his environment and that priority should be given to conquering and harnessing the physical environment rather than to inciting one class against another.

The regime rightly saw this approach as an underlying premise of Feng Ding's writing. Just as Wu Han, Feng Youlan, and Zhou Gucheng saw common values in Chinese history and thought, and May Fourth writers depicted basic human emotions shared by all classes, so Feng found a common biological drive in the instinct for self-preservation and the desire for material self-improvement. Though these views were attributed to social Darwinism, they could have been said to derive as much from the Confucian concern for man's basic well-being as from Western concepts. Feng, instead of treating selfishness and individualism as traits of the bourgeoisie, which doctrine decreed, regarded them as innate instincts of all human beings regardless of class. Consequently, his views, like those of Shao Quanlin's middle man, exposed as illusory the regime's contention that a selfless, communist spirit permeated the masses. Yet here again the regime claimed that it was Feng who was living in a world of illusions because of his disregard of man's social and class nature. His critics charged that his biological interpretation reduced humans to the level of animals and instilled the belief that revolution would lead not to communism but to personal and material satisfaction.

Whereas the party bureaucracy may have shared Mao's concern over the ideological commitment of youth, it did not go along with the accelerating effort of Lin Biao and the radical intellectuals in 1964 to give Mao a god-like aura. One remark by Feng Ding denouncing the deification of a leader was cited and not refuted: "The leader as an individual should not be considered omniscient and omnipotent. It is harmful to the development of socialism to think we can know everything and create everything simply by relying upon the wisdom and power of the individual leader."[44] Despite the more prominent role of the army and radical intellectuals in 1964–1965 and their noticeable interjections into the rectification, the rectification was very much under the control of the party bureaucrats.

Uniqueness of the Rectification

The rectification of 1964 was similar to other ideological remolding campaigns in its use of the media, sessions of criticism and self-criticism, and personalized targets. But its approach was different. Though the people in charge were for the most part the same officials from the central Propaganda Department who had conducted the campaigns of the 1950s, the rectification was less direct, less thorough, and more tolerant of its victims. Probably these officials were just as anxious as they had previously been to stop what Mao called "a slide toward revisionism," but other factors held them back: increasing bureaucratization, the fear of another full-scale campaign reeling out of control, and doubts about Mao's policies. Moreover, a rectification in which the masses were activated would be a threat not only to themselves personally, as it was in the Hundred Flowers, but to the party as a whole.

As a result, there appears to have been in some cases an inadvertent, in other cases a deliberate, misinterpretation of Mao's wishes. A speech of Mao's to the Propaganda Department, which had been delivered on March 12, 1957, in the midst of the Hundred Flowers but had never been published, appeared in June 1964 just as the rectification was about to be launched. On the one hand, it expressed Mao's desire for criticism of the party by nonparty people; on the other, it expressed the party bureaucrats' desire for criticism with restraint and understanding. The speech, given at a time when Mao was less disillusioned with the intellectuals, cautioned that criticism of intellectuals must be "fully reasoned, analytical, and convincing and should not be brutal, bureaucratic, or dogmatic." Mao advocated a moderate approach toward dissenting intellectuals: "Such people will remain for a very long time to come, and we should tolerate their disapproval."[45] This speech, as well as shorter directives of Mao's, were ambiguous as to how the rectification was to be implemented, and if anything, it advocated persuasion rather than coercion.

Whether intentionally or not, cultural officials chose to interpret Mao's words as an order for a limited rectification. As in the past, personalized targets were used as vehicles for transmitting ideological messages. But this time, instead of selecting one specific target, as in 1955, or one specific group, as in 1957, the Propaganda Department launched several different campaigns simultaneously against several related, but different, targets, thereby diffusing the movement. The campaign was broad, touching philosophy, history, literary theory, the arts, and ideology, but it was not thorough, for there was a gap between the rhetoric and the reality, between the enunciation of policy and its implementation. Moreover, the revolutionary fervor of previous movements was missing. Except possibly for the Feng Ding drive, which was directed primarily at educated youth, those affected were a small group of party intellectuals in the large cities. There was minimal effort to involve ordinary workers and peasants, and there were none of the mass meetings or emotional public denunciations that had characterized past campaigns.

Most of the rectification was carried out quietly behind closed doors, primarily in the Ministry of Culture and the All-China Federation of Literature and Art. In this campaign, unlike earlier ones, the media published few incriminating materials, so it was difficult to generate large-scale criticism. Except for a few remarks of Shao Quanlin's on the middle man, there was no published record of anyone else who spoke at Dalian. Zhou Yang supposedly stopped publication of the Dalian speeches. Except for the slogan "one into two, two into one," little effort was made to simplify the ideological themes to ensure that they could be understood by the uneducated. Most of the criticism had the character of an abstruse intellectual exercise filled with Marxist abstractions, as if to distract from its political implications. When Mao asked his nephew Mao Yuanxin what he thought of the campaign against "two into one," his nephew replied, "I have read only a little and don't understand much of what I read."[46] Although the rectification was implicitly political, the substance was explicitly academic.

The personalized targets were treated leniently. They were referred to throughout as "comrade," an appellation that had been lost by earlier targets when the initial charges were filed against them. Unlike past rectifications, this one ended without publication nation-wide of abject self-criticisms as a means of further indoctrination. No public confessions came forth from Yang Xianzhen, Shao Quanlin, or Feng Ding. Nor did individuals and journals that had not anticipated the rectification's targets suffer to any extent. In contrast to previous purges, the *Chinese Youth Daily* issued merely a mild self-criticism for having turned down the initial attack on Feng Ding, and that was all.

Nevertheless, there were signs that Zhou Yang and the cultural establishment were under pressure. Not only Shao Quanlin but also Zhou Yang's close colleagues and Jiang Qing's old enemies Tian Han, Xia Yan, and Yang Hansheng were removed from some of their positions. Mao Dun stepped down as minister of culture. The journal with which Zhou Yang and his associates were closely identified, the *Literary Gazette*, published articles criticizing itself for having praised writers like Zhao Shuli and Ouyang Shan. One such article accused the journal of being revolutionary in words but revisionist in implementation, a charge that would be leveled later against cultural bureaucrats. The journal was also accused of relying on a small group of professional writers without soliciting input from the masses.

Although the removal of some of Zhou Yang's chief colleagues marked the beginning of the breakup of the cultural machine that he had built up over almost thirty years, its operations still continued. A few high officials were removed, but most of its officials were only reshuffled, not purged. As opposed to earlier campaigns when all the disciples and associates had suffered a fate similar to that of their leader, the criticism in the rectification stopped with a small number of colleagues. Moreover, the charges against them were for the most part limited to a few specific misdeeds. Zhou's other close colleagues, Lin Mohan, Yuan Shuibo, and He Qifang, were not even criticized at the time. Kang Zhuo, who had expressed views similar to Shao Quanlin's at Dalian, was barely mentioned. Another ally, Liu Baiyu, who had been in charge of the rectification in the Chinese Writers Union, assumed Shao's place as head of the party group. Zhou's associate, Director of Propaganda Lu Dingyi, took over as minister of culture. By the spring of 1965 the criticism of Xia Yan, Yang Hansheng, and Tian Han had waned. Zhou was able to shelter most of his cultural machine from attack. Furthermore, he appears to have protected it from the infiltration of the army which had affected other bureaucracies. Whereas by the end of 1964 the establishment of political departments on the army commissar system had made some headway in the economic ministries, there was slight evidence of this system in the ministry of culture.

Although Zhou Gucheng's syncretic view of history and aesthetics was similar to Yang Xianzhen's ideological concept of "two into one," surprisingly little attention was given to Zhou in the rectification. However, one attack on him was by Luo Siding, a Shanghai writing group that was to play an important role in the ideological struggles of the post-Cultural Revolution period. This was one of the group's first appearances. Luo Siding's criticism of Zhou in the rectification was similar to Yao Wenyuan's criticism of Zhou in 1963. In opposition to Zhou's belief in the complementary nature of different ideologies in China's cultural heritage, Luo Siding asserted that the relation was one not of conciliation but of "life-and-death struggle."[47] Whereas Zhou viewed the intellectuals as a group in their own right, situated between the workers and the bourgeoisie, able to understand both sides and therefore reconcile them, Luo Siding took the standard Maoist position that the intellectuals were part of the bourgeoisie and therefore could not act as a force for reconciliation.

Similarly, Feng Youlan, though given some attention in 1964, was not a prime target. The focus for the attack was not so much on well-known intellectuals as on party members who had long careers in propaganda and ideology but were not at the very top of the cultural hierarchy. Nor were those officials who had most sharply criticized Mao and the Leap selected for criticism. Although Liao Mosha, a member of the Three-Family Village, wrote a self-criticism, it was not for his participation in the Three-Family Village or his criticism of Maoist programs. Most likely, Peng Zhen protected the Three-Family Village the same as Zhou Yang sought to ensure mild criti-

CHINA'S INTELLECTUALS

cism of his cronies. A hard-hitting campaign against their underlings would have reverberated back on them as their sponsors. Nothing was said, as in past campaigns, about the fact that the errors of the subordinates reflected those of their leaders.

Perhaps the most important difference from previous campaigns was the lack of unanimity in the negative appraisal of the scapegoats and in the imposition of one definitive line. This time there was a diversity of views, with some defense of the victims and some divergence from the party line. The attackers dominated, but the defenders and modifiers did not vanish from the scene as they had in other campaigns. All the themes that would come to dominate the Cultural Revolution—ideological class struggle, transformation of consciousness, infusion of revolutionary spirit into youth and party leaders—were present in the 1964 rectification. But the discussion was contradictory, reflecting again the differing views within the leadership as well as within the intellectual community, primarily between the liberal and radical intellectuals.

Some articles that purportedly criticized Yang Xianzhen actually defended his ideas. One such article restated Yang's condemnation of the belief that "the will can determine everything and man can do what he likes according to the dictates of his own will."[48] Similarly, though the counterargument to Feng Ding's view of happiness was that individual enjoyment must be sacrificed to the revolution, a vocal minority modified that argument by treating personal and material pleasures as secondary to the revolution rather than as destructive to it. Consequently, the revolution should not be a person's whole life but rather the major portion of it, which still left room for personal fulfillment.

Another distinctive feature of the rectification was that there was open criticism of some of the critics, particularly of the radical intellectuals. Yao Wenyuan, for example, was censured in 1964 for his earlier criticism of Zhou Gucheng. Yao's criticism was termed "self-contradictory" and "not in correspondence with the facts of history."[49] Such attacks may explain why Luo Siding rather than Yao criticized Zhou in the rectification. Some of the targets were even defended, as when Shao Quanlin's call for more realism was upheld. It was pointed out that if "only positive, advanced" characters were depicted, they would misrepresent the times.[50] The case was comparable to accepting Chernyshevsky's view that Russian literature should describe only peasants ready for revolution while ignoring

the landlords and bureaucrats of Gogol and Oblomov-type characters. Yet these countercriticisms too were not pushed far, because
Mao likewise protected the radical intellectuals and shielded them
from sharp attack. He is reported to have said of Guan Feng in this
period, "I have read He Ming's [Guan Feng's] articles; they are quite
good."[51]

By the beginning of 1965, Zhou Yang was ready to bring the rectification to a formal close. He had earlier suspended it in November
1964 in the various unions of the All-China Federation of Literature
and Art on the grounds that the members were needed in other political activities. At the end of February 1965 he called a meeting of
editors and journalists, at which he denounced the recent criticism in
the rectification as dogmatic, simplistic, and exaggerated. Subsequently the rectification faded away.

On April 15 and 16, 1965, Zhou Yang summed up the rectification, as had been his custom in previous campaigns. Though he acknowledged tardiness in criticizing revisionism, he did not admit to
any of the serious shortcomings that Mao had demanded in his December 1963 directives. Zhou agreed that his colleagues should be
criticized for some things, but he insisted that the party did not regard them as rightists: "Our contradictions with and our struggle
against them remain a contradiction among the people and an inner-
party struggle."[52] His colleagues might have deviated in the cultural
sphere, but they were not guilty of revisionism in the political
sphere. Moreover, since they had already ceased holding some of
these views, they should not be selected for criticism again.

In the sciences, as well as the arts and humanities, Mao's views
were disregarded and in some cases resisted. On February 13, 1964,
he had praised scientists who made discoveries in the course of their
everyday work, and he criticized university science departments for
being gathering places where bourgeois ideology existed in "serious
proportion."[53] Ai Siqi also argued that scientific achievement depended on the use of the Marxian dialectic and denounced those
who refused to apply it to scientific research. Yet in 1965, *Chinese
Youth* published a series of articles urging youth to become expert
without being red, advising them to disregard ideology and work
in research centers and laboratories rather than in fields and factories. The use of bourgeois experts was even encouraged precisely
because they were motivated by bourgeois values: "Some bourgeois technical experts whose world outlook has not been re-

molded can still serve socialism under proletarian leadership. Had they spent too much time on Marxism-Leninism, their expertness surely would have suffered."[54] In words that were to be heard again after Mao's death in 1976, it was asserted that neither Mao nor the party had ever said they wanted only redness and no expertise. For a scientist, redness was expressed not by attendance at meetings and in political study, but by devoting time to professional activity. "Under no circumstances," one article warned, should study, intensive research, and professional work be regarded as "a manifestation of individualism."[55]

There was reason, therefore, for Mao to be dissatisfied with the 1964 rectification. Instead of swelling into a major mass movement, it fizzled into an inconclusive affair that expressed a variety of views, some diverging from his own. The party's rhetoric intensified, but its implementation of the rectification was superficial. The central Propaganda Department, the very organization that Mao had empowered to carry out the ideological transformation, had resisted and even opposed his demands. Thus, in the fall of 1965 Mao abandoned his reliance on the party to carry out a cultural revolution and launched one of his own. In contrast to the party's rectification, Mao's Cultural Revolution sought to compel unanimity of ideology, activization of the masses, and a thorough purge of those who did not follow his orders. The concerns expressed by the liberal intellectuals since the early 1960s—on the need for stability and reconciliation, professional and intellectual standards, concurrence of ideology with reality, and recognition of the genuine demands of the peasants and the individual—were suppressed. Yet these concerns, stemming from China's Confucian and May Fourth traditions, did not die, even though some of their spokesmen were to lose their lives in the Cultural Revolution for expressing them. As throughout the course of China's volatile twentieth-century history, they were to reemerge once the turbulence subsided.

5

THE CULTURAL
REVOLUTION

Mao's Cultural Revolution began as a seemingly ad hoc effort to rekindle the ideological struggle that the party's rectification had barely ignited. But when it met with scarcely a response and then with outright opposition from the cultural and political bureaucracies, the Cultural Revolution exploded into a full-scale campaign of unprecedented ferocity and unexpected dimensions. Lasting from 1966 to 1969, it repeatedly shifted course as it encountered resistance from the liberal intellectuals, their political patrons, the party bureaucracy, and finally from Mao's erstwhile allies, the radical intellectuals themselves.

In the fall of 1965, Mao began to move the surrogate struggle from the defined limits of an intellectual debate into the open as a political struggle. In addition to the foot dragging of the party's cultural officials, a series of meetings at that time may have led him to shift the conflict from behind the scenes into the public arena. At a national conference of heads of cultural departments in September-October 1965, the party's top cultural officials pronounced the rectification a success. Zhou Yang once again described his belated discovery of revisionism in the cultural realm as nothing more than "a question of cognition."[1] Peng Zhen denied the charge of revisionism altogether contending that "the majority of cadres on the cultural front are good or basically 'good.' "[2] Some of those who had been targets, like Xia Yan and Yang Hansheng, were even seated on the rostrum, as if signifying that their rehabilitation was already underway. Yang, in fact, continued to serve as a vice-chairman of the All-China Federation of Literature and Arts. These events indicated that Peng Zhen was still supervising and Zhou Yang was still implementing cultural policy, despite the fact that during the rectification a number of their close associates had lost their positions.

There was further criticism of Mao at this meeting. Peng Zhen was reported to have said, "Everyone is equal before the truth," a phrase that could mean that Mao should submit to criticism like other officials or that Mao should be chastised for removing Peng Dehuai unfairly. Lu Dingyi was reported to have criticized Stalin's cult of the personality. Although Stalin remained a semihero in China, several liberal intellectuals had used him as a negative symbol for Mao in the aftermath of the Great Leap Forward. Tian Han had said of Stalin, "This great Marxist-Leninist in his last years departed from the masses with profound effects; he committed serious mistakes and became a great tragedy."[3] There was reason, therefore, for China's aging leader to fear that when he died, he too might be repudiated, as Stalin had been in the Soviet Union, and that the revolution for which he had fought so hard might not continue.

The Attack on Wu Han

At a work conference of the Central Committee shortly afterward, Mao instructed that Wu Han be criticized publicly for his play *The Dismissal of Hai Rui*. He pronounced this an issue of class struggle, rather than one merely of "contradiction among the people," as it had been treated by the cultural officials. Mao had previously read Wu Han's work on Ming history and talked with him about his research, and initially he appears not to have made the connection between Hai Rui and Peng Dehuai, even after his wife in 1962 had demanded the play be banned. But by 1965, perhaps because of continuing criticism of his dismissal of Peng Dehuai, he became increasingly perturbed about the connection. He appointed Peng Zhen to carry out the public criticism of Wu Han, even though Peng had just called for gentle rather than harsh treatment for dissident intellectuals: "If they had written erroneous works in the past, would it not be a good idea for them to write a critical article to put things in order? In this way, they act on their own initiative, good feelings can be maintained, and it is easier for everybody."[4] Mao's appointment of Peng despite these words is an indication that he had not yet decided to purge the party or even to launch a hard-hitting campaign. Peng Zhen, as leader of the Group of Five, which had a special mandate since 1964 to reform culture, and as mayor of Beijing, was an appropriate choice to rectify a member of his own committee.

However, in the weeks after Mao's directive, when no action was forthcoming from Peng Zhen's camp, Mao turned to his wife and her radical associates, who were ready to help with this effort. Not only had Jiang Qing in 1962 asked the propaganda officials to criticize Wu Han's play as a "feudal-bourgeois work," but again in 1964 she had tried to have it criticized, and again in vain. Finally in April 1965 she had her associates in Shanghai write such a criticism. Zhang Chunqiao helped in its preparation, Yao Wenyuan wrote it, and Mao himself went over it several times. Thus, Mao was working to silence his critics on both a formal level through the party bureaucracy and an informal level with his wife and the radical intellectuals. Jiang Qing and her associates nevertheless kept the preparation of the article secret, for fear that the cultural apparatus would suppress it before it appeared. When Mao finally gave the go-ahead to have it published, Yao was unable to gain access to the party press in Beijing. He was forced to publish the article in *Wenhui Bao*, the nonparty paper under his and Zhang's supervision in Shanghai, on November 10, 1965.

This long, seemingly erudite article charged that Wu Han's play was not about history but about the current situation. Yao Wenyuan explained that Wu Han's characterization of Hai Rui was a " 'distortion, hypothesis, or veiled criticism of contemporary people with ancient people.' "[5] When Wu Han talked of a "return of land," Yao Wenyuan pointed out, he did not mean that officials returned land to poor peasants, because officials never did so, but that individual farming was superior to the commune. And when Wu Han talked of "the redressing of grievances," he did not mean the alleviation of grievances of the peasants and workers but rather the reopening of cases of those dismissed from office and returning them to power. Yao did not yet say directly that the point of Wu Han's play was to attack Mao's dismissal of Peng Dehuai, but he implied it.

Although Yao Wenyuan's article had Mao's approval, it was not immediately republished in the party press. Mao therefore ordered it reprinted in pamphlet form, but the Beijing Party Committee refused to distribute it. When the article was finally published nineteen days later on November 30, 1965, in the *People's Daily*, it was accompanied by an editorial note that treated Wu Han's play as an academic question, in implicit opposition to Mao's treatment of it as a political question. The note asserted that the play was concerned not with current political events but with history. It called for an intellectual debate on this subject, urged freedom of criticism and countercriticism, solicited criticism of Yao's views as well as of Wu Han's, and advocated a nonideological approach of seeking the truth from facts. To support this position, the note quoted Mao: "We must learn to overcome all kinds of erroneous thinking by means of debate and reasoning."[6]

A public debate ensued. While the army's newspaper, *The Liberation Army Daily (Jiefangjun Bao)* took the offensive in criticizing Wu Han, the Beijing newspapers implicitly defended him. *The People's Daily* and *Guangming Daily* published articles both for and against him. Even *Wenhui Bao,* not yet totally controlled by the Shanghai radicals, published some articles in support of Wu Han and against Yao Wenyuan. It was later charged that the radical Zhang Chunqiao had purposedly encouraged scholars to defend Wu Han in order to smoke out the opposition. Nevertheless, although the number defending Wu Han was much smaller than the number attacking him, for several months the minority voice had the opportunity to speak out. It sought, as before, to keep the criticism within the confines of an academic debate, thus implicitly defying Mao's orders.

Using the methods of their traditional predecessors, the liberal intellectuals camouflaged their defense of their colleague Wu Han with academic debate and historical allusion. They convened symposia of cultural, educational, and journalistic groups to build support. Xu Liqun, a deputy-director of the Propaganda Department who was closely affiliated with Peng Zhen, convened a conference of newspaper editors at which he called for a reappraisal of historical plays and the traditional moral code, seemingly in an effort to turn attention away from the present. Song Shuo, a deputy-director of the

THE CULTURAL REVOLUTION

University Department of the Beijing Party Committee, stressed that *The Dismissal of Hai Rui* was an academic matter and attacked Yao for treating it as a political matter. He charged that Yao's actions had dampened the atmosphere of lively discussion that had once prevailed in academic circles. He urged that matters such as Wu Han's case not be handled in a "simple way," as Yao had done, but with caution and "proper leadership."[7] The implication was that Yao had acted without the authority of the party. Several of Wu Han's supporters decried the lack of party authorization for Yao's article and its failure to go through appropriate channels. Peng Zhen complained to the Shanghai authorities, "Where is your sense of party discipline in publishing such an article without prior communication with us?"[8]

Wu Han's most energetic defender was his closest associate, Deng Tuo. Deng convened a forum of students and newspaper editors at which he counseled against drawing any definitive conclusions on Wu Han from Yao Wenyuan's article and advised them to treat it as an academic matter. He pleaded, "Try to present facts, reason, and take a consultative attitude without giving labels to other people."[9] On the basis of Wu Han's past performance, Deng declared, "he should not be regarded as against the party and socialism, and therefore he should not be summarily condemned and liquidated."[10] Most important, Deng asked the forum members to express their ideas freely, by which he meant that they should defend Wu Han: "Have nothing to fear, whether your viewpoints differ from those of Yao Wenyuan or whether your views have something in common with those of Wu Han." The ideas of the majority were not necessarily correct, he advised, paraphrasing Mao: "Sometimes the views of individuals in the minority may be correct."[11] At a conference for amateur writers, Deng exhorted the participants to avoid rote learning of words and phrases, even from the works of Mao, and urged them to "write boldly" and not to "believe blindly in authority."[12] Deng followed his own advice. Writing under a pseudonym, he mildly chided Wu Han for promoting the traditional moral code but basically approved his work.[13]

Others openly criticized Yao Wenyuan for relating Wu Han's play to current political issues. One writer accused Yao of arrogance that had nothing in common with "the spirit of respecting the truth."[14] He insisted that Wu Han's play could not be related to the present as Yao had done, because socialist society and feudal society were fundamentally different. Another article, in direct criticism of Mao as well as of Yao, argued that Hai Rui "received some good influence from the people and did several things to betray his own class" and "perplexes only those who make use of class labels without regard to facts."[15] Some writers even contended that Hai Rui had traditional virtues which were relevant to the present. Specifically Hai Rui or Wu Han was extolled because he embodied the ideal of the scholar-bureaucrat who risked his life to expose the shortcomings of the ruler. One article quoted Hai Rui as saying, when presenting the emperor with a memorial that pointed out his wrongdoings: "I have done this out of loyalty to the Emperor and love for my country. What crime have I committed?"[16] Hai Rui thus taught, the author concluded, that when one sees mistakes committed by one's colleagues, one should not remain silent.

Mao tried to stop this subtle resistance to his order to criticize Wu Han. On December 21, 1965, he explicitly stated the connection between Wu Han's play and Peng Dehuai. As a result, Peng Zhen agreed to have Wu Han write a self-criticism. However, Wu Han's self-criticism, written with the assistance of Deng Tuo, did not acknowledge, as Mao had wanted, that his play was about the dismissal of Peng Dehuai. The only error that Wu Han admitted was the bourgeois academic one of portraying "an ancient event for its own sake," instead of "making modern use of ancient events." But, he insisted, his "class standpoint in the political field is quite solid."[17] Forums were convened to discuss Wu Han's self-criticism, which once again became a platform for his colleagues to defend him. At one public forum, the historian Jian Bozan declared, "If Wu Han is purged, all progressive intellectuals will live in fear."[18] The defense of Wu Han, however indirect and confused, undermined Mao's efforts to rebuke his critics in the cultural and academic establishment. To the informed elite, these academic discussions could readily be interpreted as implicit attacks on Mao and his authority.

Similar resistance to Mao's orders emanated from the intellectuals attached to the central Propaganda Department. Zhou Yang and his associates there, the same as members of the Beijing Party Committee, sought to limit the discussion of Wu Han's play. Although Zhou projected himself as the implementer of Mao's literary line, in a speech on November 24, 1965, nineteen days after the publication of Yao Wenyuan's article, Zhou mentioned neither Wu Han nor the play. And although he repeated Mao's demand that a writer must be a revolutionary first and a professional second, he encouraged competition between different styles and forms. As he still had the power to give prominent coverage to his own speech, it appeared in the party's national news media.

The literary and art journals under Zhou Yang's purview, which would have been expected to be among the first to attack a "revisionist" play, published only a few academic articles on Hai Rui and for the most part concentrated instead on the same targets as the 1964 rectification, particularly the middle characters and the writers Tian Han, Xia Yan, and Shao Quanlin, of whom the most disparaging epithet was still "bourgeois humanist." Their criticisms were still restrained. Tian Han's play *Xie Yaohuan* was censured, but no mention was made of the fact that this play, like Wu Han's, had a protagonist who criticized arbitrary policies and was killed in consequence. As in 1964, Zhou Yang's group trivialized the charges against their colleagues. He Qifang, for example, acknowledged that Xia Yan idealized bourgeois democracy, humanism, and the theory of universal human nature, but "His activities and works over a long period had a positive role to play during the period of democratic revolution."[19] These criticisms did not come close to the serious charges that Mao had sought against his intellectual critics. Zhou Yang, because of his long associations with the liberal intellectuals and because of his fear of self-incrimination, did not move aggressively to criticize Wu Han or to purge the members of his own group.

The debate over Wu Han went on inconclusively for over three months, primarily in the Beijing and Shanghai newspapers. Although a number of provincial papers reprinted Yao Wenyuan's criticism, it provoked little discussion. Peng Zhen, having been able to limit the criticism and divert attention from current political issues, therefore sought in February 1966 to reassert organizational leadership over the cultural realm. He invited eleven colleagues to an enlarged session of the Group of Five on February 2–5, 1966, which framed a report, titled "An Outline Report on the Current Situation," that sought to depolitize the attack on Wu Han. The report advised that the discussion of Wu Han be channeled into academic debate: "In other words, not only will we overwhelm the other side in the political field, but we will also truly and largely surpass and overwhelm the other side in the academic field and in our standard of work."[20] It invited opposing views, even anti-Marxist ones, to be expressed. If no consensus was arrived at, it recommended that conclusions be deferred. The report sought to wind down and gradually end the whole affair.

The report also rebuked Wu Han's criticis. Although Yao Wen-yuan was not mentioned by name, it condemned "scholar-tyrants," the euphemism that had been used against Yao and his associates in the 1964 rectification. The charges against them were arbitrariness, injustice, and disregard for regular procedures. The report warned against criticizing people by name, as Mao had wanted Yao to do: "Discretion must be exercised when concentrating criticism on a person and mentioning him by name in newspapers." It stressed the need to get "the permission of higher-ranked organizations," permission Yao had not sought. It asserted that, "Even a steadfast, revolutionary left-winger is not immune from making . . . mistakes."[21] There was no mention of what Mao considered to be the crux of the Wu Han play, its analogy of Hai Rui's dismissal to Peng Dehuai's dismissal. Nor was there any mention of a campaign to arouse the masses.

In the discussions that accompanied the drafting of the report, Xu Liqun, its chief author, expressed fear that if the Wu Han case became a political issue, professionals and scholars would not dare to speak out any more. In opposition, Kang Sheng charged that Xu, instead of gathering materials to be used against Wu Han, had collected materials to be used against Yao Wenyuan and other radicals. Kang then accused Xu of seeking to rectify radicals, whereas they should be the ones to be protected. Despite Kang Sheng's protest, the report was revised in its final form by the senior ideological theorist, Hu Sheng, and on February 3, 1966, the Group of Five approved it. On February 5, it was endorsed by the Standing Committee of the Politburo and distributed to the Central Committee. Up to this point Liu Shaoqi had taken no stand on the Wu Han affair, but with the Politburo's approval, he implicitly came down on Peng Zhen's side. On February 8, Peng with Xu, Hu Sheng, and Wu Lengxi, presented the report to Mao, who refused to concur in its findings. Yet despite Mao's objections, the report was officially disseminated on February 12.

The Attack on the May Fourth Writers

About the time that the party's report was being prepared and distributed, a counter document was being presented at a forum on literature and art in the army, convened in Shanghai by Jiang Qing, with Lin Biao's support, on February 2, 1966. Given the army's promotion of revolutionary culture along the lines that Jiang Qing had prescribed but the party had rejected, the alliance between Jiang Qing and Lin Biao to assist Mao in his conflict with the cultural establishment was a natural one. Mao even played a role in drawing up the report of this forum, and he, along with Chen Boda, corrected it three times. As opposed to the party's report, the forum's report called for sharp class conflict in the cultural realm. It called for debate as well, but this only reflected the radicals' weaker position in the establishment. The report's demand for "rule by many voices" as opposed to "rule by one single voice" reflected its backers' efforts to break the dominant control of the cultural bureaucracy.[22]

As Yao Wenyuan's article had sparked the attack on Wu Han, the forum report launched an all-out attack on the May Fourth writers and the Westernized cultural legacy of the 1920s and 1930s. It expressed the original intent of the Cultural Revolution, before it was eclipsed by the political power struggle. In that early stage, the movement was what its name implied—an effort to destroy the culture and ideology of both traditional and May Fourth China and to establish an entirely new ideology and culture of the Maoist era. The revolution was directed not only at the cultural officials who had been influenced by Western and Soviet literature but also at the cosmopolitan, Westernized, urban elite who still dominated China's intellectual life. The fact that a campaign had to be waged against May Fourth culture was indicative of its popularity and continuing attraction. Whereas the May Fourth writers, including the cultural officials, sought to incorporate the best of Western and even traditional culture into present-day China, Mao and his associates at this time were culturally iconoclastic. They saw May Fourth and traditional culture as representing an elite that was completely divorced from the needs and experiences of the Chinese masses.

Mao, who himself came of age in the May Fourth movement, had not always rejected Western culture. Less than two years earlier, on August 24, 1964, he had expressed a desire to assimilate some of it: "If we stick to our old ways and do not study foreign literature, do not introduce it into China, if we do not know how to listen to foreign music or how to play it, this is not good. We must not be like the Empress Dowager Cixi who blindly rejected all foreign things."[23] Most likely, it was Mao's increasing disillusionment with his cultural officials and the urban May Fourth intellectuals, who were thwarting his current policies, that turned him against Western culture itself. Moreover, Mao urged increasing class struggle, whereas May Fourth literature did not express a clear-cut class stand. Even before the forum, Mao had rejected Western culture, though not Western technology. On December 21, 1965, he rephrased the *ti* (principle/substance) and *yong* (function) dichotomy of China's nineteenth-century literati reformers, the self-strengtheners: Chinese learning for the substance; Western learning for practical application. Mao stated: "We cannot adopt Western learning as a substance, nor can we use the substance of the democratic republic. We cannot use the 'natural rights of man' nor the 'theory of evolution.' We can use only Western technology."[24]

Although Mao's repudiation of Western culture set the general tone, the Cultural Revolution's interpretation of May Fourth culture as well as the vehemence of this aspect of the campaign launched at the time of the Shanghai forum had more to do with the biases of Jiang Qing and the radical intellectuals than with Mao. What was specifically rejected and who was specifically repudiated reflected Jiang Qing's personal animus. Those singled out as the most villainous were her old enemies from Shanghai—Zhou Yang, Xia Yan, Tian Han, and Yang Hansheng. The humiliation that had festered in her for years now had an outlet. Even the Western writers singled out for attack reflected her own personal prejudices. Most of Europe's great nineteenth-century writers—Balzac, Zola, Gogol, Turgenev, Dostoevsky, Chekhov, and Tolstoy—were denounced because of the profound effect of their critical realism and Western humanism on the May Fourth intellectuals. Furthermore, their approach ran counter to the Cultural Revolution's emphasis on revolutionary romanticism and class struggle. They were accused of "glorifying" love, individualism, and alienation—values opposed to the spirit of self-sacrifice, collectivism, and ideological commitment which the revolution sought to instill.

The major thrust was directed at the nineteenth-century Russian literary critics Belinsky, Chernyshevsky, and Dobrolyubov, whose literary theories had formed a basis for May Fourth literature. The Russian critics' view that literature should denounce repression and awaken the national consciousness was interpreted as justifying the acts of the liberal intellectuals. But the focus on these particular Russian writers was also personal, as they were associated with Zhou Yang, who had translated Chernyshevksy and had been instrumental in introducing their theories to Chinese intellectuals in the 1930s.

THE CULTURAL REVOLUTION

The Soviet writers selected for attack also reflected Jiang Qing's bias. The forum report warned that even the relatively good Soviet literature and art had appeared after the Russian Revolution should not be blindly imitated. Although the less orthodox Soviet writers such as Simonov, Chukhai and Ehrenburg were criticized, the one most reviled was the more orthodox Sholokov. Jiang Qing was particularly disturbed by his *Quiet Flows the Don*, whose hero Gregor preferred to fight for his piece of bread, his strip of land, and his right to live than for the revolution. This protagonist, a poor peasant opposed to collectivization and filled with fears, was more like the middle man she intensely disliked than the heroes she sought to project in her revolutionary operas.

The attack was extended to the Soviet theater, particularly the Stanislavsky system, again a method diametrically opposed to Jiang Qing's. The Stanislavsky system was characterized as "decadent, bourgeois individualism, because it preceded from one's self rather than from society." It was contrary to the revolutionary opera's heroic approach, for instead of presenting "ugly, cruel, insidious, and reactionary" villains in order to have them stand out in relief against the proletarian heroes, Stanislavsky presented villains who had glimmers of kindness and doubt.[25]

The attack on Western culture treated the party's cultural leader in Shanghai in the 1930s, Qu Qiubai, as epitomizing the Westernized intellectual whom the Cultural Revolution sought to repudiate. He was portrayed as an intellectual who had abandoned the revolution, which supposedly China's present-day intellectuals were also doing. He, like they, had participated in the revolution, but at a critical point they had all become alienated and turned against the revolution. Qu's final statement, "Superfluous Words," written just before his death in 1935, was cited as an example of the vacillation of intellectuals toward the revolution. Actually, the statement delineated the intellectual's conflict between his revolutionary activity and intellectual endeavor, between his political views and personal life. Qu was quoted critically, "Although I have some interest in political problems, sometimes I long for literature and art and feel disappointed in my hopes." And he wrote to his wife: "I felt empty, lonely, and bored. How I wished to fly to your side."[26] During the Cultural Revolution, Qu's contradictory commitments were taken to symbolize the ambivalence not only of May Fourth writers but of all intellectuals.

Qu's friend, Lu Xun, China's most famous writer, was the exception to the rejection of the May Fourth writers. The forum report stated that Lu Xun's "militant, left-wing literature" was the only good work of the 1930s. It was ironic that Lu Xun, whose views were so contrary to Mao's, should have become the hero of the Cultural Revolution. Whereas his short stories repudiated the old society, they did not depict the new communist society. His biting satire represented an approach diametrically opposed to the heroic revolutionary opera. Furthermore, he and his disciples believed that their work should be relatively independent of political control. Although Lu Xun died in 1936, most of his disciples, who lived under the People's Republic, had been purged even before the Cultural Revolution for their refusal to accept party dictates. Like his contemporaries, Lu Xun sought out Western culture, in particular the avant-garde. Yet these fundamental qualities of his life and work were ignored in the Cultural Revolution.

It was rather Lu Xun's rebellious attitude against the party's cultural organization in Shanghai that was hailed in the Cultural Revolution. Since Mao was likewise rebelling against the party organization, particularly the very same cultural bureaucrats, Lu Xun was treated as a surrogate for Mao. Lu Xun expressed Mao's feelings about betrayal by one's own colleagues when he wrote that enemies like Chiang Kaishek need not be feared: "What is to be feared most is the so-called 'comrades in arms' who say yes but mean no . . . When a man of my own camp disguises himself and stabs me from behind, it is natural that I should hate and despise him more than I do the avowed enemy."[27] The public was urged to emulate Lu Xun's intense hatred of the internal enemy. At a rally held in Beijing in October 1966 to commemorate the thirtieth anniversary of Lu Xun's death, Chen Boda hailed his vindictive and intolerant attitude toward his enemies.

Jiang Qing also identified with Lu Xun in his battles with the same cultural officials whom she felt had thwarted her own career, and she lauded him as a fighter against bureaucratic authority. Her close associates, however, may have been less comfortable with the symbol of Lu Xun. Yao Wenyuan's father had been in conflict with Lu Xun in the 1930s, and Zhang Chunqiao had criticized one of Lu Xun's disciples, Xiao Jun, to which Lu Xun blisteringly retorted that Zhang was "one who feigns revolution in order to oppose the revolution."[28] The radicals used virtually the same charge against the liberal intellectuals in the mid-1960s. Moreover, Lu Xun's verbal abuse of the party's cultural officials as "seditious" and "rotten," reprinted at length in the Cultural Revolution, aptly expressed Jiang's own emnity toward her old adversaries.

Lu Xun was honored not only for his hatred of his adversaries but also for his "boundless esteem and love for Chairman Mao."[29] In contrast to his rebelliousness against party bureaucrats, Lu Xun was lauded for supporting Mao's policies like "a foot-soldier." At the same time, Zhou Yang was denounced because he attributed Lu Xun's attraction to Mao and the Communist Party not to his love of Mao nor to his knowledge of Marxism-Leninism, but to his absorption in Western culture. Zhou, however, was closer to the truth about Lu Xun than his Cultural Revolution interpreters, for Lu Xun was not well read in Marxism-Leninism and he was barely aware of Mao, let alone obedient to his policies. The only direct contact he was known to have had with Mao was a telegram of congratulations he sent to survivors of the Long March after their arrival in Shaanxi. The telegram was of a general rather than a personal nature.

In addition to the distortion of Lu Xun's image, his choice as a figure of emulation for the literate population was double-edged. His example might prove helpful in the attack on Zhou Yang and the cultural bureaucracy, but his immersion in Western culture and his unwillingness to accept any authority over his own work were subversive to the purposes of the Cultural Revolution. Ironically, his view of literature was even more diametrically opposed to Mao's more traditional view of literature as a tool of the political system than were the views of the cultural officials. They were willing to acknowledge and impose some controls over creative works. Few of them would have gone so far as Lu Xun, who maintained that "Good literature always refuses orders from outside; it never cares about practical considerations; it springs spontaneously from the heart."[30]

Cultural officials were made the first targets of the Cultural Revolution not only because of Jiang Qing's personal desire for revenge, but also because Mao held them responsible for the fact that, despite the years of indoctrination and thought reform, China's intellectuals still resisted his authority. They were also vulnerable in this period of repudiation of Western culture because they had participated in the cosmopolitan, relatively free, cultural life of the May Fourth movement, particularly in the 1930s. Although they were first and foremost party organization men, they had some appreciation for Western culture, particularly Western literature. Although most of their careers in the People's Republic had been spent imposing a utilitarian view of literature and culture, at brief intervals they, like the dissident writers whom they purged, articulated and kept alive values and literary standards that they had learned in their earlier days.

The Attack on the Liberals' Political Patrons

The ostensibly ideological campaign against the May Fourth writers and Wu Han was intertwined with a submerged power struggle which burst forth to the surface in the spring of 1966. For almost four months, Peng Zhen had been able to control and divert it but not to suppress it. Even if he had fulfilled his obligations to Mao rather than to his subordinates, the power struggle could not have been avoided, for it would have been impossible to carry out Mao's orders to repudiate Wu Han without also repudiating Wu Han's close associate Deng Tuo and then the Beijing Party Committee with which they were enmeshed. Once the campaign against Wu Han had been set into motion, it would have inexorably reached Peng as head of the committee. Thus, Peng tried desperately to protect Wu Han, because he was ultimately protecting himself. But without the active support of the party bureaucracy, he could only blunt the attack, not stop it.

At a March 28, 1966, Politburo meeting, Mao openly criticized Peng Zhen, the central Propaganda Department, and the party's outline report. He directly stated that since 1962 his orders had not been carried out by the party's cultural officials: "In 1962, the Tenth Plenum passed a resolution concerning class struggle. The central Propaganda Department had not had a single word with Wu Han, who had written so many reactionary articles. Yet they wanted other people to have a prior word with them on publication of Yao Wenyuan's article . . . The central Propaganda Department is literally 'the imperial court of Hades,' and we are duty-bound to overthrow it."[31] Shortly after, in the first week of April, two articles against Wu Han that the Propaganda Department had blocked from publication since 1964 were published in the national media. They were by the radical intellectuals Qi Benyu and Guan Feng. These articles, as opposed to those sponsored by the Beijing Party Committee and the Propaganda Department, made a direct connection between *The Dismissal of Hai*

Rui and the dismissal of Peng Dehuai. Given Peng Zhen's power in the media, these articles could never have been published without Mao's intervention.

With these attacks, Peng Zhen realized that he could no longer help Wu Han, but he still tried to protect Deng Tuo. Peng had the Beijing newspapers include an editorial note that only two members of the Three-Family Village, Wu Han and Liao Mosha, had "consciously opposed the party, socialism, and the thought of Mao Zedong"; there was no mention of Deng Tuo.[32] But on May 8, 1966, the *Guangming Daily* featured an article by Guan Feng, under his pen name He Ming, accusing the Beijing Party Committee of shielding the Three-Family Village. Within days these charges were repeated in the media by Yao Wenyuan and Qi Benyu. With the onslaught against his bases of support accelerating, Peng Zhen realized that the forces arrayed against him were overwhelming. On the eve of his fall, he called some of his associates to his home and pleaded, "I look up to you kind friends to help me now."[33]

Liu Shaoqi, Deng Xiaoping, and members of the Politburo were not among Peng Zhen's friends at that moment. Until then, they had appeared to give tacit support to his efforts to suppress the radical intellectuals, as indicated by their approval of the party's outline report. Though Liu may not have been as willing as Peng to tolerate the expression of diverse views, he and the party bureaucracy had shared Peng's interest in maintaining party discipline and regularized procedures. But with Mao's open repudiation of Peng and the Beijing Party Committee and with the army's clear support of Mao, these top officials affirmed their primary loyalty to Mao rather than Peng. The radicals had only defied party discipline, but Peng had defied Mao's instructions. Liu was also not altogether satisfied with the cultural establishment, whose senior officials in September 1965 he had called "incompetent."[34] In May 1966, the Secretariat, presided over by Deng, dissolved the Group of Five and repudiated the party's outline report.

Without the support of the party bureaucracy, Peng Zhen had no choice but to fall back on his own network of supporters in the Beijing Party Committee and Propaganda Department, but their limited power base in Beijing and in the media and cultural circles was no match for Mao's radical intellectuals and, particularly, the army. In May 1966 Peng was purged, and the campaign turned ferociously against Deng Tuo, the Beijing Party Committee, the Propaganda Department, and the whole academic and artistic community. No words, not even subtle analogies, were heard in their defense. Their political protectors could no longer shelter them.

It is likely that when Mao had called for ideological class struggle at the Tenth Plenum in 1962 and even when he had called for criticism of Wu Han in the fall of 1965, he had intended the removal of some cultural officials, but not the overthrow of the whole cultural bureaucracy and open political struggle. However, the resistance of the cultural officials and the initial neutralization of the party bureaucracy led him to rely increasingly on the radical intellectuals under his wife's patronage and the army under Lin Biao, which led inexorably to that result. Jiang Qing's group, as well as Lin Biao, sought open conflict not only to retaliate against those who opposed them but also to expand their own influence. Their alliance with Mao against his critics thus set in motion a movement whose momentum and direction Mao could not wholly control.

With the purge of Peng Zhen, the Cultural Revolution shed its cultural image and became an open political struggle, goaded to increasing ferocity both by the radical intellectuals, who took over the *Red Flag*, and by Lin Biao through the *Liberation Army Daily*. The shift was marked by the issuance on May 16, 1966, of a circular that denounced Peng Zhen and revoked the party's outline report. Although the circular was not released publicly for a year, its content was known by the party hierarchy. Written on Mao's instructions by Jiang Qing, the circular called not only for criticism of the prevailing ideas in academia, journalism, literature, art, film, drama, and publishing but also for seizure of the cultural sphere from "party people in authority taking the capitalist road."[35] A *Liberation Army Daily* editorial of May 4, 1966, declared that because people looked to academic authorites with "blind faith" and because these authorities could remold public opinion to stage a counter-revolution, it was imperative to wage "an extremely sharp class struggle" against them.[36] The struggle against intellectuals and cultural officials built up in intensity and shrillness until by June 6, 1966, the Cultural Revolution had become a movement without "parallel in scale, in sweep, in strength, or in momentum."[37]

Left powerless by the purge of their political protectors, the liberal intellectuals became the most abused victims of the movement. Beginning in the spring of 1966, a reign of terror engulfed China's most eminent professors, university presidents, editors, journalists, musicians, actors, film directors, writers, and artists. Shortly after he was attacked in the press in May 1966, Deng Tuo was killed at the age of fifty-four, significantly just the day after the issuance of the May 16 circular. Wu Han's wife, daughter, and brother were persecuted to death. Wu himself endured fierce meetings against him and was sent to the countryside, where he died of medical neglect in 1969. The playwright Tian Han was arrested, tortured, and died in prison in 1968. The literary critic Shao Quanlin suffered a similar fate in 1971. Zhao Shuli, a creator of middle man characters, was arrested and died of beatings he suffered at meetings convened against him. The verbal attacks on the economist Sun Yefang and the ideologist Yang Xianzhen, which had been relatively mild in the 1964 rectification, became ferocious in the Cultural Revolution. Sun was imprisoned and spent a number of years in solitary confinement. Although most of the liberal intellectuals' political patrons did not die violently, Peng Zhen, Lu Dingyi, Zhou Yang, Lin Mohan, Xu Liqun, and others were forced to stand before rallies of thousands of people with heavy boards hung from their necks bearing such inscriptions as "Anti-revolutionary, revisionist element." Those who were not arrested, persecuted to death, or did not commit suicide were sent to work camps. The persecution drove some of their family members to mental breakdowns from which they never recovered.

The only May Fourth writer to emerge unscathed was Guo Moruo, the friend with whom Mao exchanged poetry. In anticipation of what was to happen to his colleagues, he produced a groveling self-criticism on April 14, 1966, in which he stated that, "Examined by today's standards, all that I have written in the past should strictly speaking be burned to ashes, for it has not the slightest value."[38] He blamed the worthlessness of his work on the fact that, unlike the workers, peasants, and soldiers, he had not studied the thought of Mao and not worked with his hands. In this respect, the Cultural Revolution demanded that writers, as prescribed by the early Marx, should use the plough and the gun as well as the pen.

Similarly in academic institutions not only were the professors who had directly or indirectly criticized Mao's policies repudiated, such as the philosopher Feng Youlan and the historian Jian Bozan, but the overwhelming majority of senior professors were removed from their positions. Jian met death because of persecution. Much abuse was heaped on university presidents, particularly those who headed their university's party committee. Singled out as the archetype anti-Maoist, antirevolutionary university administrator was Lu Ping, president of Beijing University, who in the early months of 1966 had blocked the efforts of a group of radical junior faculty, led by the philosophy professor Nie Yuanzi, to organize criticism of Wu Han's play and had then sent the organizers to the countryside.

Nie Yuanzi had a history of conflict with university administration. For years, she had been demanding that the university give greater importance to ideology in the curriculum. Although Lu Ping was an old revolutionary who had taken over when Ma Yinchu was removed in 1959 for advocating birth control, he had come to see the university as a place for academic study rather than political struggle. He and other Beijing University administrators, with the implicit support of Peng Zhen, an old comrade, not only disregarded Nie's demand for greater ideological emphasis but in 1964 had her confined for seven months in a Beijing hotel for interrogation about her activities. Thus, Nie, like the radical intellectuals, had a personal interest in taking advantage of the Wu Han campaign to counterattack her superiors.

With the purge of Peng Zhen, Lu Ping was stripped of his political protection. Taking advantage of his weakened position, Nie Yuanzi, with six of her radical colleagues in the Philosophy Department, on May 25, 1966, mounted the first wall poster of the Cultural Revolution outside a Beijing University dining hall. It traced Lu's close relationship with Peng Zhen and the Beijing Party Committee and denounced the repressive acts of the party authorities at the university. Lu had the poster torn down, and he mobilized a counterattack through the China Youth League. The poster might have received little notice, except that Mao ordered Kang Sheng to broadcast it on June 1, 1966, and to publish it in the *People's Daily* on June 2, 1966. Mao's endorsement and the prominent publicity given the poster in effect countenanced attacks on university administrators by disgruntled professors and students. These actions unleashed an outburst of wall posters and student demonstrations against university authorities.

In July 1966, when these attacks had extended to party officials and party organizations in the universities, the party bureaucracy under Liu Shaoqi and Deng Xiaoping sent in work teams to reestablish discipline. These teams, composed of party cadres, suppressed the students rebelling against the party's authority, but they also continued the ongoing attack on all intellectuals. Their harsh treatment of the students was not because they had harassed the intellectuals but because they had upset party control over the university. What began as an effort to reestablish order ended with an equally massive attack on the intellectual community as well as on the radical students and professors.

Though it was charged at the time that there was a conspiratorial connection between the party bureaucracy and the intellectuals, this episode demonstrates that the connection was one not of conspiracy but of practical expedience and was only temporary. In the early 1960s the party bureaucracy had shared with the intellectuals an interest in rebuilding China after the Leap, but as the economy revived and the bureaucratic leadership went along with Mao's plan to suppress divergent views, its interests no longer coincided with those of the intellectuals. The bureaucracy reimposed party control on all who deviated or resisted, no matter what their political bent. However, Mao and the bureaucracy's interests did not completely coincide either. Liu Shaoqi, Deng Xiaoping, and the bureaucracy, like Peng Zhen earlier, had followed Mao's instructions only in part. Whereas Mao encouraged an uninhibited mass movement to overthrow the cultural establishment, they limited the movement by banning wall posters, open meetings, and demonstrations. Furthermore, their curbing of rebellious students was in opposition to Mao's view of youth as the vanguard of the Cultural Revolution. Mao expressed his disapproval by calling their actions "a white terror."[39] In late July, he ordered the work teams withdrawn.

Despite strong opposition, Mao retaliated against the bureaucratic leaders at the Eleventh Plenum of August 1, 1966, by demoting Liu Shaoqi from the second to the eighth position in the Politburo. The party leadership was weakened, but not yet overthrown. A directive, known as the Sixteen Points, which emerged from the plenum, envisaged a more limited movement. It decreed a Cultural Revolution from below against the party bureaucracy, but one that did not interfere with industrial and agricultural production or with science and technology. Scientists were exempted from the Cultural Revolution. All that was required of them was to work energetically and not to be antiparty, antisocialist, or engage in illicit relations with foreign countries. Scientists had been relatively exempt from the mass attack on the Westernized intellectuals in the spring and summer of 1966. Because scientists worked with slide rules and equations, their work was ostensibly less related to political issues than was that of writers and social scientists which, by its very nature, challenged political control. Moreover, Mao and the radical intellectuals did not claim to have the knowledge of science that they did of history, philosophy, and literature. They thus were willing at first to allow it more independent inquiry into its own subject matter. Most important, science was of more practical use to the immediate aim of industrialization.

Thus, high academic standards were still fostered in science, and scientists were still to master the most advanced technology of foreign countries. As late as July 23, 1966, a *People's Daily* editorial declared, "To learn with modesty from the advanced experience in science and technology of other countries is an important task for Chinese scientific workers."[40] Although Mao and his allies used student activists, known as the Red Guards, to intimidate nonscientific intellectuals and party officials, the Red Guards were initially restrained from attacking scientists and scientific instututions. Zhou Enlai, who was allied with Mao in the Cultural Revolution, nevertheless shared the more pragmatic approach of the other party leaders, and he warned the Red Guards against intrusion into scientific research centers. While nonscientific and creative intellectuals were being reviled by the Red Guards and denounced in posters, the official press continued to praise scientists for their contributions to China's development.

However, the purges of Liu Shaoqi, labeled "the first capitalist roader in the party," Deng Xiaoping, "the second capitalist roader," and the party bureaucracy in the winter of 1966–1967 removed the official protectors of the scientific community. Just as the nonscientific intellectuals were linked to Peng Zhen and the Propaganda Department, the scientists were linked to the party bureaucracy. Like the scientists, Liu Shaoqi and his associates purportedly fostered theoretical work divorced from practice and handed over the leadership of science and technology to bourgeois intellectuals. They gave high salaries and bonuses that further divorced the scientists from the masses. Yet the charge of an identification of interests between the bureaucracy and the scientists was only partly correct, for the bureaucracy had promoted theoretical science in the early 1960s not because of its intrinsic interest but because of its ultimate practical results. The bureaucracy may have allowed some discretion to the scientists in their individual research and provided increased salaries, but it maintained tight control over the kind of research they did.

The linkage of the scientists with the party bureaucracy spurred the Red Guards to disrupt high-level ministries concerned with science and technology. Not even the ministries involved in defense were unscathed. The Seventh Ministry of Machine Building, which directed aircraft and missile production, came to a standstill because of Red Guards' rampages through the ministry. There were some exceptions, but most scientists at research institutes and universities were sent with other intellectuals to factories and farms to learn through practice. In the face of an accelerating, runaway movement, even Zhou Enlai, who sought to curb the excesses of the Cultural Revolution and restrain the attacks on intellectuals and officials, was unable to protect the scientists from Red Guard abuse. Moreover, he was not always consistent in his efforts to shield them from political interference. On January 25, 1967, for example, he stated that scientists "must take part in the class struggle . . . and establish ties with the workers and peasants in society."[41]

Not only had scientists lost their official protectors but the nature of their work now made them vulnerable. Despite the supposedly nonideological character of their research, they were tainted as elitists and specialists in a movement that ennobled amateurs and generalists. The New China News Agency announced on October 17, 1966, that China had embarked on a new and unique road to scientific development in that the scientists, like other intellectuals, were to rid themselves of Western and bourgeois thought. China's scientific development could no longer rely on advanced Western technology and a handful of Western-trained scientists cooped up in laboratories, unaware of the needs of the masses. Instead, it would rely on Mao's thought to inspire the Chinese masses to create their own innovations. Mao's views thus assumed religious dimensions. A Shanghai *Liberation Daily* (*Jiefang Ribao*) editorial prophesied that, when Mao's thought was used to direct science and technology, the result would be the "creation of a host of miracles."[42] Whereas before the Cultural Revolution Mao's thought had been a guide, now it was to be the major source for scientific research. Workers who rejected "reliance on experts" and "discarded all foreign conventions and rules" in favor of Mao's thought were reported to produce thousands of technological innovations.[43]

During the Cultural Revolution China announced the development of synthesized insulin and the establishment of China's first synthetic benzene plant, but these were isolated achievements whose groundwork had been laid before the Cultural Revolution. In most areas, scientific research stagnated and even retrogressed because of disruptions, isolation from world scientific development, and the closure of universities in order to politicize their curricula. A generation of scientists was lost. Even China's nuclear weapons program, which Mao tried strenuously to insulate, was upset by Red Guard interference. Mao authorized Zhou Enlai in April 1968 to stop the disruption caused by the Red Guards in the defense agencies, but to no avail. In the following month, Red Guards again attacked leading scientists and ransacked their offices.

Among the scientists, as well as throughout the rest of the intellectual community, the threat of often violent disruptions created an atmosphere of fear and silence, which retarded their work as much as the disruptions themselves did. Intellectuals refused to speak out at political meetings, and the apathy apparently extended to their own work as well. At a study class of the Department of Mathematics and Mechanics at Qinghua University, for example, participants just stared at one another and did not talk. When asked to explain the silence, one person said: "Who dares to tell the truth at such meetings? If you reveal what is in your mind, don't you give others a chance to find fault with you?"[44] Fearing to express their own views, scientists, like their nonscientific colleagues, fell silent.

Again, Mao may not have anticipated that the overthrow of the party bureaucracy would result in the repression of scientists. Whereas Mao in December 1965 had complained that "Philosophers can't turn out philosophy, writers can't write, and historians can't produce history," he did not say the same of scientists.[45] Though he wanted them to do applied rather than theoretical work, his actions indicated that he also wanted to shield them from the kind of violent attacks that hit nonscientific intellectuals. Nonetheless, his stated distrust of experts obscured his position on scientists. Once the party bureaucracy had been purged, there was no longer a buffer between the scientists and the rampaging Red Guards, who associated the scientists with the bureaucracy they were directed to overthrow.

THE CULTURAL REVOLUTION

The Struggle Against Radical Intellectuals

With the ruthless purge of the liberal intellectuals and their political patrons, a new group, the Cultural Revolution Group, assumed direction of China's cultural life. Though formally established in August 1966, the group had already made its appearance at the time of the May 16 circular that dissolved the Group of Five. It took over control of the cultural realm, which had previously been in the hands of the Propaganda Department and the Beijing Party Committee. Unlike these organizations, which functioned under the party bureaucracy, the Cultural Revolution Group was directly responsible to Mao. It reflected Mao's desire for an organization responsive to his wishes, unlike the cultural bureaucrats.

Chen Boda was the director of the group, Jiang Qing was first deputy, and Zhang Chunqiao and Lin Jie were deputy directors. The majority of its members were radical intellectuals who had coalesced around Jiang Qing and attacked the liberal intellectuals prior to the Cultural Revolution. It included Guan Feng, Qi Benyu, Yao Wenyuan, Wang Li, who had worked in propaganda since the 1940s, and Mu Xin, a journalist for communist newspapers since the 1940s. Tao Zhu and Kang Sheng were advisers. Except for Chen Boda, who was a member of the Politburo, none of the members of the group held high party positions. The Cultural Revolution gave them the opportunity to assume informally positions held formerly by their rivals, the liberal intellectuals and their political patrons. Furthermore, when Mao forced the work teams to withdraw from the universities and the party bureaucracy lost control over higher education, the Cultural Revolution Group expanded its influence to the universities and research institutes.

With the removal of the bureaucratic leaders in the winter of 1966–1967, the Cultural Revolution Group, along with Lin Biao, purged entrenched party bureaucrats on an increasingly massive and turbulent scale. In contrast to the party bureaucracy, the group members were committed to uncontrolled rather than controlled mass movements and unlimited rather than limited power seizure. Their agents in the field were the more radical Red Guard units, to whom they were connected by old school ties.[46] For example, the Red

Guard unit at the Philosophy and Social Sciences Department was led by Guan Feng's old colleague Wu Chuanqi who, along with Zhang Chunqiao, had defended Mao's Leap policy in the late 1950s. Lin Jie, a graduate of Beijing Normal University, was close to the Jinggangshan Red Guard unit at that university. Wang Li and Guan Feng were in touch with the Earth faction, the most radical Red Guard unit in the universities in Beijing.

While the Cultural Revolution Group, with the army under Lin Biao, became the dominant political force in the Cultural Revolution, its most direct impact was in the area of its expertise, the media and academia. With its Red Guard agents, it extended the purge from Beijing to the universities, propaganda offices, and journals in the provinces. The Beijing and important provincial newspapers were temporarily suspended in order to replace their editors with associates of the group. The national media—the *People's Daily, Guangming Daily, Red Flag,* and New China News Agency—continued, as did the *Liberation Army Daily,* but with new staff dominated by the radical intellectuals. At *Red Flag,* Chen Boda became editor-in-chief; Wang Li became the first deputy editor; and Guan Feng, Qi Benyu, and Lin Jie became deputy editors. Mu Xin, deputy editor of the *Guangming Daily* at the time of the antirightist campaign in 1957, became chief editor of that paper in 1965. They all had a hand in running the *People's Daily.* Yao Wenyuan dominated literature and art.

Virtually all academic and scientific journals stopped publication, and virtually all universities, libraries, and museums were closed. Only Mao's book of quotations was to be bought in the bookstores. With a few exceptions, such as the work of the "peasant" writer Hao Ran, the major form of literary activity was collective and amateur writing. Whereas in the Leap a group of amateur writers had existed side-by-side with professionals, now amateurs were substituted for all professionals and instructed to create collectively under an assigned leader. In the early stages, the army's writers and drama troupes were quickly absorbed into the collective productions under Jiang Qing's direction. The predominant culture to emerge in the Cultural Revolution was Jiang Qing's model revolutionary works that she had begun in 1964.

In the initial period of the Cultural Revolution, radical intellectuals in the Cultural Revolution Group shared Mao's vision of the revolution. Like their liberal intellectual adversaries, they combined

THE CULTURAL REVOLUTION

a traditional Chinese and a Marxist-Leninist approach, but with different emphases. They put much greater stress on class struggle and mass mobilization than the liberal intellectuals. Whereas the liberal intellectuals looked to the distant past as an abstract source of inspiration, the radicals sought literally to repeat the immediate past. As Mao had used the peasant uprisings in south China in the 1920s to try to overthrow the landlords, the radicals advocated a similar release of mass discontent to overthrow the party bureaucrats. They also sought to perpetuate some of the revolutionary practices developed in the guerilla days at Yanan and in the Base Areas. Following the model of the schools established in the 1940s in the Base Areas to imbue students with revolutionary ideas, the radicals sought to transform the universities from centers of academic study into centers of indoctrination in the thought of Mao.

As in the tradition of the Confucian literati, the radical intellectuals much more than the liberals stressed ideology and motivation. Whereas the liberals accepted the conventional Marxist view that economic change preceded ideological change, they, like their qingyi predecessors, believed that the revival of ideological principles must precede all other changes. As a Wang Li article, written with two collaborators, pointed out, the Cultural Revolution was "a great revolution to remold the souls of the people and promote revolutionization of people's thinking, which inevitably touches every aspect of society in the political, economic, and cultural sphere."[47] The original guerrilla spirit of the Long March and Yanan had to be reinstilled in the masses in order to overcome the bureaucratic and economic obstacles to continuing the revolution. They, like Mao, held a vision of attaining a communist society by stressing human will over material limitations, revolutionary virtue over professional merit, and ideological mobilization over political organization.

In a further departure from traditional Marxism, they charged that a new class had emerged in China based on political and professional rather than economic position. Economic relations had changed, but the ideological superstructure had not. The unchanged superstructure promoted specialization and professionalization within the party and among intellectuals, divorcing both groups from the masses. This elite obstructed revolution and produced revisionism, as in the Soviet Union. It had originally been thought that when the party seized power, the ideological and political structure would be revolutionized along with the economy, but this had not happened because, according to Wang Li, "the overthrown exploiting classes have been using the relative superiority they still possess in the ideological and cultural spheres . . . to poison people's minds in order to extend their own positions and create public opinion for staging a restoration."[48] To rid China of this new or old class, the radical intellectuals called for a system of general elections to be held in all organs of power leading the Cultural Revolution. The masses would thus have the power to replace officials through election or to recall any official, supposedly making it impossible for this elite to hold onto its power.

These views sparked conflicts both within the Cultural Revolution Group and with its mentor Mao. The first major conflict centered on Tao Zhu, first secretary of the Central-South Region. In the early stages of the Cultural Revolution, Tao Zhu had continued to express the radical position he had advocated in the 1964 controversy over opera reform. In April 1966, in the midst of the Wu Han campaign, Tao Zhu bemoaned the elitist nature of the academic community. He demanded that philosophy and social sciences associations be transformed into elected organizations and that professional unions, such as the All-China Federation of Literature and Art or the Chinese Journalists Association, be "changed into an extensive revolutionary mass organization." He recommended that an internal publication be established to communicate and organize this transformation. And he proposed the revolutionizing of the universities, because a university training turned one into "a bourgeois intellectual."[49]

However, Tao Zhu also echoed Peng Zhen's policy of restraint in treating intellectuals. He cautioned that "Middle-of-the-roaders are temporarily not wanted, but this must not be made public." In fact, what he suggested was a rectification behind closed doors along the lines of the party's 1964 rectification. He warned that "the scope must not be too wide."[50] Although influential intellectuals such as Wu Han and Jian Bozan should be treated as guilty of "antagonistic" ideological contradictions, they should not be criticized too sharply. They could retain their official positions. Tao recommended that the unorthodox philosopher Liu Jie not be thrown out of the Philosophical Association. Although "right wingers" were not wanted in professional organizations, Tao advised that if they were already in such organizations, they should not be purged. Thus, while he called for

THE CULTURAL REVOLUTION

revolutionizing the intellectuals, he sought to do so without intense public struggle, preferring the party-approved method of behind-the-doors criticism. His approach was consistent with his views of the early 1960s which expressed distaste for public humiliation, particularly of intellectuals.

Despite his known desire for restraint, which was in opposition to Mao's demand for open, expanded struggle, Tao Zhu became director of the Propaganda Department in June 1966, replacing Lu Dingyi. His appointment, along with Liu Shaoqi and Deng Xiaoping's support of Mao's purge of the Beijing Party Committee and the old Propaganda Department, indicated that Mao and the party bureaucracy still sought to work together. Tao may also have endeared himself to Mao because of his active role in opera reform and because of the fact that in the spring of 1966 the newspapers from his area of Guangdong echoed the slogans of the radical intellectuals. Yao Wenyuan later described Tao's switch to the radical position: "When the masses rose up to criticize, with a twist of the body he made a sudden change and appeared in the guise of an ultra 'left' anarchist."[51] Apparently, his sudden switch further enhanced his standing in Mao's eyes, because at the Eleventh Plenum in August 1966 he was ranked fourth in the political hierarchy, just behind Mao, Lin Biao, and Zhou Enlai.

However, just as dramatically as Tao Zhu rose, he fell. The reasons for his fall are complex, but they stem from his previous views and actions. In line with his call for restraint, he sought to dampen the struggle against the intellectuals. He went along with Liu Shaoqi and Deng Xiaoping in sending work teams to the universities. He also supported Xiao Wangdong, who became Minister of Culture when Lu Dingyi was purged. Xiao, though a high army political official, was a follower of Liu's and had advised the work teams to limit their own actions. Tao, as his superior, had shielded Xiao from attack for his restraint. Tao was also charged with manipulating the media in order to protect the party bureaucracy. He supposedly joined two different news pictures together so that Liu was placed beside Mao, and in another picture Deng's head was placed on the body of Chen Yi, who was positioned closer to Mao. Furthermore, Tao sought to protect the provinces, particularly his regional power base in the Central-South Region, from the disruptions of the uncontrollable Red Guards.

Therefore, the radicals could not completely seize power from the party bureaucracy without first removing Tao Zhu, the last remaining spokesman for the party leadership. In January 1967 Tao, along with an associate, Wang Renzhong, and his administrators in the Central-South Region, were removed and imprisoned. With Tao's purge, the radical intellectuals were fully in control of the Cultural Revolution Group and China's cultural and intellectual life. Tao died in prison in 1969 under harsh circumstances. Before his death, he left a poem that revealed the despair of a revolutionary who gave his life for a cause which had rejected him:

My hair turns white as the seasons pitilessly pass;
My remaining life in shame, my bitterness I suppress.
A sick horse neighs in the stable, too late to join the battle;
A withered palm tree fears the onslaught of the frost.
All one's past exploits forgotten, vanished like the mists;
Yet wide the world before me, my heart free of selfish desires.[52]

Whereas Tao Zhu's alliance with Mao had been based not on ideological commitment but on political expediency, that of the radical intellectuals was based on an ideological commitment to Mao's revolutionary vision as well as on the desire for power. Yet as the Cultural Revolution unfolded, Mao retreated from this vision, while they upheld it. They were more committed to their patron's vision than he was. As in the traditional qingyi movements, political pressures forced the ruler to play down and then oppose the ideological demands of his idealistic intellectual allies.

The divergence between Mao and the radical intellectuals started with the establishment of a commune in the radicals' stronghold in Shanghai. In January 1967, an alliance of students overthrew the old Shanghai Party Committee, and in February it proclaimed the establishment of the Shanghai People's Commune. On February 6, thirty-eight Shanghai rebel groups announced that the Shanghai People's Commune had established a steering committee as its highest organ, staffed by representatives of mass organizations. Zhang Chunqiao, along with Yao Wenyuan, arrived from Beijing to head the commune as its first and second secretaries. It was patterned after the Paris Commune of 1871, which was greatly admired by the radical intellectuals because it was thought to have practiced mass participatory democracy. The Shanghai Commune similarly sought to overthrow the bureaucratic authorities, allow the masses direct participation in government, and prevent the emergence of a new elite. The establishment of the commune transformed the Cultural Revolution from a purge of the existing system to an all-out assault on the system itself.

Such a radical action had been inherent in the Cultural Revolution virtually from the start. The Sixteen Points issued at the Eleventh Plenum specifically called for a system of general elections and the right of recall on the order of the Paris Commune. Even before the Cultural Revolution, these principles had been repeatedly proclaimed by Chen Boda and the radical intellectuals, particularly Guan Feng and Lin Jie. Although Mao had made only passing reference to the Paris Commune in his writings, at the time the first wall poster went up at Beijing University in June 1966, he described it as "a declaration of a Chinese Paris Commune for the sixth decade of the twentieth century, the significance of which surpasses that of the Paris Commune itself."[53]

The Shanghai Commune, therefore, was the ultimate result of both Mao and the radical intellectuals' inciting the revolutionary masses to seize power from below, overthrow the office-holders, and create a new revolutionary organization on the order of the Paris Commune. The establishment of the new political structure, however, was accompanied by conflict between the old Shanghai leaders and the rebels, as well as among the rebelling groups themselves. As some groups of workers and students participated in large-scale demonstrations in support of the commune, other groups of workers and students protested by cutting off the electricity and water. The factories ceased functioning. Shanghai virtually came to a standstill. The mass movement was out of control and wreaked havoc in China's most industrialized center.

Although in January 1967 Mao had praised the upsurge of revolutionary power in Shanghai as an example for the whole country, after the establishment of the commune in February, he sought to dampen the upsurge. The Shanghai Commune created such chaos and concern in the army that Mao had little choice but to restore order if he were to maintain his rule. On February 12, he asked Zhang Chunqiao and Yao Wenyuan to come to Beijing, where he informed them that the Shanghai Commune's slogan of "overthrow everything" was "reactionary" and its demand to do away with all "heads" was "anarchism."[54] Mao revealed that although many areas had asked for permission to establish their own people's communes, he had refused because he considered the commune too weak in suppressing counter-revolutionaries. He therefore directed the Shanghai Commune to dissolve itself into a Revolutionary Committee.

Mao's rejection of the commune demonstrated that he wanted mass movements to overthrow his bureaucratic enemies, but not to overthrow all authority. It was not leadership but particular leaders that he opposed; he did not oppose mass mobilization but did oppose mass participation. Thus, on February 24, 1967, on Mao's instructions, Zhang Chunqiao and Yao Wenyuan dutifully replaced the Shanghai Commune by a Revolutionary Committee, a political structure based not just on representatives of the masses but on a three-way alliance that included the army and revolutionary party cadres as well as the masses. The effect was to suppress the masses. Power shifted to the army and the cadres in the Revolutionary Committee. The one representative of the masses to be retained was Wang Hongwen, a middle-level cadre of the Shanghai Seventh Textile Mill, who became a member of the Shanghai wing of the Cultural Revolution Group. Thus, after only nineteen days the commune ceased to exist, and other areas canceled plans for similar communes. This denouement marked the beginning of Mao's disillusionment with extensive democracy and his retreat from the initial goal of the Cultural Revolution to establish a new kind of society. It also marked the beginning of his break with the radical intellectuals. While the Shanghai contingent obediently carried out Mao's bidding, the contingent connected with the Philosophy and Social Sciences Department of the Academy of Sciences in Beijing was less willing to retreat from Mao's initial goals.

This break, however, was not immediately apparent, because the Cultural Revolution turned shortly afterward to a formal denunciation of Liu Shaoqi. Until this time, Liu had been denounced only with the euphemism "the first capitalist roader," but on March 30, 1967, the radical intellectual Qi Benyu launched the first outright attack on Liu in *Red Flag*. Mao had gone over the manuscript and added passages. The article did not discuss Liu's pragmatic economic policies or his emphasis on bureaucratic controls, which had already been criticized informally. Instead, as befitted Qi's and Mao's concern with ideological issues, it attacked Liu's historical views. The focus was on the film *The Inside Story of the Qing Court*, which Lu Dingyi, Zhou Yang, and the ideological theorist Hu Qiaomu had approved for showing in 1950 against Jiang Qing's protests. On October 15, 1954, Mao had denounced the film, along with another film, *The Story of Wu Xun*, and ordered Liu to stop its showing. But Liu and the others disregarded Mao's order. Their noncompliance apparently still rankled with Mao after ten years, because on December 21, 1965, he referred to the film as "treasonable—out-and-out treason."[55]

In 1967, Qi Benyu set out to prove Liu Shaoqi's treasonous nature by analyzing the film's treatment of the Boxer uprising. Although the Boxer sequence in the film was a minor episode, Qi treated it as if it were the major theme. In an effort to equate the Boxers with the Red Guards, Qi praised the Boxers as revolutionary because they had opposed the prevailing system. One's attitude toward their movement was therefore "a touchstone to distinguish genuine revolutionaries from fake." Since Liu had approved a film that disparaged the Boxers as "ignorant people engaged in 'witchcraft,' " he was a fake revolutionary. At the same time, because the film glorified the Hundred Days of Reform of the emperor and the Westernized literati reformers, Liu was supporting a similar kind of "bourgeois reformism." Qi repudiated this approach of trying to make China "rich and strong" by means of constitutional reform and economic modernization rather than revolutionary struggle.[56]

While Qi and his associates continued to incite the Red Guards in clashes and violence on the order of the Boxers, their political patron, Mao, despite his help in writing the article, sought to bring them under control. Power in the Revolutionary Committees he had ordered established gravitated toward regional military commanders and experienced party cadres and away from representatives of the masses, whose number was drastically reduced. Since the radicals were the political sponsors of the representatives of the masses, this shift threatened not only their ideology, but also their power. Although they had become a political faction as well as an intellectual faction, with the possible exception of Zhang Chunqiao, they had no administrative, organizational, or economic experience. Rather, like the nineteenth-century qingyi literati, they were imbued with a sense of mission to purify government by their beliefs. They regarded themselves as the transmitters of the true values. Mao had needed their talents in the early stage of the Cultural Revolution when he sought to take over the propaganda, media, and cultural spheres, to incite the masses against the party leadership, and to regenerate a revolutionary spirit. But as these goals were achieved and as Mao retreated to a more limited ideological and mass campaign, he no longer needed their literary skills, ideological polemics, and moral fervor. In fact, these very qualities undermined his current effort to reestablish order and control.

By the spring of 1967, even the media dominated by the radical intellectuals was filled with articles denouncing anarchism. A New China News Agency release described anarchist thought as "the enemy of the proletarian revolutionaries."[57] The *Guangming Daily* asserted that anarchism was opposed to the correct view of the revolution because it aimed at "overthrowing all authorities."[58] Even radical Red Guard newspapers condemned anarchism for causing disunity within the revolutionary movement.

However, alongside these denunciations of anarchism and affirmations of authority, the very same papers continued to include articles articulating the original ideals of the Cultural Revolution which Mao had begun to compromise. They still spouted the slogans "Rebellion is justified" and "Destruction before construction," which Mao in early 1967 had rejected. By the summer of 1967, the papers were inciting rebellion not only against party bureaucrats but also against military leaders and even Zhou Enlai, holding them responsible for the suppression of the masses. On July 19 and 20, 1967, Lin Jie coined the slogan "Seize the small handful of those in authority in the army who take the capitalist road." Jiang Qing on July 26, 1967, summoned Maoist groups in Honan to take up arms against the military.

These calls to arms by such authoritative figures as members of the Cultural Revolution Group appeared to signal a purge of the military comparable to the purge of the party. Accordingly, Red Guards attacked various regional militay commanders and army units and seized weapons, which they used to oppose the restoration of order. The army defended itself by instigating other groups to attack Red Guards, which resulted in increasingly violent confrontations. The radicals, as editors of the major national newspapers, sent journalists to report on these attacks, provoking further confrontations and a return to chaos in certain areas. These events climaxed with the Wuhan mutiny of late July 1967, in which several hundred thousand steel workers and militia, euphemistically called the "One Million Heroes," supported by the regional military commander Chen Zaidao, clashed with an alliance of younger radical workers and Red

Guard groups. This clash erupted into a large-scale battle. When Mao's emissaries, Wang Li and Xie Fuzhi, were sent to investigate, they were taken into custody by the "One Million Heroes" and forced to parade through the streets of Wuhan and endure the abuse of onlookers in the same manner as they themselves had earlier humiliated their victims. They were not released until gunboats and paratroopers threatened the city. Chen Zaidao was relieved of his post but not made an object of attack.

The radicals nevertheless continued to incite Red Guards to attack regional military commanders. The national media from late July through early August was filled with calls to purge ideologically impure military as well as party leaders. On August 1, 1967, Wang Li, in collaboration with Guan Feng and Lin Jie, proclaimed a mass criticism movement throughout the country against a handful of power-holders taking the capitalist road in the army and party. And at a Red Guard rally on August 7, Wang Li called for a purge of the army and of regional commanders in Guangzhou, Nanjing, and other areas.

At the same time that they were fomenting attacks on the army, the radicals continued to instigate the Red Guards against the remaining government bureaucracy. Zhou Enlai was besieged for eighteen hours in his office on August 26. The radicals regarded him as a major obstruction to the Cultural Revolution because he condemned the seizure of government offices and the humiliation of old comrades. This was not the first clash between the radicals and Zhou. In April 1967, the radicals had instigated Red Guards to occupy the Foreign Ministry under Zhou's jurisdiction, and in May 1967 Red Guards took over and burned the British chargé d'affaires office. The radicals' purpose was to turn embassies into centers of agitation against the host governments. They also incited Red Guards to attack Mao's old comrade, the former Foreign Minister Chen Yi. More disruptive even than the Red Guards' abuse of Mao's few remaining comrades was their subjection of military commanders to the same public humiliation and physical assault that they had once used against the intellectuals and party officials.

As the scale and scope of the violence escalated and the specter of civil war and economic chaos loomed, the regional military commanders, the central military under Lin Biao, and the veteran bureaucrats under Zhou Enlai were galvanized into a united front against the radicals. Under pressure from these groups and on a tour at this time of central and eastern China, where he must have seen at first hand a situation bordering on anarchy, Mao apparently concluded that there was no alternative but to curb the Cultural Revolution before it degenerated into civil war. Even though he had called for "bombarding the headquarters," his goal from the start had been to revolutionize the existing ruling structure, not to destroy it. Suddenly in mid-August the call to purge the military leaders ceased in the media. In September, there was a purge of most of the radical intellectuals in the Cultural Revolution Group, primarily the branch associated with the Philosophy and Social Sciences Department. Guan Feng, Lin Jie, Mu Xin, Wang Li, and their ideological colleagues, such as Wu Chuanqi and Lin Youshi, were imprisoned.

The Shanghai contingent—Zhang Chunqiao, Yao Wenyuan, and Jiang Qing—who had previously compromised on the Shanghai Commune, quickly and visibly disassociated themselves from their former associates. On September 5, Jiang Qing repudiated the attacks on the military commanders and the seizure of weapons and sought to distinguish between attacks on party leaders and on military leaders: "We can talk only about dragging out the handful of party capitalist roaders in authority and nothing else." She failed to mention that she previously had called for an attack on military leaders, nor did she mention that the "ultraleftists" she now denounced were her former allies. Pressure must have been put on her to condemn them because, she said, "Old Kang [Sheng] just dragged me here." Yet she also had a personal grievance against the "ultraleftists" for collecting dossiers on her as well as Zhou Enlai. Although she had been instrumental in fomenting factions, she now accused the "ultraleftists" of fomenting factions which would lead to anarchism and counter-revolution: "We oppose people who oppose the leadership group of the party Central Committee headed by Chairman Mao either from the left, the extreme left, or the right side." She now proclaimed, "The revolution cannot proceed without leaders!"[59]

Jiang Qing's Shanghai supporters followed suit. The Shanghai newspapers in the fall of 1967 condemned "ultraleftists" for interference in state affairs. Yao Wenyuan was also prominent in attacking his radical colleagues: "Using slogans that sound extremely 'left' but in essence are extremely right, they have stirred up evil gusts of 'doubting everyone' while bombarding the proletarian headquarters, creating dissension, and exploiting confusion."[60] These were the very same "crimes" that he and his radical colleagues had earlier attributed to the liberal intellectuals and their political patrons.

The purged radicals were identified as leaders of the May 16 Group, named after the circular of May 16, which had announced the end of the Group of Five and the establishment of the Cultural Revolution Group. It was an appropriate name for a group which had sought to achieve the original goals of the Cultural Revolution. Yao Wenyuan, in an effort to disassociate himself from his one-time allies, charged that the Philosophy and Social Sciences Department was the stronghold of the May 16th Group, whose followers were hidden underground in Beijing where, at night, they put up posters and planted slogans. Others charged that the group's rank and file were students of varying ideologies in universities in Beijing, particularly the Beijing Normal University, Beijing College of Geology, and Beijing Aeronautic Institute, which were also centers of radical Red Guard action. The ties between the May 16th Group and the purged radicals were never proven. The group's leaders and members were never specifically identified. Most likely, the regime sought to associate the purged radicals with the May 16th Group in order to separate them from the Cultural Revolution Group, which was so closely identified with Mao. To condemn that group was to condemn Mao and his closest advisers. Identifying the purged members instead with the May 16th Group was a means of shielding Mao.

Ironically, it is precisely because the purged members of the Cultural Revolution Group had carried out Mao's original orders to rebel against authority and to galvanize mass discontent that they became the scapegoats for the anarchy which inevitably resulted from such policies. But they were now expendable in Mao's effort to reestablish order, because their impact was essentially destructive, even though they sought also to construct a new society. They exacerbated Mao's relations with the bureaucracy and especially with the military commanders, whom he needed to reassert control. Although Chen Boda, Kang Sheng, and the Shanghai group had also continued to pursue divisive policies after Mao's moderation of his, they escaped blame this time because, unlike their radical allies, whose only weapons were ideological and intellectual prowess, they were higher-level officials and closer to Mao.

Probably because he was more closely connected to Jiang Qing than the other members of the Philosophy and Social Sciences Department, Qi Benyu was not purged until December 1967. He had been a favorite of Jiang Qing's since his indirect criticism of Peng Dehuai in his attack on the Taiping general Li Xiucheng in 1964. More recently, in addition to launching the formal attack on Liu Shaoqi, Qi had praised Jiang Qing's pet projects, such as the model revolutionary operas, and denounced her pet peeves, such as the Russian literary critics and nineteenth century European literature. In the summer of 1967, Qi had also incited his fellow revolutionaries to do battle with the capitalist roaders in the military. Although delayed, his purge, when it came with his imprisonment in early 1968, was no less harsh.

With the purge of their colleagues, the Shanghai contingent retreated somewhat. Their media outlets were temporarily curtailed. *Red Flag*, their chief mouthpiece, was suspended from November 1967 to June 1968. The introduction to the materials criticizing the writer Hu Feng, which had launched the 1955 campaign against intellectuals and was now attributed to Mao, was reprinted on September 6, 1967, as part of the effort to condemn intellectuals who interfered in politics. This was another irony, because Hu Feng was a disciple of Lu Xun, the symbolic hero of the Cultural Revolution. The introduction stated: "In the past, it was said that they were a group of simple cultural people. This is wrong, because they have worked their way into the political, military, economic, cultural, and educational establishments."[61] With this warning against intellectuals interfering in politics, the Shanghai group turned once again to the performing arts. Jiang Qing in November 1967 apologized that over the past two years she had neglected her work in transforming opera, music, and film. From this point on, the Cultural Revolution began to wind down.

Still, the "ultraleftists" had a lingering influence, which blossomed briefly in the spring of 1968. Given the powers arrayed against them, including that of their patron Mao, and their lack of organizational roots, the radical intellectuals in the Philosophy and Social Sciences Department had been easy to purge. Although some of their followers were involved in armed skirmishes, they too were not difficult to suppress once their instigators had been removed. But it had not been these disruptive actions so much as the ideas of the radicals that undermined the reestablishment of order. Although their spokesmen were purged, the ideas continued to be expressed indirectly in the Shanghai newspapers. While repudiating the May 16th Group in particular, the Shanghai newspapers urged restraint toward radicals in general. The *Liberation Daily* issued a warning on September 12, 1967, that, "We should never allow the handful of party persons in authority taking the capitalist road and the remnant conservative forces holding fast to the bourgeois reactionary line to launch revengeful counterattacks against the proletarian revolutionaries under the camouflage of 'opposing the trend of the extreme "left" thought.' "[62]

More significant, radical Red Guards continued to put up posters and circulate pamphlets which preached, now unofficially, the principles of the Cultural Revolution that had been abandoned. Though it was charged that the purged members of the Cultural Revolution Group were the theorists behind these groups, no direct connection was specified. Nevertheless, the sense of betrayal expressed by these semiclandestine groups echoed ideas that the radical intellectual had once articulated officially.

The most articulate of these radical Red Guard groups was the Hunan Provincial Proletarian Revolutionary Great Alliance Committee, abbreviated as Sheng-wu-lian. It was an alliance of about twenty Red Guard groups in Hunan which had liaison with groups in other parts of the country. In January 1968, one of its pamphlets charged that although the Cultural Revolution had purged officials, the bureaucratic machinery and military establishment remained to perpetuate the old state and privileged system that repressed the masses. If the Cultural Revolution were truly antiorganizational and antibureaucratic, it would attack not only the party but the powerful military establishment as well. Sheng-wu-lian still held, as did the radical intellectuals and at one point Mao himself, a utopian, antibureaucratic vision. They were most critical of Zhou Enlai and the leaders of the army for repressing the Cultural Revolution, but they also expressed disillusionment with Mao for purging the radicals and retreating from the revolution's goals. Despite Mao's rejection of the idea, they still looked to a commune-style government as the model for a new type of political system in which the masses could participate fully.

Sheng-wu-lian regarded the establishment of the Revolutionary Committees as tantamount to reinstating the bureaucracy and repressing the masses. Specifically, the group criticized the leaders of the Hunan Revolutionary Committee, one of whom was Hua Guofeng, who was to become prime minister in January 1976. Although Mao had sanctioned these Revolutionary Committees, Sheng-wu-lian blamed Zhou Enlai and party officials for their establishment all over the country. They viewed the crushing of the attacks on the military and bureaucracy and the purge of the Cultural Revolution Group as an indication that one type of bourgeois rule had been replaced by another. The addition of a few representatives of the masses was merely window-dressing. The Cultural Revolution, the group declared, should not be merely a matter of dismissing officials or a purely cultural revolution, but should be "a revolution in which one class overthrows another."[63] Therefore, they urged the forceful overthrow of the prevailing system. Sheng-wu-lian compared themselves to the Russian Soviets, those councils of workers, peasants, and soldiers, established in 1917, which were embryonic communes. Their purpose was to carry out a pure revolution in a localized area as the first step toward revolutionizing all of China, a task that they believed had been abandoned.

An indication that these ideas were held by more than a few groups of youth and indeed had widespread lingering influence can be seen in the sharp opposition to Sheng-wu-lian at a high level. Within a week of expressing these views publicly, Sheng-wu-lian was disbanded. Once again, the few remaining members of the Cultural Revolution Group were prominent in repudiating this radical group. At a meeting to denounce the group in Beijing on January 21–24, 1968, Kang Sheng hurled vituperative charges at it, calling it an ally of American imperialists, Soviet revisionists, Trotskyites, and the Guomindang. Jiang Qing and Yao Wenyuan were a bit more restrained. Jiang Qing limited her condemnation to the leaders and absolved the "hoodwinked" masses.[64] Pressure from Zhou Enlai for criticism of the radical group was suggested in Yao's statement, "The Premier wants me to say a few words and that is all I have to say."[65] Despite Yao's apparently reluctant repudiation of Sheng-wu-lian, his public remarks in 1968 followed the Mao-Zhou Enlai line. He praised the leadership of the Revolutionary Committees and criticized "intellectuals" for inciting "civil war."[66] However, none of the critics of Sheng-wu-lian and of other leftists groups responded to Sheng-wu-lian's fundamental critique of the Cultural Revolution as a movement that merely purged officials but did not create a new structure which would eliminate the evils of bureaucracy.

Outbreaks of rebellious Red Guards and the appearance of wall posters expressing the ideas of radical intellectuals continued into 1968, but they were brief and sporadic. The purge of the Cultural Revolution Group had removed the political group that encouraged radical activities, and in the summer of 1968 their agents, the Red Guards, were disbanded and sent to the countryside. Mao himself authorized the Red Guards' dispersion. Their exit reflected his disillusionment not only with radical intellectuals but also with youth as the embodiment of revolutionary virtue. In a meeting of Red Guard leaders in July 1968, Mao reportedly broke down and wept as he condemned their disunity and failure to achieve his revolutionary objectives. Worker and army propaganda teams were ordered to take over their duties and reestablish authority in institutions of higher learning.

The radical intellectuals became the scapegoats in the Cultural Revolution not only because Mao lacked a plan for the realization of his vision, but also because he did not fully comprehend the implications of his vision. He had not anticipated the consequences. He himself admitted on October 24, 1966, "One big-character poster, the Red Guards, the great exchange of revolutionary experience, and nobody—not even I—expected that all the provinces and cities would be thrown into confusion."[67] Mao compromised his revolutionary vision both because of outside pressures and because of his own unwillingness to accept its inherent anarchy. Thus, as the turmoil and factionalism implicit in the revolution's rhetoric intensified, Mao betrayed its ideals as well as its spokesmen, the radical intellectuals, who had assumed the responsibility for fulfilling those ideals. But even if Mao had not betrayed them, the radical intellectuals were ill equipped by experiences and skill to go beyond the overthrowing of authority to the establishment of a new order. Like their qingyi predecessors, the radicals' alliance with the ruler was short-lived, because the disruption that ensued from their ideological fervor forced their political patron to retreat from ideals they shared.

6

IDEOLOGICAL
DIVERGENCE
OF THE SHANGHAI
GROUP

When the Cultural Revolution was concluded in 1969, the remnant of the radical intellectuals, the Shanghai group, appeared to be at the height of their political power. Although Jiang Qing, Zhang Chunqiao, and Yao Wenyuan, the group's top leaders, never had been members of the Central Committee, at the Ninth Party Congress of April 1969 they became members of the Politburo. Despite their previously close relationship with Lin Biao and Chen Boda, they now joined with Mao, Zhou Enlai, and the regional military commanders to oppose Chen and Lin Biao, who had gained increasing power and obstructed the reestablishment of party and civilian authority. Chen was imprisoned in the late summer of 1970, culminating the purge of the radical intellectuals associated with him in running the *Red Flag*. A year later after an abortive coup against Mao, Lin Biao reportedly died in an airplane crash while trying to escape to the Soviet Union.

Although ostensibly a powerful political faction, the Shanghai group in reality was much weaker than they had been as an informal political body of the Cultural

Revolution Group, which had been abolished at the Ninth Party congress. Despite their alliance with the party bureaucratic leaders in the struggle against Lin Biao, they were excluded from the task of rebuilding the party and government. This task was carried out by rehabilitated party bureaucrats, under the leadership of Zhou Enlai and, later, Deng Xiaoping, who after seven years in disgrace was brought back from exile in 1973 when Zhou became fatally ill with cancer. Except in the cultural and educational realm, where the Shanghai group still predominated, the distribution of power once again became more favorable to the veteran leadership, who returned in increasing numbers from exile, prison, farms and factories to fill the party bureaucracy, economic ministries, and military hierarchy.

Whereas some Cultural Revolution programs associated with the Shanghai group were continued, such as the forced indoctrination of officials and intellectuals in Mao's thought and the dispersion of urban youth to the countryside, other programs associated with them were gradually diluted, even in the universities and performing arts, the areas of their dominance. Political correctness and work experience, which had been established during the Cultural Revolution as the criteria for entrance to the universities, remained, but academic criteria were reintroduced. Jiang Qing's model revolutionary productions still dominated opera, film, dance, and music, but a diversity of local operas reappeared. There was greater variety not only in the performing arts but also in literature. Although material incentives were still ritually denounced, they slowly reemerged. The Shanghai group became increasingly on the defensive as they were isolated more and more, not only from the centers of political and economic power, but even from their own power base in the cultural sphere.

While remaining a political faction, the Shanghai group reassumed in the early 1970s some of the characteristics of an intellectual group, even though their more intellectual members, those associated with the Philosophy and Social Sciences Department, had been purged in the Cultural Revolution. The ability of the group's members to express themselves publicly, and even their very existence, were dependent on their political patron, Mao. Although they maintained their predominance in Shanghai, their support there was superficial. Their bases of power were primarily in the universities, the arts, and the media—the very areas from which they had ousted the liberal intellectuals. Since their power lay in the cultural realm, they fought back in the manner of intellectuals by means of ideological and intellectual persuasion expressed in the central media, which they still dominated: the party's official paper the *People's Daily*; its ideological journal, the *Red Flag*; and the *Guangming Daily*. They also used the same camouflage that they and the liberal intellectuals had employed in the first half of the 1960s—the traditional methods of historical and philosophical analogy, ideological debate, and literary criticism. No longer able to engage openly in name-calling and purges because of strong opposition, they expressed themselves once again through allusions, analogies, and allegories. They sought through these traditional devices to influence public opinion and sway policy makers to continue the programs of the Cultural Revolution.

The actions of the Shanghai group, however, tended to be more negative than positive. Through their domination of the media, they were able to prevent the party bureaucracy from defending its views publicly in a sustained way and to block initiatives abolishing Cultural Revolution programs. They denied coverage to the bureaucracy's reports, conferences, and positions. But they could create the impression of popular indignation against party policies and leaders more easily than they could generate popular support for their own policies. Although they were able to obstruct their bureaucratic adversaries, they were less able to revive the impetus for a new revolutionary drive. They could no longer provide the revolutionary ideology that had appealed to large numbers of idealistic youth and workers in the Cultural Revolution. Because of the loss of the contingent from the Philosophy and Social Sciences Department which had provided the major ideological arguments, and because of their own compromises, the Shanghai group's ideological appeal was weakened. Despite their rhetoric, they were concerned more with the struggle for power than with the implementation of principles.

The Shanghai group undertook several initiatives to organize a mass base among workers, women, and youth, most of which failed. Wang Hongwen, the worker member of the Shanghai group leadership, organized the first urban militias in Shanghai and sponsored this model throughout the country. But in most other places these militias came under the sway of the army's regional commanders. The Shanghai group could get only a small number of their followers into provincial posts with authority. Whereas during the Cultural Revolution they had been able to mobilize a popular base to support the purge of the party hierarchy, the chaotic nature of the revolution had dissipated its base. They also lacked the organizing skills and resources to consolidate a mass base.[1] Their support was superficial, limited to pockets of radical students and professors in elite universities in Shanghai, Beijing, Guangzhou, and Liaoning and to a small number of young, relatively unskilled workers.

Although their bases of support in the media, culture, and the universities were in no way comparable to the forces arrayed against them, the Shanghai group created the impression that they had more power than they actually possessed. The group's control of the media in particular gave their pronouncements an aura of legitimacy, for the population had grown accustomed to trusting the media's pronouncements as an accurate reflection of official policy even though that was no longer true. Since the early 1960s the media had expressed a variety of views—those of Mao, the bureaucracy, the liberal intellectuals, and the radical intellectuals, among others—but the shades of distinction among these views may have been too subtle for the average person to comprehend. The Shanghai group's domination of the media was thus sufficient to enable it to project a seemingly national ideological tone.

Using the traditional mode of dissent, the Shanghai group launched three different media campaigns from 1973 until the death of Mao in 1976—on Confucianism, the dictatorship of the proletariat, and the Chinese tale *Water Margin*. A media campaign was the most intensive, direct means of political communication by which the population learned of policy directions, priorities, and "enemies." It was therefore the Shanghai group's sharpest weapon in their effort to regain the initiative from their bureaucratic rivals.

However, the bureaucratic leaders subtly thwarted these campaigns, even as the Shanghai group with less subtlety thwarted the bureaucratic leaders. Zhou Enlai's authority made it possible to interject the bureaucratic view at critical points in the media, in spite of the Shanghai group's domination. Thus, when the Shanghai group launched a campaign, the bureaucracy deflected its blows, redirected its goals, and reinterpreted its slogans to communicate a contrary political message. Just as the Shanghai group used the campaigns to continue Cultural Revolution policies and oppose the bureaucracy, the bureaucratic leaders used them to discontinue Cultural Revolution policies, reassert their own power, and return China to more conventional administrative, economic, and educational practices. Similarly, as the Shanghai group used the campaigns to espouse revolutionary values of struggle, mass mobilization, and ideological commitment, the bureaucratic leaders used them to espouse opposing values of unity, discipline, and production.

The effect of these opposing signals was to obscure the message. The media campaigns, once the most direct form of political communication, now expressed contradictory values and a variety of views, as in the pre-Cultural Revolution period, which confused rather than indoctrinated the public whose support each side sought. The disguised polemics of both sides were so shrouded in symbolism that they could barely be understood by the elite, let alone by the workers and peasants. The abstruseness of the debates discouraged the involvement of the masses on either side, perhaps purposely in order to limit disruption. This seemingly controlled arrangement reflected not a compromise, but a stalemate, created by fear of provoking again the open disruption and near anarchy of the Cultural Revolution.

Although the media campaigns were widespread and intensive, extending down to the villages and factories, they were not emotional and uncontrolled like the Cultural Revolution. They were more in the nature of nationwide study movements, carried out through reading and commenting on ancient texts and ideological doctrine. Instead of swelling into purges against living figures, these campaigns chose their victims only from the dead. As in the pre-Cultural Revolution period, it was as if both sides accepted certain defined limits within which to wage the political struggle.

The conflict was also contained because both factions spoke primarily through groups of intellectuals rather than through individuals. As opposed to the early 1960s, the major spokesmen for the two sides were not famous intellectuals with reputations and constituencies of their own. With a few exceptions, such as Yang Rongquo, a professor of philosophy at Zhongshan University, and Feng Youlan of Beijing University, the spokesmen were anonymous writing groups. Whereas the bureaucratic leaders used a variety of pseudonymous spokesmen, the Shanghai group used a more consistent body of writing groups, which turned out hundreds of articles. The Luo Siding writing group, which had been in existence since before the Cultural Revolution and was comprised of intellectuals from Fudan University in Shanghai, came under the patronage of the Shanghai group in the early 1970s.[2] The writing group Liang Xiao, which suddenly appeared in late 1973, was made up of about thirty people from Beijing University and Qinghua University. The writing group Chi Heng was controlled by Yao Wenyuan and some of his followers on the editorial board of the *Red Flag.* Another writing group, Chu Lan, was under the leadership of one of the followers of the Shanghai group, the former opera singer Yu Huiyong, who was to become minister of culture in 1974.[3] It wrote particularly about the arts. The Shanghai group also controlled other writing groups at the universities of Beijing, Qinghua, Fudan, Nanjing, and Liaoning.

Jiang Qing and Zhang Chunqiao worked closely with these writing groups, particularly with Liang Xiao, but it was Yao Wenyuan who personally supervised most of their writing, determining their subject matter, content, structure, and pseudonyms. The Shanghai group communicated with their collective spokesmen either in person or by letter, phone, courier, or confidant. The relationship, however, was not all one-sided. At times the writing groups acted in an advisory capacity. They reported findings and made suggestions. They also compiled dossiers on leading party and military officials. Circumventing bureaucratic procedure, they worked in secrecy. They did not always conform to the dictates of the Shanghai group, as their loyalty was sometimes bought by presents and promises of official position.

Still another reason for the stalemated character of the conflict between the Shanghai group and the bureaucratic leaders was Mao's ambivalent role. He remained the political patron and protector of the Shanghai group, supporting their opposition to the reemergence of material incentives and intellectual and cultural elites. Nevertheless, he identified at times with the bureaucratic leaders whose goal, like his, was to reestablish unity and end divisions. At the Ninth Party Congress on April 28, 1969, he asked: "Which is better, to unite more people or less people? It is always better to unite more people. Some people's opinions differ from ours, but it is not a case of the relationship between us and the enemy."[4]

There was an inherent tension in Mao's relationship with the Shanghai group. His concern was to maintain revolutionary principles; the group's was to continue the power struggle. He sought to revive the party organization, while the group sought to block the return of party officials. Consequently, at times Mao clashed with and reprimanded members of the Shanghai group. In the summer of 1971 his remark with reference to Lin Biao's wife could easily have been interpreted as a criticism of Jiang Qing, with whom he was upset for assuming too much power and disobeying his orders: "I have never approved of one's wife becoming the office manager in one's own work unit."[5] And a 1966 letter to Jiang Qing advising her, "You should remind yourself often of your weak points, shortcomings, and mistakes," published in 1972, served to put a further distance between Mao and his wife.[6] Although Mao's real power had been weakened by the factionalism and chaos of the Cultural Revolution, his history, prestige, and charisma were still of such a magnitude that he could tip the political balance, at least temporarily. Therefore, as his support for the Shanghai group fluctuated, the bureaucratic leaders found it possible to debate and challenge the views of the Shanghai group in their very own domain, the media.

The Revival of Science

The ambiguity of Mao's role was evident in the discussion of scientific research that occurred in the media in 1972. Zhou Enlai and his bureaucratic associates, who had turned their attention increasingly to economic revival and modernization, saw the need for more conventional scientific practices, particularly for basic research. Accordingly, a spate of articles appeared in the national media, explicitly demanding that scientific theory be taught in the universities and that laboratory experiments be conducted in research institutes rather than in fields and factories. These demands implicitly condemned the harm done to scientific development in the Cultural Revolution. Such criticism of Mao's practices could have been presented publicly only through the initiative of an official of Zhou's stature. Indeed, on numerous occasions Zhou urged that universities revise their curricula so as to give more attention to theoretical science and the training of scientists. He also proposed that universities enroll students in science, engineering, and foreign languages directly from senior middle school rather than having them work first, which had been another practice during the Cultural Revolution.

Although Zhou Enlai consulted with the scientific community and was made aware of its problems by individual scientists, his concern with scientific theory and education did not necessarily reflect the importance of the scientific community at this time. The scientists, who, like intellectuals in the humanities and social sciences, had been demoralized by the Cultural Revolution, were still too weak to exert pressure as a group. Most universities still did not have courses in scientific theory. Biology departments did not teach genetics. The Chinese Academy of Sciences was virtually nonfunctioning, and many research laboratories were either destroyed or obsolete. The scientists had not gained a strong enough base in their own institutions, associations, or government agencies to impress their priorities on the regime. They were unable to put forth their priorities without the initiative of China's top leaders. But once the leadership decided to give attention to science and education, the areas on which they focused reflected the interests of the scientific community. Hence the scientists must have convinced Zhou Enlai of the importance of theoretical science as a prerequisite for economic development, a concept that is not readily apparent to nonscientists. Political factions used the intellectuals, but the intellectuals intermittently were able to use the factions for their own purposes as well.

The input of the scientific community was evident in newspaper articles written in 1972 by representative scientists in order to build support for Zhou Enlai's scientific initiative. A number were written by education groups at various universities, including Fudan University in Shanghai, which indicated that the control of the Shanghai group over education, even in Shanghai, was not as complete as they or their opponents claimed. These pieces were not shrouded in the historical and philosophical imagery that characterized more directly political discussions. They forthrightly argued that, without research in theoretical science, China would be unable to achieve modernization: "We can only crawl behind others and have to start from the very beginning in solving every production and technical problem."[7] In an implicit reference to the Shanghai group, the articles denounced the "short-sighted" view that theoretical science was a useless study. One article, explained that "at the present stage, the interference comes from the 'left.' "[8]

In opposition to the Shanghai group's view that scientific knowledge could be acquired only through practice, the scientists' articles asked that theoretical and experimental work be separated from practical application and be studied in universities and conducted in laboratories. Such work required more intense education and training for longer periods of time. With these changes, production would take "a new flying leap forward."[9] Leaps forward were therefore no longer to be effected solely by mass movements but also by scientific research to increase production, which in turn would lead to further scientific research. Not only mass movements but also class struggle were downgraded relative to scientific experiment and production: "If class struggle is grasped exclusively at the expense of struggle for production and scientific experiment, the socialist revolution and construction will be weakened."[10]

The physicist Zhou Peiyuan, who was rehabilitated in the early 1970s as vice-chairman of the Science and Technology Commission and vice-president of Beijing University, was the most authoritative scientific voice on these issues. He called the lack of distinction between science and engineering in the universities "very harmful." These disciplines were complementary, not synonymous. Whereas engineering might satisfy current needs, the function of science was not immediately apparent. Sometimes "no connection can be seen between some branches of abstract mathematics and production practice," but "care must be exercised in dealing with some specialties which are more or less abstract and for which no application can be found at present." Although there was no way to predict when the transition from pure to applied science would take place, theoretical work could have practical spinoffs. Zhou pointed out that scientific work in universities and research institutes was more important to economic development than applied science in the fields and factories, because the university "assembles together a large number of scientific and technical personnel and is continuously supplied with reinforcements by admitting new students."[11] The concentration of specialists from different disciplines made possible the integration of other disciplines in scientific experiments, which in turn might develop branches of scientific knowledge that could enhance China's economic development.

These proposals provoked retaliation from the Shanghai group which hindered the efforts to regenerate scientific theory and education. Although Zhou Peiyuan's article was written in the spring of 1972, its publication was delayed by the Shanghai group until the fall of 1972. In the meantime, Yao Wenyuan and Zhang Chunqiao organized forums to criticize Zhou Peiyuan's views and his "behind-the-scenes boss," Zhou Enlai. When Zhou's article was finally published, it did not appear in the party paper, the *People's Daily*, which had requested it originally, but in the intellectuals' paper, the *Guangming Daily*. After its appearance, party committees at a number of factories in Shanghai warned against the "traditional prejudice" of distinguishing between practice and theory.[12] In mid-1973, a quarterly journal, *The Dialectics of Nature*, was founded in Shanghai with the specific purpose of publicizing the Marxist, or political, view of the physical and biological sciences and repudiating the Western view.

Along with their attack on theoretical science, the Shanghai group blocked retreat from the Cultural Revolution in higher education. In 1973 they instituted another wave of anti-intellectualism at the universities. At Qinghua University, for example, once again scores of professors were investigated and hundreds became the focus of criticism. Zhou Enlai's proposal for the entrance of students directly into the universities was not implemented. Political standards of admission were reaffirmed with the case of the youth Zhang Tiesheng. Instead of completing his entrance examination to the university, Zhang wrote to the examiners complaining that his work as a laborer had prevented him from studying for the exam. When Mao's nephew Mao Yuanxin, an associate of the Shanghai group in Liaoning, heard of Zhang's complaint, he had it published in the *Liaoning Daily* and the *People's Daily*. His purpose in publicizing this incident so zealously was to evoke criticism of academic authorities for discriminating against working people. The affair mushroomed into a countermovement against the efforts of the party bureaucracy to reintroduce academic criteria for admission to higher education.

The Shanghai group probably would not have been able to waylay the move toward greater attention to scientific theory and education if Mao had fully backed the move. Although Mao was disillusioned with expertise and specialization, he was concerned with China's scientific and technological development. In 1972, in fact, after meeting with the Chinese-American scientist C. N. Yang, a Nobel-laureate who deplored China's scientific state, Mao had assented to Zhou Enlai's effort to train personnel in scientific theory and upgrade scientific education. Yet Mao's interest was apparently not strong or sustained, because when Zhou Enlai's efforts were hindered by the Shanghai group, Mao did not come to his assistance.

His inaction may have been due to his increasing enfeeblement as well as to his continuing resistance to the development of a scientific elite to achieve China's scientific modernization.

The Anti-Confucian Campaign

Shortly after the move to revive theoretical science and education became stymied, a campaign was launched in the fall of 1973 against Confucianism. At one level, the attack on Confucianism was what it appeared to be, a continuation of the effort to eradicate traditional habits and attitudes that had persisted despite the Cultural Revolution. It was a movement against bureaucratism, contempt for physical labor, and the inferior position of women. Most important, it called for rejection of the Confucian values of idealism, humanism, and conservatism. At another level, however, the campaign became a vehicle through which the Shanghai group and the party bureaucratic leaders, by means of historical analogy and symbolism, carried on their personal and ideological power struggle. They debated the fundamental issue of the Cultural Revolution, whether China should give priority to class struggle and continuing revolution, or to national and social unity and economic and scientific development.

The campaign followed a vacillating course, which confused the public to whom it was addressed. This vacillation reflected the conflicting views not only of the groups but also of Mao. As opposed to the other campaigns, in this one Mao did not issue relevant quotations, an indication that he may have sided with both factions. He supported the use of the anti-Confucian campaign to oppose the remnant of Lin Biao's followers and to restore unity and order. But at the same time he had not forsaken his commitment to struggle and continuing revolution. Thus the campaign reflected the contradictory nature of Mao's own position as well as that of the opposing factions. Even more confusing to the public to which the campaign was addressed was the fact that the views of the Shanghai group were themselves contradictory. At times, their writing groups expressed the opinions of the bureaucratic leaders as well as themselves within one piece. They may have been trying to gain legitimacy by projecting themselves as responsible leaders willing to undertake some conventional political and economic practices. Whatever the reason, this conveyed a jumble of contradictory political messages and gave a bifurcated, counterpoint quality to the campaign.

The Shanghai group and the bureaucratic leaders expressed their contending views within the context of a discussion on the conflict between the Confucian and Legalist thinkers in Chinese history. Both modern groups used differing interpretations of the ancient conflict to hit at each other. The discussion went through several phases. Though the campaign appears to have been launched by the bureaucratic leaders, it was soon taken over by the Shanghai group, whose interpretation dominated the media in the early months of 1974.[13] Yet the bureaucratic interpretation was interjected increasingly by mid-1974. The same analogies were given opposite interpretations by each group. The Shanghai group, for example, used anti-Confucianism to attack Zhou Enlai, Deng Xiaoping and their pragmatic economic policies and to promote the revolutionary fervor, continuing struggle, and anti-intellectualism of the Cultural Revolution. Similarly the bureaucratic leaders used anti-Confucianism to attack disruptive groups such as Lin Biao's military followers and, by implication, the Shanghai group and to promote unity, institutionalization, production, and science.

This was not the first time that the denunciation of Confucianism and praise of Legalism were chosen as the medium for a political movement. The conflict between the Confucians and the Legalists had been treated as analogous to the present since the May Fourth movement, because the initial conflict between the Confucians and the Legalists in the fourth and third centuries B.C. was, like the twentieth century, regarded as a time of transition from one system to another. In ancient times, the transition was from slavery to feudalism; in modern times, from capitalism to socialism. Supposedly the Cultural Revolution also represented a transition from one phase to another. Whereas after the Great Leap Forward, Confucianism and the Confucian values of harmony and compromise had been used by the liberal intellectuals to promote stability and unity and Legalism had been criticized for increasing the antagonisms between the rulers and the ruled, after the Cultural Revolution, the roles of these historical movements were transposed. The Legalists were praised for introducing universal law, centralization, and unification, and the Confucians were criticized for emphasizing spirit, decentralization, and factionalism. A positive view of an historical character could thus be changed to a negative one, depending on the political circumstances. Neither the interpretation nor even the historical record were consistent or historically accurate. Historical truth was secondary to the appropriation of China's past for current political purposes, a traditional Chinese as well as a Communist use of history.

Even though Mao was a part of the May Fourth generation which had denigrated the Confucians and praised the Legalists, his view of Confucianism was mixed. At times he extolled Confucius; at other times he criticized him. Shortly before the Cultural Revolution, on February 11, 1964, Mao said approvingly that Confucius was of poor peasant stock and did not have a higher education: "He was raised among the masses, and he understood their sufferings."[14] Yet many times in Mao's march to power he had also identified with the strong, unifying first Legalist emperor Shi Huang of the Qin dynasty (221–202 B.C.).

The choice of Shi Huang as the specific hero and Confucius as the specific villain in the anti-Confucian campaign appears to have been sparked by the use of these figures in the "571 Documents," allegedly drawn up in 1971 by Lin Biao and his military associates to resist Mao's efforts to curb their power. Using the traditional description of Shi Huang as a tyrant, these documents attacked Mao as a contemporary Shi Huang: "We cannot deny Mao's historical function of unifying China, and this is why we have given him his rightful place in revolutionary history and the support he deserves. But now he has abused the confidence and status given him by the Chinese people and in historical terms he has become retrogressive. In fact, he has become the Qin Shi Huang of modern times." Furthermore, "He is not a true Marxist-Leninist, but the greatest feudal tyrant in Chinese history; he practices the teachings of Confucius and Mencius, puts on the cloak of Marxism-Leninism, and exercises the laws of Qin Shi Huang." Yet Lin Biao expressed his own determination to follow the Confucian dictum, "Die to preserve virtue."[15] While ignoring the Confucian characterization of Mao, the campaign used the Shi Huang association with Mao as positive and the Confucian association with Lin Biao as negative. Consequently, Shi Huang and Legalism were identified with Mao and the post-Cultural Revolution consolidation, while Confucius and Confucianism were identified with Lin Biao and those who opposed consolidation.

Even before the anti-Confucian campaign, there had been periodic attacks on Confucianism that could be interpreted as criticism of the bureaucratic leaders. A Luo Siding article in 1971 portrayed Confucius as two-faced, a quality that the Shanghai group privately attributed to Zhou Enlai: "Did Confucius not take to tempering severity with gentleness, tempering gentleness with severity ... a peaceful and pleasant appearance with one face and imminent bloodshed with the other?" Luo Siding charged "Liu Shaoqi and his ilk" with endorsing the Confucian theories of "the dying-out of class struggle" and "inner-party peace," which was an implicit criticism of the efforts of Zhou Enlai and his associates to moderate the conflicts of the Cultural Revolution and reunite the party.[16] Similarly, Luo Siding attacked the Confucian elitist idea of education, which was analogous to attacking the bureaucracy's effort to revive education. The group's most blatant analogy was embedded in their criticism of Confucius for calling to office "those who retired to obscurity," a charge that could easily have applied to Zhou Enlai's reinstatement in the early 1970s of party administrators, managers, and scientists who had been purged in the Cultural Revolution. Moreover, in early 1973 the Shanghai group were able to distance themselves from Lin Biao by switching his designation from "ultraleftist," meaning that he had supported the Cultural Revolution, to "ultrarightist," meaning that he had opposed it.

The submerged conflict between the Shanghai group and bureaucratic leaders surfaced at the Tenth Party Congress in August 1973, which also witnessed the phenomenal rise of the Shanghai group member Wang Hongwen to the first vice-chairmanship of the party, just below Mao Zedong and Zhou Enlai. At the congress, Zhou called for party discipline, whereas Wang called for rebellion against authority, supposedly against the bureaucratic leaders, by echoing the Cultural Revolution phrase "Going against the tide." These contradictory strands were expressed in the anti-Confucian campaign, which was launched in the wake of the congress.

The contradictions were especially pronounced in the work of one of the few well-known writers in the anti-Confucian campaign, Yang Rongguo, a scholar of the Confucian-Legalist conflict.[17] In the early 1960s, Yang had acknowledged that some Confucian concepts, such as *ren* or human kindness, served the ruling class, but like Feng Youlan, he believed that this concept also had potential for progress and positive influence. In December 1972, Yang compared the Confucian "villains" to the Shanghai group and the Legalist "heroes" to the bureaucratic leaders. Whereas he accused the Confucians of divorcing themselves from reality, he praised the Legalists for pragmatism. Yang interpreted the Legalist Han Fei's remark, "Cite the facts, do away with what is useless, and do not talk about perfect virtue and righteousness," to mean that "one should seek truth from facts and follow the contemporary course . . . One should not cherish any metaphysical viewpoints, nor should one hold that there exists what is termed eternal truth."[18] Yang lauded the Legalists for their concern with production and economic development, while he chastized the Confucians for their disregard of these questions. He pointed out that Shi Huang had been able to reach his greatest achievement, the unification of China, because he based his rule on realistic economic practices and the centralization of political authority. These pragmatic policies were associated with the party bureaucratic leaders and opposed by the Shanghai group.

On August 7, 1973, however, just as the anti-Confucian campaign was to be launched, another article by Yang Rongguo appeared much more in line with the Shanghai group. What produced this switch is not clear, but the reasons may be similar to those that also led Feng Youlan at this time to join the Shanghai camp. When the writing groups at Beijing University and Qinghua University had started to criticize Confucius, Jiang Qing asked Feng to become their adviser. Given Feng's past efforts against great pressure to uphold the integrity of his non-Marxist interpretation of Confucianism, he probably gave in this time only because of his advanced age and the harsh physical and mental abuse he had suffered at the hands of the Red Guards in the Cultural Revolution. With yet another campaign about to be launched, this time against Confucianism, the field to which Feng had devoted most of his scholarly life, he perhaps thought he had no choice but to compromise his views in order to survive.

Yang Rongguo, too, had been manhandled and humiliated by the Red Guards. A wall poster described "a deep scar left on his neck by hanging a board inscribed with 'Counter-revolutionary, Black Hand.' "[19] Perhaps fearing a repeat of the abuse, Yang now carried out the bidding of the Shanghai group. He criticized the Confucians for recalling "to office those who had retreated into obscurity," a key phrase that, by analogy, accused the bureaucratic leaders of seeking to restore the pre-Cultural Revolution system and officials.[20] He also charged the Confucians with believing that "exploitation was justified and rebellion was a crime," a charge that the Shanghai group later leveled against the bureaucratic leaders.

Although the Shanghai group had initiated previous attacks on Confucianism, when the anti-Confucian campaign began in earnest in September 1973, it appears to have been the work of the bureaucratic leaders. They linked the denunciation of Confucianism with the denunciation of Lin Biao, as if aiming to divert the Confucian attack away from themselves and toward the last remnants of Lin Biao's followers and military regional commanders who had grown in power during the Cultural Revolution. The campaign initially praised Shi Huang, an analogue to Mao, and his prime minister Li Si, an analogue to Zhou Enlai, for fighting against the aristocrats, Confucian scholars, and military warlords, and for unifying China. The implication was that Mao and Zhou Enlai, too, had collaborated to consolidate the country after a period of disunion.

In the beginning of the anti-Confucian campaign Lü Buwei, a premier in the early days of the Qin, was depicted as the major villain. Apparently he was an analogue for Lin Biao. When Lü had called for the revival of separatist states, Shi Huang dismissed him. Lü then established a secret faction and plotted revolt, allegedly in collusion with restoration forces inside and outside Qin. This allegation referred to Lin's supposed collusion with the Soviet Union.

However, the theme of Shi Huang and Li Si working together for unity was quickly overwhelmed by an increasingly loud counterpoint from the Shanghai group. Their writing units in late 1973 and early 1974 emphasized that the major contradiction in history was not so much between disunion and union, depicted by the bureaucratic leaders, as between the rising landlord class, represented by the Legalists, and the remaining forces of the slave-owning class, represented by the Confucians. The primary object of the rising class was to destroy the declining class. This interpretation, viewed as a reflection of the present, indicated that the rising class, the Shanghai group, would overpower the declining class, the bureaucratic leaders, by increasing class struggle and violent measures.

The conflict between the two groups was described with a myriad of historical analogies. In opposition to the party bureaucracy's view that modernization would be achieved by introducing technology and increasing production, the Shanghai group allegorically presented the view that modernization would be achieved by breaking the power of the old elite. Thus, Luo Siding asserted that "after the shackles of the system of land ownership by slave-owners were smashed, a new prosperity was necessarily brought to the landlord economy."[21] Luo Siding described the bureaucratic leaders' resistance by charging the Confucians with spreading an eclectic philosophy under the name "miscellaneous schools," the term that had been used by Deng Tuo in the early 1960s to encourage the leadership to listen to different viewpoints.

Luo Siding also treated Lü Buwei as the villain, but the characterization had more resemblance to Zhou Enlai than to Lin Biao. Lü had considerable strength among large numbers of Confucian scholars who tried to infiltrate government and cultural departments. Dissatisfied with the new system, a metaphor for the Cultural Revolution, "they started a new polemic on whither the Qin dynasty?" Because their activities undermined the new system, Shi Huang suppressed them by the forceful measures of "burning books and burying scholars alive," not because he was "ruthless," but because it was "the inevitable trend of class struggle."[22]

As if in direct reference to Mao, Luo Siding pointed out that Shi Huang had been "more fond of literature than other sovereigns" and did not aim at "destroying literature." He was not against all scholars, or even all scholars with divergent views. Among the seventy scholars of the Qin, at least eight were kept alive because they did not covertly plot against the ruler. Only those who engaged in conspiratorial activities were buried alive, an allusion to Mao's concern with conspiracy since the criticism of Peng Dehuai. Nevertheless, whether secretly or openly, those who resisted Shi Huang's new system were treated harshly because, "If they were not sternly suppressed, the economic status and state power of the newly emerging landlord class could not be consolidated, and a general retrogression toward slave society would take place all over China."[23] Metaphorically, Luo Siding threatened harsh actions against those who sought to return to the pre-Cultural Revolution era.

Confucius, ostensibly like Zhou Enlai, when confronted with monumental changes in society, concocted the "doctrine of the mean," a middle way, in order to achieve a compromise between the conflicting forces. He complained that "there is no law and order," a complaint also expressed by the bureaucratic leaders and even by Mao.[24] The doctrine of the mean was attributed by Luo Siding to those who blasphemed progressive movements like the Leap as "going too far"; by implication, it was attributed to people who attacked the Cultural Revolution as "going too far."[25]

The Shanghai group also used Confucianism, as in 1971, to accuse a small number of people of opposing, in the manner of Liu Shaoqi, Mao's educational reforms of the Cultural Revolution. These people were charged with fostering the "Confucian" practices of separating learning from productive labor and training officials in specialized skills rather than in ideology, although Confucianism in fact stressed ideology not skills. They were also accused of using the Confucian principle that "in teaching there should be no distinction of classes" to discriminate against workers and peasants' children in favor of children of officials and the middle class.[26] Even the advocacy of professional leadership of the academic community, a practice associated with Western educational thinking, was attributed to Confucius, whose followers spread the view that "people outside the professions are unable to lead those inside the profession."[27]

Despite the harshness of their allegorical attacks, the writing units of the Shanghai group also expressed some views espoused by the bureaucratic leaders, thereby weakening their own impact. Liang Xiao, for example, praised Shang Yang's Legalist doctrine of "governing by law," as opposed to the Confucian doctrine of "governing by rites." Shang Yang had held that, "when the law was enforced, the state was governed well."[28] Luo Siding quoted the Song statesman Wang Anshi's defense of Shang Yang to the effect that "people of this age should not vilify Shang Yang, who administered the government by emphasizing law and order."[29] Although the Shanghai group's interpretation of law had more to do with the imposition of class dictatorship than with the Western concept of impartial administration and equal treatment, their attribution of terms used by bureaucratic leaders to the Legalists with whom they themselves supposedly identified and their attribution of ideological fervor that they themselves had espoused in the Cultural Revolution to the "hated" Confucians must have been bewildering, even to the knowledgeable.

Even more confusing was the writing units' stress on economic priorities in relation to ideology. Luo Siding criticized Lü Buwei because "he violently opposed the traditional policy of the Qin state to invigorate the foundation and enfeeble the secondary."[30] In Luo Siding's view, to stress ideology, "the secondary," and to ignore the economy, "the foundation," was an inversion of priorities. Shi Huang was praised for adopting "the political system of pragmatism."[31] Though the term "pragmatism" was used in a political rather than an economic context, it was regarded as a bureaucratic, not a radical, value. In fact, the Shanghai group in its later campaign on the dictatorship of the proletariat directly condemned pragmatism as antithetical to its revolutionary goals.

Adding further confusion to the issues, Liang Xiao stressed the value of profit, material incentives, and economic development, an approach associated with the bureaucratic leaders, not the Shanghai group. For example, they ridiculed the Confucians for upholding the traditional principle of "valuing virtue while despising profit; attaching importance to righteousness while neglecting fortune." Confucius was attacked for saying that "the mind of the superior man is conversant with righteousness; the mind of the mean man is conversant with gain." Sang Hongyang, adviser to the Han emperor Wu, was praised for expounding the Legalist concept of "doing things in a practical manner" in order to develop agriculture, industry, and commerce.[32] Perhaps in the wake of the economic difficulties caused by the Cultural Revolution, the Shanghai group wanted to present themselves as concerned with economic and financial affairs, but in view of their former disparagement of such concerns and their ruthless attacks on those involved in economic affairs, these articles may have confused readers and even caused them to support the bureaucratic leaders rather than the Shanghai group.

The articles must also have caused confusion on foreign policy issues. They praised historical figures who had strengthened China against foreign invasion and mobilized the country's vast economic, political, and military forces against the Huns, a euphemism for the Russians. Sang Hongyang was again extolled because he "expounded the thinking of preparedness against wars of aggression" and called for "building fortresses for defense and setting up plants to produce arms." By contrast, the Confucians criticized these actions as showing a "disregard of morality." Their concern with morality weakened the nation in "the just war of resistance against Hun aggression."[33] Because of the Confucians' efforts to cease hostilities, they fostered capitulation. With increasing hostilities with the Soviet Union along the border in 1969 and the early 1970s, here again, the Shanghai group may have wanted to be associated with military preparedness, but in view of their weakening of military defense in the Cultural Revolution and the bureaucratic leaders' consistent concern for defense, it is likely that these articles helped the bureaucratic rather than the Shanghai group.

In November 1974, Luo Siding accused the Confucians of having betrayed the nation to the northern barbarians because they preferred a return of the old system instead of the internal reform needed to make the nation strong, an analogue to the Shanghai group's stress on internal reform as the prerequisite for external strength. Yet Luo Siding's arguments against the Confucians were in some respects more applicable to the Shanghai group than to the bureaucratic leaders. For example, the Confucians were accused of treating the threat of foreign aggression as a "small matter along the border, a matter that does not deserve much attention," which was far more applicable to the foreign affairs approach of the Shanghai group than of the bureaucratic leaders. At the same time, the chief opponent to the Confucians, the Song "Legalist" statesman Wang Anshi, was portrayed in the guise of the bureaucratic leaders. For example, Luo Siding disparaged the Confucians led by Sima Guang for emphasizing "spirit," whereas Luo praised Wang for his concern with financial affairs and military modernization and preparedness. Moreover, Wang had appreciated the need to build a strong economy in order to stand off foreign aggressors: "As a result of Wang Anshi's reforms, the economy and military power of the Song dynasty were markedly strengthened."[34] Yet it was not the Shanghai group but the bureaucratic leaders who were concerned with economic modernization and weapons technology.

Upon the death of Wang Anshi's patron, Emperor Shenzong, Sima Guang and his group had assumed power and overturned Wang's reforms "with the support of the Empress Dowager Gao who opposed the reforms," a statement that could be an allusion to Jiang Qing.[35] As the aggressors closed in, the Confucian faction made concessions by ceding them territory. A folksong of the time denounced this unrealistic and capitulationist approach to foreign policy:

The well-being of the country is no concern of theirs, but Con-
fucian learning is.
They bother not about guarding against the autumn offensive
[by the Jin troops], but about "Chunqiu" [Spring and Autumn
Annals of Confucius].
They turn not against the enemy, but against Anshi.[36]

Luo Siding criticized the Confucian faction for being so absorbed in
personal vendettas and ideological questions that they neglected the
country's defense against the enemy, an approach that could be attributed more to the Shanghai group than to the bureaucratic leaders.

Despite the overlapping of some of their arguments with those of
the bureaucratic leaders, the Shanghai group's writing units inevitably called for radical reform of the whole structure and personnel of
government. Liang Xiao observed that during the period when Shang
Yang had carried out his pragmatic reforms, he dug out all parts of
the old foundation, not only in the economic structure but also in the
political, economic, ideological, and cultural spheres.[37] Thus the
public was confronted by the writers of the Shanghai group with the
views of both that group and the bureaucratic leaders.

The Bureaucratic Counterefforts

At the same time, the public was presented with dissenting arguments that expressed the views of the bureaucratic leaders, primarily
on scientific and economic development. A writing group at
Qinghua University portrayed the Legalists as advocates of scientific
thinking because their respect for materialism had given impetus to
the development of Chinese science. By contrast, the Confucians had
inhibited science because they believed in apriorism and considered
mastery in scientific fields as "skills of no significant value."[38] The
Confucians' contempt for technological innovation was held responsible for the stagnation of iron production, water conservation, and
canal and dam building. Moreover, the Qin metallurgical craftsmen,
by increasing their knowledge of copper alloys and iron casting, had
developed the metallurgical industry.

The Shanghai group, too, sanctioned applied science, but they
opposed emphasis on scientific theory. Yet the Qinghua spokesmen
also extolled the Legalist scientists for having been at the forefront in
theoretical attempts to understand the laws of nature. They lauded

the ancient scientist Zhang Heng because he had spent his life studying astronomy, geography, and mechanical structures, which had no immediate practical application but led eventually to the invention of the celestial globe and the seismoscope. The Confucian scholars accused Zhang Heng of playing with "skills to slaughter a dragon," that is, with useless activities. In response, Zhang Heng ridiculed them as "pedants who did not know the world was changing all the time and were unable to adapt themselves to the changing world."[39] A reader of this article might have found it difficult to associate the "pedants" with the bureaucratic leaders, who fostered science, and would have been more likely to associate them with the Shanghai group, who hampered the development of science.

Discussions of scientific and economic development in the anti-Confucian campaign also touched on the issue of foreign assistance. The campaign coincided with China's increasing interest in better relations with the West, particularly for the importation of Western skills and technology. Like other aspects of the campaign, the discourse on foreign assistance reflected an internal debate.

Although in early 1974 the *People's Daily* warned against faith in foreign products and reliance on Western technology to modernize China's industry, some participants in the Confucian-Legalist discussion expressed a willingness to accept foreign assistance and criticized those who objected. A group of writers at Wuhan University described a debate during the reign of Shi Huang over whether to appoint officials on the basis of merit or favoritism. The prime minister, Li Si, had advised that the government employ a wide range of reformers with expertise, and even foreigners, in order to strengthen the state. This could be interpreted as representing the Shanghai position that younger people outside the inner circle be given higher positions. However, the writers went on to present the bureaucratic interpretation of self-reliance, which did not mean isolation and self-sufficiency, as in the Shanghai group's interpretation, but contacting the outside world and acquiring foreign products in order to develop China's own. Li Si had welcomed not only skilled foreigners but foreign products and culture, pointing out that things used by the Qin were determined "by whether or not they were useful to the Qin and not by whether or not they were produced in the Qin."[40] Jade, pearls, horses, music, and other products popular in the Qin were of foreign origin. Li charged that the faction at court which opposed this opening to the outside world was hindering reform.

The debate over history and will that had obsessed Chinese thinkers since the late nineteenth century and which reemerged periodically in the People's Republic, most prominently in the Leap and the Cultural Revolution, reappeared in the Confucian-Legalist discussions. There was some agreement on this issue. The spokesmen of the Shanghai group as well as the bureaucratic group stressed the objective laws of historical development, independent of the subjective will. This seeming agreement may have been due to Mao's criticism in the early 1970s of the view that genius and heroes were responsible for change, although in the Cultural Revolution Mao had gone along with Lin Biao and Chen Boda's efforts to project him as such a genius.

In contrast to the emphasis on the subjective will in the Cultural Revolution, the will's power to make history was now downplayed. Even Luo Siding regarded the immutable laws of history as determining historical stages: "The feudal system would inevitably replace the slave system; this is a law of historical development independent of man's will."[41] Whereas in the Cultural Revolution, revolutionary leaders, principally Mao, were thought to lead history onto "the correct path," now the leaders had to allow history to take its own course. To deemphasize the subjective will, Yang Rongguo contrasted the thought of the Confucian thinker of the Han, Dong Zhongshu, who had believed that the process of man's cognition moved from the subjective to the objective, with the iconoclastic thinker Wang Chong, who had insisted on deriving truth from fact. Yang concluded that thinkers like Dong were "vainly turning back the wheel of history."[42] Subjective will could no longer telescope stages of history. The Shanghai group's rejection of the subjective will—a concept extolled by them in the Cultural Revolution—and their affirmation of the objective laws of historical development—a view associated with their bureaucratic rivals—must have perplexed those to whom they looked for support and have inadvertently aided their rivals.

Despite their agreement on the need to conform to the inexorable laws of history, there was a subtle distinction between the Shanghai group and the bureaucratic leaders. The Shanghai group stressed that the movement from one stage to another was through class struggle. By contrast, the bureaucratic spokesmen emphasized that the traditional Marxist technological-economic causation and traditional Chinese emphasis on unity were the moving forces of history.

They argued that history moved not so much through continued struggle as through economic development and unity. Even a Shanghai writing unit noted that unity had been "the basic trend of the historical development of the country."[43]

In late 1973, the bureaucratic leaders' stress on unity and the centralization of authority in the Confucian-Legalist discussion was reflected in a shift of eight of the eleven regional military commanders from their regional bases to other regions, where they assumed military responsibility but relinquished their political responsibility. Deng Xiaoping, with Mao's acquiescence, appears to have played a major role in this reshuffling of the military and in the reestablishment of civilian control. In December, he also became a member of the Politburo and vice-chairman of the Military Affairs Commission of the army. Anticipating death, Zhou Enlai actively promoted Deng as his successor. Zhou could not have done so without the sanction of Mao, who apparently appreciated the need for Deng's organizational skills and old party ties to reinvigorate the party and reestablish central party control over the regions and the military.

Despite the regime's emphasis on unity and Deng's return to power, the *People's Daily*, the supposedly authoritative voice of the party, continued to call for struggle. On February 2, 1974, it reiterated the revolutionary slogan "Going against the tide" and presented Mao as the exponent of continuing struggle. Mao's words in big, black characters proclaimed: "I CARE NOT THAT THE WIND BLOWS AND THE WAVES BEAT: IT IS BETTER THAN IDLY SITTING IN THE COURTYARD."

Conflict in the Performing Arts

Whereas the anti-Confucian campaign gave forth conflicting signals in the political, economic, and foreign policy areas, the signals in the cultural arena sounded much clearer. In contrast to the other areas, the performing arts were virtually dominated by the Shanghai group. Thus their views on cultural matters were expressed with less equivocation, fewer interjections from the bureaucratic side, and only passing reference to the Confucian-Legalist discussion.

Whereas the anti-Confucian campaign presented divergent approaches to Western influence, the cultural realm categorically rejected Western influence. The Shanghai group's first public attack on the opening to the West began a short time after the visit of the Philadelphia Symphony Orchestra to China in September 1973, when the writing group Chu Lan addressed the seemingly innocuous issue of juvenile songs. The group acknowledged that such songs might be "healthy in content," but their music "transplants in toto the tunes and methods of expression of foreign dance music."[44] The incongruity between content and form was due to "an uncritical, mechanical application and imitation of foreign things," which Mao had denounced.[45]

Chu Lan's subsequent articles expressed a distaste for Western culture that resonated with Jiang Qing's views, even though she personally enjoyed Beethoven and American musicals, such as *The Sound of Music*. It decried the view, attributed to Zhou Yang, that foreign classical music had no social content and could therefore not impose bourgeois ideas, because such a view "would make people blindly worship foreign bourgeois culture and assume a nihilistic attitude toward our own national culture."[46] Chu Lan considered program music, which included Soviet socialist realist music, to be as pernicious as symphonies and sonatas. Such music insinuated Western culture into China, rejected the Cultural Revolution in the arts, and resurrected the "cosmopolitan" culture that prevailed before the Cultural Revolution. The discussions on Western music were in fact tied in with the debate over continuing the Cultural Revolution.

An invitation in 1972 to the Italian director Michelangelo Antonioni to make a film on China, like the invitation to the Philadelphia Symphony Orchestra, was attacked by the Shanghai group as a device to undermine the Cultural Revolution. Since both invitations must have had the approval of Zhou Enlai, the attack on them could be construed as criticism of Zhou. The denunciation of Antonioni's film had the earmarks of Jiang Qing, for the *People's Daily* used arguments against Antonioni similar to those that Jiang Qing had used against pre-Cultural Revolution Beijing operas and films. The newspaper criticized Antonioni's selection of drab subjects filmed in dim light from low angles, which evoked in the audience "a forlorn, gloomy, melancholy, and somber impression." Instead of reflecting the new spirit of China, Antonioni showed only old-style phenomena. Even worse, he did not "shoot a single scene of China's model revolutionary theatrical works, but unscrupulously ridiculed the arias."[47] That Antonioni was allowed to affront Jiang Qing's work was interpreted as a rejection of the Cultural Revolution.

The Shanghai group also attacked the performance of nonrevolutionary operas as subversive of the Cultural Revolution. In the spring of 1974, they launched a minicampaign against theatrical works that did not follow Jiang Qing's model revolutionary productions. The same people responsible for the infiltration of Western bourgeois culture were charged with allowing the nonrevolutionary operas. Jiang Qing's productions, which had dominated stage, screen, ballet, music, and the airways for over eight years, though initially well received, had apparently become tiresome to Chinese audiences. A number of provincial theatrical companies began to revive local operas. Jiang Qing regarded these operas as a threat to her authority and her model productions. Chu Lan complained that, "in some places, there are still people who stage bad plays, tell bad stories, sing bad songs, and covertly and overtly compete with the proletariat for ideological and cultural ground."[48]

The Shanghai group concentrated their attack primarily on pre-Cultural Revolution issues and villains like Liu Shaoqi and his associates, in particular Zhou Yang. They paid only scant attention to Lin Biao, since he was associated with the Cultural Revolution, and criticism of him implied criticism of their own radical values. By contrast, to criticize Liu Shaoqi was to reject Liu's more pragmatic approach of the early 1960s that was being revived in the early 1970s. The group's major focus was a local opera, *Three Visits to Taofeng*, which allegedly defended Liu Shaoqi. This opera, written collectively by a creative group in Shanxi, was performed in several provinces and presented in January-February 1974 at the North China Drama Festival, sponsored by the cultural group under the State Council. On February 28, 1974, ten days after the close of the festival, the opera was attacked by Chu Lan in the *People's Daily*.

Since the opera has not been published, its plot must be gleaned from the criticism. The story concerned the Jinling Production Brigade, which sold a sick horse to the Taofeng Production Brigade for the price of a good horse. When this was discovered, the secretary of the party branch of the Jinling Production Brigade made three visits to Taofeng to apologize and return the money. Apparently the opera had been written in the summer of 1965 under the auspices of the purged central Propaganda Department. In its original form, entitled *Three Visits to Taoyuan*, it had praised the achievements of the socialist education campaign in Taoyuan in order to honor Liu Shaoqi and his wife Wang Guangmei. The charge was then made in the Cultural Revolution that Liu had sent his wife to learn about the Taoyuan

Production Brigade in Hebei in order to use that experience to subvert Mao's call to learn from the more radical commune Dazhai. Supposedly *Three Visits to Taoyuan* was restaged in 1974 in order to reverse the condemnation of Liu and his wife. Although the theme remained the same, superficial changes made the connection to Liu and his wife less overt. The name of the production brigade was changed from Taoyuan to Taofeng; the time period was moved back from 1965 to 1959; and a female magistrate named Wang was omitted.

Chu Lan's criticism of the new production again reflected Jiang Qing's biases. Like her impromptu speeches before Red Guards during the Cultural Revolution, Chu Lan expressed great personal animosity toward Liu Shaoqi's wife. They claimed that the opera had been "created to adorn Wang Guangmei."[49] They charged that the original version had been the work of Xia Yan, Tian Han, Yang Hansheng, and Zhou Yang—Jiang Qing's old enemies from Shanghai in the 1930s. They criticized the play for presenting nonantagonistic middle characters and ideological compromise, approaches of the Liuist era of the early 1960s that had provoked Jiang Qing to produce her revolutionary operas. Instead of conflicts being resolved through struggle, they were resolved through negotiation and good deeds. The misdeed of selling the sick horse was handled by a mere apology rather than a struggle against those who did wrong. Chu Lan regarded this opera as a direct challenge to the standardized formula of struggle in Jiang Qing's model works.

Chu Lan compared *Taofeng* to Wu Han's *The Dismissal of Hai Rui*. Since the Hai Rui play criticized the Leap and sought to reverse the decision on Peng Dehuai, *Taofeng* by implication criticized the Cultural Revolution and sought to reverse the decision on Liu Shaoqi. The most disturbing feature of *Taofeng* was the symbolism of the sick horse. Although the horse was suffering from disease, it was made to gallop at such a high speed that it died of exhaustion. By analogy, the opera was saying that the nation, like the sick horse, neither too healthy nor too strong, had been pushed in the Cultural Revolution to the point of collapse. Chu Lan therefore saw the criticism of *Taofeng* as "not just an ordinary academic debate over literature and art or over some problem of creative writing" but as "a cardinal issue" in defending the Cultural Revolution.[50]

The criticism sparked a movement against the Shanxi opera that spread to a number of provinces in the north and south in the spring of 1974. Other provincial plays were criticized. One was the Hunanese opera *The Song of the Gardener*, supposedly produced with Hua Guofeng's knowledge because he was head of the Hunanese Revolutionary Committee. It was condemned because it focused on a teacher who advocated the pre-Cultural Revolution emphasis on academic achievement. The condemnation was meant to intimidate not only those who produced nonrevolutionary theatrical works but also those who sought to improve academic standards. Another opera, *Life*, was criticized because it portrayed poor peasants as uninterested in taking a strong class stand, an attitude associated with Liu Shaoqi's de-emphasis of class struggle in the countryside.

Accompanying the attacks on *Taofeng* and other operas was a defense of the model revolutionary works. Any criticism of these works was treated as an offense against the left, the Cultural Revolution, and Jiang Qing. Despite their unique characteristics, local operas were to follow Jiang Qing's model. The argument, later attributed to Deng Xiaoping, that the fierce struggles depicted in the model works evoked nervous tension in the viewers was repudiated. Chu Lan retorted that "revolutionary literature and art are not something meant for entertainment alone but are powerful weapons . . . for attacking and destroying the enemy."[51] In contrast to the more academic tone of the anti-Confucian campaign, the controversies in the cultural arena displayed more of the crusading zeal associated with the Cultural Revolution.

The movement to criticize *Taofeng*, however, faltered by the summer of 1974. In July, Chu Lan attempted to revive the criticism, but whereas their initial attacks on *Taofeng* had aroused support outside cultural circles, they now elicited little response. By the fall of 1974, this counteroffensive, emanating from the cultural realm, had become no more than a skirmish. The controversy over opera, music, and film was just a diversion from what had become the main focus of the anti-Confucian campaign, the question of succession.

Conflict over Succession

With Mao aged eighty-one and increasingly enfeebled, an allegorical debate over the succession to Mao was conducted in the summer and fall of 1974 by means of interpretations of the succession crises in Chinese history. A number of articles on succession criticized Mao indirectly. On July 23, 1974, the *Guangming Daily* reprinted the essay "Solitary Indignation" by the Legalist thinker Han Fei Zi, which could have been interpreted as the bureaucratic leadership's criticism of Mao. The essay described an aging ruler, conniving courtiers, and capable administrators—a situation that resembled China's current political scene. It denounced the ruler who, because of arbitrariness and an inability to quell factions at court, had brought about the destruction of the legal institutions. Han Fei's description of the ruler's courtiers resembled the bureaucratic view of the Shanghai group. They were "not necessarily intelligent" but "cater to his taste." As a result, they rose high in the hierarchy. They "deceive and fool the ruler, violate the laws, and harass the people, giving rise to the danger of the state being weakened." In contrast, the administrators, who resembled the bureaucratic leaders, were described as intelligent and good at maintaining legal institutions.

These two "irreconcilable enemies" were locked in a power struggle. Han Fei warned that, "If the ruler does not reward people according to their character and skills and does not investigate before making decisions about people's misconduct, but only listens to and trusts close aides, then those who serve the royal court are men without talent and those who occupy office are a bunch of fools." A state so ruled could not "avoid destruction." Lest the reader fail to make the correct associations, an editorial note stressed the point that Han Fei's advocacy of "rule by law" and "rule by skill" were "of realistic significance today." Even more pertinent, the note explained that, because of the weakened authority of the ruler, careerists and conspirators could virtually hold the ruler captive.[52]

Although the original edition of the *Guangming Daily* with this essay was quickly withdrawn and a new one appeared without it, this and other Han Fei essays were referred to frequently and positively in the press. Whereas only indirect allusions were made to the weak, inadequate ruler in "Solitary Indignation," a number of articles praised Han Fei's advocacy of a strong central government, restating his belief that "All officials and military forces must be put under the unified management and command of the state."[53] They echoed his call for vigilance against those who sought to usurp political power by conspiracy. And they extolled those who followed the "observance of the law in fulfilling official duties" and showed "courageous spirit" in carrying out reforms "without fear of incurring the displeasure of those in power."[54] Deng Xiaoping would later describe himself as one who implemented reforms without fear of antagonizing others.

The discussion of Han Fei was even carried down to the factory level. A group of workers at the Tangshan Cogwheel Plant, after reading "Solitary Indignation," denounced those in power who "act arbitrarily without orders, breech the law for selfish ends, and enrich their families at the expense of the state." Unlike Han Fei, these workers shifted the blame from the ruler to the courtiers, who played a "double game to hoodwink the sovereign and sabotage the rule of law, thus enfeebling and endangering the state and bringing disgrace to their sovereign."[55] The workers vowed "to break up the factionalism." Instead of allowing offices to go to "stupid and corrupt officials," they demanded a policy of "putting the capable into office . . . so that people could be appointed on their merit and stern and fair rule of law could be practiced."[56]

The Shanghai group likewise expressed indirect criticism of Mao and fear of the takeover of power by an opposing faction. Luo Siding in August 1974 rejected the traditional Chinese view that the Qin dynasty had fallen because of Shi Huang's violent policies. They also rejected the Marxist explanation that the dynasty had fallen because of irreconcilable differences between the landlords and peasants. Rather, the Qin had fallen because "hidden traitors" had usurped the throne, for which Shi Huang was to blame. The eunuch Zhao Gao, an apparent analogue to Deng Xiaoping, after having been sentenced to death, had been reinstated by Shi Huang and put in an important position, even though Shi Huang knew of his crimes. This gave Zhao the opportunity to launch a coup after Shi Huang fell ill.[57] Thus Shi Huang "neither hit hard enough nor thoroughly suppressed those restoration forces."[58] Luo Siding also indirectly criticized Zhou Enlai through criticism of Shi Huang's prime minister, Li Si, for refusing to oppose the restorationists. When Zhao Gao had planned his coup, Luo Siding pointed out, Li Si was the only person who could have exposed and resisted him. Instead, he wavered and compromised. Although he helped Shi Huang consolidate power, Li Si made concessions to the restorationist forces of Zhao Gao. Consequently, Shi Huang and Li Si's failure to suppress the restorationist forces allowed Zhao Gao to engineer a counter-revolution, restore the old ways, and abolish the Legalist line and its supporters. The Shanghai group feared a similar fate would befall them.

At the same time, Luo Siding extolled Jiang Qing through their portrayal of Empress Lü, wife of Liu Bang, the Han dynasty's founder. Lü was depicted as crucial to Liu Bang's success. In his struggle for power, Liu Bang had suffered repeated defeats at the hands of his rival Xiang Yu, until Empress Lü and an aide, Xiao He, came to his rescue. Even after Liu Bang wiped out his challenger, there was still resistance, but together Liu Bang and Empress Lü quashed the opposition.[59] Although Jiang Qing was allegorically presented as a great help to Mao in his march to power, in actuality she had played virtually no role. Luo Siding also analogized Jiang Qing's help to Mao in the struggle with Lin Biao. The Han official Han Xin, an analogue to Lin Biao, helped the emperor destroy the enemy but subsequently instigated a rebellion against the regime. Empress Lü assisted the emperor in getting rid of Han Xin, an apparent effort to separate Jiang Qing from her former ally Lin Biao.

The Shanghai group praised the political competence of empresses such as Lü and Wu of the Tang dynasty, in order to enhance Jiang Qing's status and prepare the population for a female ruler after Mao died. Lü was extolled because of the capable way she had taken over the government after Liu Bang's death. She enlisted officials committed to her husband's policies and guarded against any deviation. Although before her reign the masses had led hard lives, afterward they had "plenty to wear and eat and the criminal code was seldom applied."[60] In reality, however, the historical record, itself often biased, depicts Lü as concerned primarily with power, not with benevolent deeds. Nor did Liu Bang suggest her as a suitable successor. Rather, after his death in 195 B.C. her family launched a coup and placed its members in key positions, causing turmoil until it was finally overthrown. This scenario was much closer to what actually happened to the Shanghai group than Luo Siding's scenario.

As in the early phase of the anti-Confucian campaign, a contradictory interpretation was interjected, presumably by the bureaucratic leaders. The reason for Liu Bang's victory over his opponent Xiang Yu was not his wife's assistance, as Luo Siding stated, but his policy of unity and centralization, which was more popular with the people than Xiang Yu's policy of conflict and disunity, the approach associated with the Shanghai group. Liu Bang appointed "people on their merit," whereas Xiang Lu placed his trust "either in his own brothers or in the brothers of his wife, and persons with rare talents could not be used."[61] Liu Bang's appreciation of expertise was an allusion to the bureaucratic leaders, and Xiang Yu's dependence on a small ingrown group was an allusion to the Shanghai group and possibly Mao.

At best, the public must have been bewildered by an official campaign in which it received contradictory signals from the Shanghai group and bureaucratic leaders. Even more mystifying must have been the Shanghai group's portrayal of the "hated" Confucians in tones that resembled their own political patrons and the "praiseworthy" Legalists in tones that resembled their own bureaucratic opponents. Given such conflicting, inverted messages, neither side was able to build up a body of political opinion that would support its position. Moreover, since there were no quotations from Mao in the anti-Confucian campaign, he did not, as in the past, provide the authoritative interpretation. Although such a lengthy and widespread campaign, sputtering along for more than a year and extending to rural as well as urban areas, had to have Mao's approval, Mao was disturbed by some of its aspects. According to later accounts, at a Politburo meeting on July 17, 1974, in the midst of the anti-Confucian campaign, he said of Jiang Qing, "She does not speak for me; she only speaks for herself."[62] Mao himself pinned the label of a faction of "four" on the Shanghai group at the time.

Although the anti-Confucian campaign was the most widespread campaign since the Cultural Revolution, perhaps because of its contradictory character and Mao's ambivalence it did not swell into a full-scale offensive against specific political figures, nor did it assume the uncontrolled fervor of the Cultural Revolution. The Shanghai group used it for its own purposes, but there were no rampaging Red Guards or independent factions, such as the Cultural Revolution Group, to usurp the direction of the campaign. Wall posters denounced top leaders like Zhou Enlai along with a number of regional military leaders, but their impact seemed minimal. Rather, the Shanghai group and the bureaucratic leaders expressed their divergent views within the official limits of a discussion of Confucianism, Legalism, history, and culture.

In this nationwide study movement, carried out through reading and commenting on ancient texts, the public were exposed to a series of opposing concepts. They were told to rebel against authority at the same time that they were told to accept the imposition of political authority. In the course of the campaign, Wang Hongwen's slogan of "Going against the tide," a sanction to rebellion, was given the reverse meaning. One writer explained that "Going against the tide seeks to oppose the unauthorized alteration of the party's basic line and policies."[63] Thus, the public were encouraged to struggle and disobey at the same time that they were advised to unify and obey. Alongside exhortations to continue Cultural Revolution policies were instructions to discontinue them.

Such contradictory pronouncements led to a questioning of official policy. Even the *Red Flag* acknowledged that nonparty people were asking why the media pointed in one direction while party directives pointed in another direction.[64] According to Kenneth Lieberthal, the discrepancies in emphasis between the official communications and the national media allowed officials to modify the messages by adjusting the tones to their own individual wavelengths.[65] Likewise, the contradictory arguments in the national media led the public to make their own individual adjustments.

Even more than the contradictory nature of the anti-Confucian campaign, its very obscurity had the potential for individual interpretation. The style of communication, as well as the subject matter, was dense. Since its ideological disputes were designed not only to debate fundamental issues but also to fight political battles, they had an opaqueness and subtlety that, as Franz Schurmann observes of earlier disputes, turned them into a "closed communications system," impenetrable to the uninitiated who did not know "the code of ideas."[66] Because of the camouflaged nature of the communication, the uninitiated sometimes made interpretations that were the reverse of what either the Shanghai or the bureaucratic group expected.

The resurrection of the traditional thinkers, many of them previously repudiated, may have further undermined China's ideological unity. The works of the Confucians, the Legalists, and even the Daoists, the other major school of traditional thought, were not only read in the libraries and sold in the bookstores, but also read in schools, factories, and communes. They appeared in their original versions as well as in translations into the modern vernacular. The journals of Beijing, Fudan, and Qinghua universities were devoted to their analysis. Scholars who had worked in these areas before 1949 but had since been forced to write on contemporary affairs returned to their prerevolutionary scholarship. For the generation born after 1949, who knew virtually nothing about their history, and even for those born after the May Fourth movement, when the past had been rejected, this campaign must have been a sharp awakening. What was essentially a political movement took on a decidedly academic character as scholars and students in the universities went back to the original texts.

A variety of interpretations was evoked by the return to the original sources. Even the journal of the Shanghai group, *Xuexi yu Pipan* (*Study and Criticism*), printed letters questioning the Shanghai group's as well as the bureaucrats' interpretations of history. One writer suggested that Confucianism rather than Legalism was more appropriate for the times: Confucianism was used "to suppress the military and enhance the civilian," whereas Legalism was used "to exercise the art of surveillance and manipulation." Another writer presented a positive rather than a negative view of Lü Buwei. Instead of being a renegade during his thirteen years in power, Lü had enacted progressive political measures.[67] The significance of these expressions of diversity was not so much that they defended either Lin Biao or Zhou Enlai as that they differed from the interpretations of either the Shanghai or the bureaucratic groups.

In addition to being exposed to divergent interpretations, the public was made aware of concepts antithetical to those of either group. For example, selections of the Daoist philosopher Zhuang Zi ridiculed the Confucian concern with bureaucracy and showed the hypocrisy of the Confucian view of altruism. But Zhuang Zi also advocated a laissez-faire form of government and preached that the best kind of government was the least government. His society was one in which the individual mind was free to roam. Such views were opposed to both the Shanghai and the bureaucratic groups.

Even more than Daoism, the resurrection of Legalism had the potential for unexpected results. The reaffirmation of China's Legalist tradition provoked a discussion of Western legalism in the unofficial media of wall posters and pamphlets. The focus on legalism reflected the symbiotic relationship between the official and unofficial acts. The discussion of China's Legalist tradition in the official media stimulated demands in the unofficial media for legal guarantees in the Western sense, which diverged from what both the Shanghai group and the bureaucratic leaders desired. The most significant example was a wall poster by Li Yi Zhe, a collective pseudonym for a group of disaffected students, which was drafted in the fall of 1973, revised several times, and finally appeared on November 7, 1974, in Guangzhou. Containing 20,000 characters and extending 100 yards, it echoed the Legalist concern for legal institutions and material incentives, but it was written more in the spirit of the Western-

CHINA'S INTELLECTUALS

oriented critics of the Hundred Flowers campaign than of Qin Shi Huang, whom it denounced as dictatorial, or of the party, to whom it addressed its plea. In some ways, it voiced the views of the liberal intellectuals of the early 1960s and expressed the disillusionment of youth who initially had been inspired by the Cultural Revolution.

The poster called for legal guarantees of democratic and individual rights. Since the Cultural Revolution, it charged, China had been governed by the "Lin Biao system," a euphemism for the Shanghai group, since Lin Biao had been dead for three years. That system was defined as one of "lawlessness and recklessness, gangsterism and killing, kidnapping of males and grabbing of females, and the total rejection of the rule of law."[68] These abuses were inherent in the system: "The bad habits of autocracy and despotism are deeply imbued in the minds of the masses, even in those of the Communists in general."[69] Although the constitution guaranteed democracy and protection against arbitrary attack, torture, and interrogation, these rights had not been upheld. Even more disturbing was the lack of any consistent, regularized system of laws and policies. In the name of Mao, one could take power into one's own hands. Furthermore, there were frequent and unfathomable shifts of policy: "orders issued in the morning are changed in the evening." This made people "very much confused, even to the degree of doubting the party."[70]

The poster separated Mao from the "Lin Biao system," although the acts it condemned, such as criticism of Hai Rui and the unleashing of the Red Guards, were personally associated with Mao, and thus it implicitly attacked him. It compared the Cultural Revolution to a religious frenzy and worship of Mao to a religious cult. The daily readings of Mao's Little Red Book "resembled the incantation of spells."[71] Although Mao had denounced the worship of "genius," the cult of the personality had destroyed China's intellectual life: "No one is allowed to think; no one is allowed to study; no one is allowed to do research; and no one is allowed to ask a single 'why' on any question."[72] The poster advocated a system in which both sides of the class struggle "should have democratic rights; to have one faction overcome the other will not work."[73] The proposal for something other than a one-party government was a suggestion that neither the Shanghai group nor the bureaucratic leaders desired.

There is no way to measure the prevalence of such views or to know whether the poster represented more than a group of alienated students. Yet a postscript pleading for paper in order to mimeograph and distribute the poster indicated that such views were being spread by a Chinese samizdat. Moreover, the official response on the local level was not totally negative. Although the poster was condemned and the leader of the group, Li Zhengtian, was arrested and denounced at a mass meeting, he was allowed at the meeting to debate with his critics, thereby reaching an even wider audience than would have read his poster. In fact, he may have been permitted to refute his critics at such length and before such a large audience because his denunciation of the "Lin Biao system" increased the opposition to the Shanghai group, which the Guangdong officials themselves may have endorsed but could not express publicly.[74]

Confronted with a campaign that communicated divergent views, opaque messages, alternative ideas, and multiple symbols, the public was uncertain which course to follow. Individuals selected concepts that fit their own predilections. Despite its rejection of pluralism and scholarship, the anti-Confucian campaign inadvertently produced a more varied intellectual and ideological climate than China had experienced since the early 1960s, a result counter to what the Shanghai group wanted and perhaps to what the bureaucratic leaders had anticipated.

The Dictatorship of the Proletariat Campaign

In early 1975, as the anti-Confucian campaign petered out, the Shanghai group launched a new campaign in its continuing struggle against the bureaucratic leaders. Now the conflict was masked as a doctrinal debate over the theory of the dictatorship of the proletariat. The campaign was sparked by the Fourth National People's Congress, held in January 1975, which endorsed Zhou Enlai's efforts to restore stability and modernize the economy. At the congress, Zhou set forth as China's goal by the end of the twentieth century the Four Modernizations—in agriculture, industry, science and technology, and defense. Along with its endorsement of this relatively pragmatic program, the congress gave major positions in the government to party officials who had been purged in the Cultural Revolution. Those associated with the move away from the Cultural Revolution and with Zhou Enlai rose to the top positions. Deng Xiaoping, who just before the congress had been made vice-chairman of the party and a member of the Standing Committee of the Politburo, at the congress was made first vice-premier, just behind Mao and Zhou Enlai, and chief of staff of the army. Whereas the Ministry of Culture was headed by the Shanghai group's associate, the opera singer Yu Huiyong, the Ministry of Education—supposedly another preserve of the Shanghai group—was headed by Zhou Rongxin, an associate of Zhou Enlai and a former vice-minister of education.

The Shanghai group maintained their positions in the Politburo, and one of their members, Zhang Chunqiao, ranked just below Deng Xiaoping as vice-premier and was made head of the General Political Department of the army. Nevertheless, those associated with the group were given few other official positions in the government. Thus, the group was weakened by the make-up of the new government, but their bases in the cultural and ideological spheres were not shifted from under them. They still had access to the system and still maintained a major voice in the media, which they used to attack the pragmatic program of the party leaders by means of a new campaign reinterpreting the concept of the dictatorship of the proletariat.

The campaign began with a series of quotations from Mao on material incentives and differentiated wage systems. After the Cultural Revolution, Mao had approved of renewed emphasis on economic development. However, this emphasis rekindled the old fear, which had obsessed him since the Leap, that material incentives would produce an elite of intellectuals, specialists, and administrators who would undermine the revolution. Mao had expressed this concern in April 1969 when decrying party leaders who "were all for material incentives. They put profits in command and did not promote proletarian politics."[75] He expressed similar views in late 1974, but they did not appear in the *People's Daily* until February 9, 1975, shortly after the close of the National People's Congress. Although ambiguously worded, Mao's remarks showed concern with economic inequalities: "Why did Lenin speak of exercising the dictatorship over the bourgeoisie? This question must be thoroughly understood. Lack of clarity on the question will lead to revisionism. This should be known to the whole nation." He continued: "China is a socialist country. Before liberation she was much the same as capitalism. Even now she practices an eight-grade wage system, distribution to each according to his work and exchange by means of money, which are scarcely different from those in the old society. What is different is that the system of ownership has changed." Bourgeois rights, Mao pointed out, "can only be restricted under the dictatorship of the proletariat."[76]

Taking off from these quotations, followers of the Shanghai group warned that the emphasis on economic modernization would ensure the continuation and even increase of bourgeois rights, which they defined as greater use of material incentives to increase productivity. This practice would enrich the old bourgeoisie and produce a new elite of skilled workers, cadres, intellectuals, and well-to-do peasants, which would hinder China's transition to a revolutionary, egalitarian communist system. This view was similar to the view first enunciated by Milovan Djilas in 1957, that party control over a centrally directed administration and economy produced a new ruling and exploiting class. The Shanghai group referred to this new class as a new "bourgeoisie" even though it had little to do with capitalism. Whereas the bureaucratic leaders accepted the new class as the price of industrialization, the Shanghai group, perhaps for power reasons, and Mao for ideological reasons, refused to acknowledge its inevitability.

The day after the publication of Mao's quotes, Liang Xiao proclaimed in the *People's Daily* that to reach communism, "the proletariat must carry out the most radical rupture with traditional property relations." But Liang took an unhurried view of the time required to make the rupture: "The socialist society cannot all at once and completely get rid of the traditions and birthmarks of capitalism."[77] In the interim, the change must be prepared for ideologically, because that was where the bourgeoisie still exerted the most influence. In addition, ideological incentives instead of material ones should be used to encourage productivity. Zhou Si, another Shanghai writing group, recommended symbolic incentives and volunteer labor as a means to inspire workers with such idealism that their collective interest would override all thought of their individual gain. Unlike the Leap, "volunteer labor" did not mean an uncontrolled mass movement from below but an organized labor movement with firm leadership from above. However, Zhou Si stopped short of calling for full adoption of ideological incentives, even though it was "the first step" toward communism: "Today, it is still necessary to apply the principle of 'to each according to his work.' "[78]

Indirectly acknowledging that their proposals might be unpopular, several supporters of the Shanghai group vowed that their de-emphasis of material incentives did not mean a lack of concern for the material well-being of the working people. On the contrary, material well-being was to be raised by increasing production, but this increase would be accomplished by ideological rather than material means. As one writer explained, "Our party has never used [material incentives] as a means to stimulate production but has given priority to carrying out education on socialism and communism for the masses of the people."[79]

At the end of February, Yao Wenyuan published his first signed article in seven years. The article was greeted with fanfare in the media, for this was the first time since the Cultural Revolution that members of the Shanghai group had spoken in their own names rather than through writing groups. Yao revealed the factional disputes going on behind the veil of ideological discourse. He predicted that unless "the new bourgeoisie" were suppressed, it would usurp power, as it had done in the Soviet Union. The new bourgeoisie was really "the old bourgeoisie," a euphemism for the pre-Cultural Revolution leaders returning to power, who were directing their activities: "Inexperienced, newly engendered bourgeois elements openly break the law while cunning bourgeois elements of long standing direct them from behind the scenes—this is a common occurrence in class struggle in the society today." With a premonition of what might happen to his associates and himself if "the old bourgeoisie" gained full power, Yao warned that they "will first of all carry out a bloody suppression."[80]

To counter these forces, Yao Wenyuan called for a struggle to whittle away bourgeois rights. But Yao's concept of this struggle, unlike the earlier pronouncements of his followers, went beyond the ideological sphere to the political. He explained, "We must carry out such class struggle and two-line struggle and continually defeat the bourgeoisie and its agents working for revisionism, for a split, and for intrigues and conspiracy"—the very charges that the bureaucratic leaders, and even Mao, had directed against his own group.[81]

Yao Wenyuan leveled a new charge against the bourgeoisie, that of empiricism. Pointing out that Mao had declared in 1959 that "the main danger lies in empiricism" and had subsequently warned of this danger many times, Yao implied that Mao was alarmed by the same danger in the present.[82] Yao did not define empiricism, but he claimed that Mao sought to overcome it by having the Central Committee and senior and intermediate-level party cadres act on the basis of Marxism-Leninism, which by implication defined empiricism as a disregard for ideology, and defined those who disregarded ideology as high party administrators. Following Yao Wenyuan's signal, other writers associated with the Shanghai group attacked empiricism. Those guilty of empiricism were accused of despising theory, or ideology, as "outdated." In true qingyi tradition, a commentator in the *Red Flag* of April 1975 accused "empiricists" of rejecting the view that "the correctness or incorrectness of the ideological and political line decides everything."[83]

A number of writers called for even more radical action than had Yao Wenyuan. Whereas Yao demanded struggle under party direction, others called for struggle arising from the masses in the manner of the Cultural Revolution. One of these pointed out that Mao "inspired a vast number of the masses to expose our dark side in an open, all-around way and from the lower levels upward."[84] Whereas Yao cautioned that the suppression of bourgeois rights should be done gradually and in the ideological-political realm primarily, a new Liang Xiao article in March 1975 called for a struggle against bourgeois rights in the economic sphere, with little mention of the gradual approach they had espoused earlier.[85] Some writers used quotations that recalled the uncontrolled revolutionary fervor of the Cultural Revolution. The phrase "No construction without destruction" was repeatedly cited, as well as Mao's quotation, "Before a brand new social system can be built on the site of the old, the site must be swept clean."[86]

There was a demand to return China to the revolutionary spirit of the guerrilla days, which was reminiscent of similar calls in the Leap and the Cultural Revolution. Like the qingyi, some writers of the Shanghai group contrasted an ideal past with a decadent present. Much attention was given to Mao's report of March 5, 1949, expressing the fear that, once the party was in power, feelings of arrogance, inertia, love of pleasure, and distaste for hard work would emerge. He urged his comrades to continue "to display the same vigor, revolutionary enthusiasm, and death-defying spirit." In contrast to the guerrilla days, one writer observed, contemporary people "do not compare their work, zeal, and contributions to the revolution with those of others; they only compare with others for wages, treatment, and material comforts, chasing after and extending bourgeois rights in every way."[87] Some comrades preferred to make revolution peacefully, which would eventually mean the end of the revolution. These demands for mass movement, a return to the guerrilla spirit, and radical change in economic relationships were nevertheless minor counterpoints to the campaign's dominant tone of controlled ideological and political struggle.

Another minor counterpoint of the dictatorship of the proletariat campaign subtly expressed the views of the Fourth National People's Congress and the bureaucratic leaders. The difference between their views and the dominant line of the Shanghai group was one of emphasis. With some exceptions, most writers approved of the gradual whittling away of bougeois rights. But a number of them, instead of emphasizing the inevitable overthrow of the bourgeoisie and the establishment of an egalitarian society, stressed the inevitability of inequality at the beginning of socialism, as at present: "these shortcomings are unavoidable in the early stages of communist society—the socialist society that is just born out of capitalist society ... The principle of each according to his work in the historical period of socialism still has its historical functions which must be implemented."[88] As opposed to the writers of the Shanghai group, these writers emphasized material incentives rather than ideology as the stimulus to productivity.

A *People's Daily* editorial of February 22, 1975, was more specific. It explained that in the near future the small commodities producers "cannot be driven out or crushed; we must live in harmony with them." They could be transformed "only by very prolonged, slow, cautious organizational work." The editorial's description of the ordinary worker resembled "the middle man" in that, though he wanted revolution, he was not yet ready to carry it out. Revolutionary action was therefore inappropriate at present: "The worker is building the new society, but he has not yet become a new person who wipes out the mire of the old society. He is still standing in the mire of the old world. We can only dream of making a clean sweep of this mire. If we think that this can be done immediately, it is nothing more than a most stupid pipe-dream, which is in practice a pipe-dream of moving the socialist world into mid-air."[89]

As if in response to these two opposing counterpoints, Zhang Chunqiao in April 1975 also published his first signed article since the Cultural Revolution, which was given prominent and widespread coverage in the press and radio similar to Yao Wenyuan's. The article was presented as the authoritative interpretation of Mao's views on bourgeois rights. Although Zhang sought to direct the dictatorship of the proletariat campaign along the "correct" path, he was somewhat defensive. He rejected the call for an immediate radical rupture in property relations, perhaps reflecting Mao's own reservations about moving too fast economically. Apparently he was also responding to expressed fears of another Leap that were aroused by the campaign. He accused others of sabotaging the movement by spreading rumors of "communization," a reference to some of the radical practices introduced during the commune movement of the Great Leap, such as abolishing private plots. As if to dispel the fear and rein in more radical cadres, Zhang vowed that "the wind of 'communization' . . . shall never be allowed to rise again." He promised that even when the commune, instead of the production team, was finally made the basic accounting unit, it would remain under collective leadership, thereby continuing "commodity production, exchange through money, and distribution according to work."[90]

Zhang Chunqiao denounced the Leap's voluntarist approach of achieving communism economically in a short period of time. There would be no quick transition to common ownership and the abolition of private property; in the short term, no basic change would occur. Instead, Zhang presented the more traditional Marxist approach, affirming that communism would come only when an abundance of goods existed. Change would be slow, because "our country does not yet have a great abundance" of commodities.[91] Hence, in the pursuit of communism's economic goals, Zhang was more cautious than some of his associates. He was willing to tolerate the "harmful" effects of bourgeois rights in the economic sphere in order to develop the economic potential necessary to ensure the transition to communism. Still, he warned, there could be no backsliding or widening of the gap in the distribution system. He sought to block further wage differentiation but did not seek an immediate leveling of wages.

Although Zhang Chunqiao cautioned against radical action in the economic sphere, he was not so cautious about radical action in the political and social arenas. His main concern was not so much with economic class enemies as with political enemies within the leadership. He warned that "the 'bourgeois' wind blowing from among those Communists, particularly leading cadres . . . does the greatest harm to us." They are "Communists in name but new bourgeois elements in reality."[92] With the moral indignation of his qingyi predecessors, he regarded this new class as perpetrators of evil ways and ideological hypocrisy.

Returning to the guerrilla paradigm, Zhang Chunqiao compared the attack on the present-day bourgeoisie to the attacks on counter-revolutionaries in the guerrilla bases in the 1930s. He cited an incident Mao had described, when a fortified village close to the party's headquarters at Baoan, held by a handful of counter-revolutionaries, was finally stormed and destroyed in 1936 by the Red Army.[93] Whereas Mao had mentioned a handful of enemies, Zhang spoke of numerous enemies: "Today there are still many 'fortified villages' held by the bourgeoisie; when one is destroyed, another will spring up, and even when all but one have been destroyed, this last one will not vanish of itself if the iron broom of the proletariat does not reach there."[94] The struggle against China's bourgeois enemies, he implied, would be protracted and violent.

Zhang Chunqiao's milder attack on bourgeois rights in the economic sphere, coupled with his intensified attack on the bourgeoisie in the political sphere, was subsequently echoed in the press. The Shanghai writing groups at Beijing University and Qinghua University explained that the "New bourgeois elements have an exceedingly greedy appetite, and they are not merely after economic interests. There is no doubt that they also try to take over political power."[95] The writing groups accused these elements of using the tactics of the Monkey King, who wormed into the belly of his adversary and took over leadership, a charge that Mao had leveled at Liu Shaoqi and his associates in the Cultural Revolution.

The Shanghai group's purpose was to create a hostile public opinion against both the old and the new elites. This was succinctly spelled out in the Red Flag in April 1975: "We simply want to create a strong public opinion among the masses to intimidate the class enemies and all social forces and social groups who oppose socialist revolution and hate and sabotage socialist construction. We want to create such an opinion so that we can keep the capitalist forces from surfacing and make them give up hope."[96]

Although Mao may have used Zhang Chunqiao, Yao Wenyuan, and their writing groups to limit material incentives and economic inequalities, they in turn took advantage of Mao's apparent blessing to influence public opinion in a direction that he did not intend. They reinterpreted his quotes for their own purposes. Where Mao was primarily concerned with bourgeois rights in the economic sphere, Zhang Chunqiao and his followers were concerned primarily with expelling the bourgeoisie from the political sphere. Whereas Mao spoke of only a small number of bourgeoisie in the party, the Shanghai group saw the bourgeois class usurping political leadership. After the Cultural Revolution, Mao, along with the bureaucratic leaders, favored the more traditional Marxist approach to change in the economic base in order to change the superstructure; the Shanghai group reiterated this doctrine but at the same time continued to express the Cultural Revolution's voluntarist view of changing the superstructure in order to change the substructure.

The Shanghai group attributed views to Mao that he had not even expressed and indeed opposed. Yao Wenyuan implied that condemnation of empiricism was in line with Mao's thinking, whereas not only Zhou Enlai but also Mao were now concerned with pragmatic economic policies, although Mao's concern did not include material incentives. Mao in fact criticized Yao for calling empiricism the main danger. At the end of March 1975, Yao revised a press report to include a condemnation of empiricism and sent it back to Mao for approval as an official document. On April 23, Mao responded by declaring that revisionism was not just empiricism but also dogmatism: "It seems the formulation should be: Oppose revisionism which includes empiricism and dogmatism. Both revise Marxism-Leninism. Don't mention just one while omitting the other. Not many people in our party really know Marxism-Leninism. Some who think they know it in fact do not know very much. They consider themselves always in the right and are ready at all times to lecture others. This in itself is a manifestation of a lack of knowledge of Marxism-Leninism."[97]

One indication that Mao's statement was an attack on the Shanghai group was the fact that Yao Wenyuan and Wang Hongwen blocked dissemination of the statement at the time with the excuse that it had not been formally transmitted as a document. The Shanghai group's attack on empiricism and their advocacy of struggle against the bourgeoisie in the political sphere were clearly not in conformity with Mao's other quotations in the dictatorship of the proletariat campaign, and his rejection of Yao Wenyuan's statement on empiricism signified his active disagreement. Whereas Mao had turned his attention to economic matters, the Shanghai group persevered in his Cultural Revolution vision of ideological transformation as the prerequisite for economic transformation. Again, as in traditional times, practical necessity forced the political patron to separate himself from the idealistic vision he had once enunciated and from his ideological allies who continued to perpetuate it.

As in the anti-Confucian campaign, in the dictatorship of the proletariat campaign the message became bifurcated. Although Mao's comments on empiricism were not relayed to the public at the time, criticism of empiricism gradually petered out. The bureaucracy's quiet counterpoint of the winter became louder in the spring of 1975 as much sharper criticism was directed against those who acted radically or arbitrarily in the economic sphere. Whereas Zhang Chunqiao called the cadres who had curbed bourgeois rights merely "overzealous," an April *Red Flag* article called these cadres "leftists." It charged that those who advocated the outright abolition of material incentives, rural private plots, private side-line enterprises, and free markets committed "leftist" mistakes. It acknowledged that material incentives caused inequality and a gap between mental and manual labor, but it rejected the Cultural Revolution's approach of an all-out effort to close these differences. Instead, it proposed a traditional Marxist approach to restrict bourgeois rights by producing favorable economic as well as ideological conditions that would abolish them gradually in the distant future. At present, pressures to change the existing economic relations should not be encouraged but resisted: "Attention must be paid to guard against such sentiments, which are divorced from reality."[98] Bourgeois rights were to be not only recognized but also safeguarded for a protracted period.

While Zhang Chunqiao also sought to move slowly in economic relations, another part of the bureaucratic counterpoint, the emphasis on unity, was antithetical to his stress on political and ideological struggle. People were advised by an article in the *Red Flag* in June 1975 to analyze the impact in their areas of the negative factors of the dictatorship of the proletariat campaign, those that "adversely affect stability and unity."[99] In contrast to its role in the initial stage of the campaign, the theory of the dictatorship of the proletariat was used by late spring 1975 to promote, not undermine, stability and unity. Mao's Three Directives issued at the start of the campaign—study the dictatorship of the proletariat, achieve stability and unity, and promote the national economy—were now listed together, giving each equal importance, instead of just stressing the ideology of the dictatorship of the proletariat. By mid-1975, unity and economic modernization rather than struggle and ideological exhortation became the predominant themes of the campaign.

Although the reasons for the labor unrest that erupted in localized areas in the late spring and summer of 1975 are unclear, the contradictory arguments of the dictatorship of the proletariat campaign may have aggravated an already factionalized conflict in some industries. The opposing signals may have activated, on the one hand, managers and skilled workers who identified with the bureaucratic leaders, and on the other, cadres and unskilled workers who identified with the Shanghai group. As the unrest grew and troops were dispatched to quash labor disputes, the campaign virtually died out.

From the very beginning, the campaign organizers, if not all of their followers, had accepted certain inherent limitations. Most of the writings of the Shanghai group, including those of Yao Wenyuan and Zhang Chunqiao, did not express the messianic quality of the Cultural Revolution nor the bitterness of the later campaign against Deng Xiaoping. With some exceptions, the Shanghai group advocated a "step-by-step" narrowing of economic and social inequalities. The complete elimination of money, wages, and all forms of private property were long-range goals that were not to be implemented overnight. Although both Yao and Zhang criticized the bourgeoisie in the party, they had not yet incited, through their writing groups, mass movements against the bourgeoisie. Both talked more of study than of action in the implementation of ideas. Consequently, when the campaign provoked more disruptive action in the economic realm than Mao and perhaps even its organizers had originally intended, it was terminated.

The Water Margin Campaign

The Shanghai group launched its next campaign against the popular tale *Water Margin*. This campaign, which dominated the nation from August through December 1975, turned away from the broad economic and social issues of the dictatorship of the proletariat campaign to focus more narrowly on factional issues. It used the discussion of a classic tale to attack more directly than in the anti-Confucian campaign specific individuals, such as Zhou Enlai, Deng Xiaoping, and the rehabilitées of the Cultural Revolution.

Deep as were the ideological disputes between the Shanghai group and the bureaucratic leaders as revealed in the dictatorship of the proletariat campaign, their personal animosities were even sharper. The *Water Margin* campaign allegorically depicted the intensification of these factional rivalries in anticipation of Zhou Enlai and Mao's deaths.

A cause of the campaign was the acceleration earlier in the summer of 1975 of the rehabilitation of officials purged in the Cultural Revolution. Deng Xiaoping had reappointed a sizable number of his old associates to government and party positions and to provincial posts. Several members of Peng Zhen's former Beijing Party Committee were seen around Beijing. As these rehabilitées had personally been persecuted by the Shanghai group during the Cultural Revolution, the group had every reason to believe that the rehabilitées might retaliate against them. They used *Water Margin* to defend themselves as well as to attack their opponents.

Like Robin Hood in the West, *Water Margin* had fired the imagination of generations of Chinese. For centuries its heroes were sung about in operas and its tale retold by storytellers in villages and marketplaces. Based on a series of popular stories and legends which had been gradually compiled during the Yuan dynasty (1279–1368), the story concerned a peasant uprising in the early twelfth century, led by a group called the 108 Heroes, comprising peasants and ex-government officials who had been persecuted by corrupt officials. Their original leader was Chao Gai, who had built up a base in the area of a swamp, the water margin. After Chao's death, he was succeeded by Song Jiang, who led the water margin rebels to victory over a group of corrupt officials led by Qao Jiu. Subsequently, Song Jiang accepted amnesty from the emperor and helped the regime quell other rebellions. So went the original version. At the end of the Ming dynasty, the scholar Jin Shengtan condensed the novel from one hundred to seventy chapters and deleted the section where Song Jiang accepted amnesty from the emperor and suppressed other rebellions. Jin's version was used in the People's Republic until the Cultural Revolution.

Reinterpreting the classics was a convenient means for changing attitudes, because they were known by all, literate and illiterate alike. The sense and characters of a story would be distorted in order to communicate a particular political message. For example, the party's reinterpretation of *The Dream of the Red Chamber* in 1954 had

been used to indoctrinate the population in the value of class struggle. However, there had been no long exegesis or campaign to rein-
terpret *Water Margin* in Marxist-Leninist terms. It was accepted for
what it was, a romantic account of heroic peasant rebels who waged
battles against corrupt officials. *Water Margin* was one of Mao's favorite stories because of its description of peasant rebellion, and it
was one of the few books he carried with him on the Long March.
When denouncing Peng Dehuai on July 23, 1959, Mao praised Song
Jiang, who "robbed the rich to help the poor and could take what he
wanted since he had justice on his side."[100]

During the Cultural Revolution, as part of the renewed effort to
reject China's traditional past, *Water Margin* was subjected to only
mild criticism. Song Jiang was portrayed as a dual personality who
was both revolutionary and compromising. Then in 1972 *Water
Margin* was recirculated as a favorable example of peasant rebellion
against corrupt bureaucrats. Although Song Jiang was criticized in
some respects, *Water Margin* continued to be treated as progressive.

Suddenly, in the late summer of 1975, *Water Margin* was used to
arouse popular hostility to the bureaucratic leaders and their policies. Yao Wenyuan orchestrated this reinterpretation from a few
chance negative comments on *Water Margin* that Mao had made on
August 13, 1975, in response to a teacher's request for his appraisal
of a number of classics. Two days later, on August 15, Yao sent to
the national media and the writing groups in Beijing and Shanghai
Mao's comments, with accompanying instructions on how to interpret them. Thus, in less than two weeks after Mao had made his remarks and without the apparent knowledge or approval of the Central Committee, Yao was able to arrange a rapid series of articles
depicting Song Jiang as a traitor and *Water Margin* as a reactionary
novel. Because Mao was in failing health, Jiang Qing and her friends,
especially Mao's nephew Mao Yuanxin, had greater access to him
and could communicate his words more readily than could the bureaucratic leaders. Moreover, Yao, with his editorial abilities and
journalistic connections, could take quick advantage of Mao's ellip-
tical comments for his own purposes.

Accordingly, on August 23, 1975, a new bimonthly column, called
"Literature," appeared in the *Guangming Daily*, portraying Song Jiang
no longer as a hero or even as a dual personality but as a betrayer of
the revolution because he had capitulated to the emperor and suppressed peasant rebellion. His battles against corruption in govern-

ment were no longer praised, because he had only eliminated corrupt officials and had not changed the political system. An editorial note explained that the story of *Water Margin* demonstrated how a revolution could end in failure when it "opposed only corrupt officials and not the emperor."[101] Unless the top leadership was overthrown, revolutions were bound to fail.

"Capitulation" was defined further in the next column, which appeared on August 30. Written by Liang Xiao, it attacked the view that "as long as we pledge allegiance to the emperor, oppose corrupt ministers, and rely on several 'good officials,' all contradictions will be wiped out and all problems will be resolved." Liang Xiao pointed out that the top leadership in *Water Margin* had tolerated corrupt officials. Qao Jiu, apparently a stand-in for Liu Shaoqi, committed his crime under the "indulgence and connivance" of the emperor. Nevertheless, the "emperor was invariably embellished as the wisest and most august ruler."[102] These articles could be interpreted as a condemnation of Mao as well as of the bureaucratic leaders.

Following the Liang Xiao piece, the *People's Daily* carried several articles, personally revised by Yao Wenyuan, which presented the power struggle in *Water Margin* so that it resembled the current power struggle. After Song Jiang, analogous to Zhou Enlai and Deng Xiaoping, had been given amnesty by the emperor, "he used persuasion and force to suppress and reject the revolutionaries." At the same time, "he recruited deserters, renegades, hereditary aristocrats, generals of the royal court, and landlords and assigned them important positions."[103] These articles warned that capitulationists like Song Jiang, who looked like revolutionaries but were actually counter-revolutionaries, had appeared in revolutionary ranks throughout history and into the present. The reader would have had no trouble, as he might have in the more complex anti-Confucian campaign, connecting these *Water Margin* counter-revolutionaries to presentday counter-revolutionaries. Zhou Enlai and Deng Xiaoping had suppressed the radicals and brought back purged officials, whom they appointed to high posts. The description of Song Jiang and his associates was thus more obviously analogous to Zhou, Deng, and their associates than were the more erudite allusions of the two previous campaigns.

Finally, on September 4, Mao's chance comments on *Water Margin* in August were published in the *People's Daily*. The first quotation merely summarized what had already appeared in the "Literature" column: "The fine point of this book *Water Margin* is its description of capitulationism. Using it as teaching material by negative example will enable the people to know the capitulationists." But the next quotation ensured that Mao would be identified not with the emperor but with Chao Gai, the original founder of the peasant movement before it had been taken over by renegades such as Song Jiang: "*Water Margin* only opposed corrupt officials but not the emperor. Chao Gai was excluded from the 108 Heroes." Mao then expressed the negative view of Song Jiang that had been presented in the column: "Song Jiang capitulated, practiced revisionism . . . The struggle between Song Jiang and Qao Jiu was a struggle of one faction against another within the landlord class." Mao's quotation, which charged that Chao Gai's principles had been changed by his successor Song Jiang, appeared to accept the Shanghai group's charge that Mao's successors, like Chao Gai's, would pervert his revolutionary principles.

Still, the editorial in which Mao's remarks were presented was more moderate in tone than the column. It expressed a desire to limit the campaign and to keep it strictly under the control of the party, an approach which more likely reflected Mao's wishes than those of the Shanghai group. It warned against turning the campaign into another Cultural Revolution, citing another of Mao's quotations: "Practice Marxism and not revisionism, unite and don't split, be open and aboveboard, don't intrigue and conspire."[104] This quotation was later cited as an example of Mao's effort to rein in the radicals.

The *Water Margin* campaign, however, was less moderate in tone than Mao's quotations. It, like the dictatorship of the proletariat campaign, diverged from the sense of Mao's remarks and even distorted his meaning. There is evidence that, although Mao was once more becoming disenchanted with Deng Xiaoping, he did not seek to attack Zhou Enlai. But as the *Water Margin* campaign progressed, there is little doubt that it was directed against Zhou as well as Deng. For example, Mao did not mention the character Lu Junyi in his quotations, but much attention was given to him in the campaign. It was stressed repeatedly that Song Jiang had put Lu Junyi, a "reactionary big landlord," into the number two position in the political hierarchy to "consolidate the rule of the capitulationist line of the *Water Margin*."[105] Song Jiang promoted Lu "not for the sake of transforming him into a leader of the revolutionary peasant army, but precisely for the sake of making use of his reactionary character and using him as the chief accomplice to push his capitulationist line."[106] Originally Song Jiang had wanted to put Lu in the number one position, but the opposition of Chao Gai and especially of his followers compelled Song Jiang to place Lu second.

Allegorically, this interpretation of *Water Margin* charged that Zhou Enlai brought in Deng Xiaoping to help him retreat from Cultural Revolution policies and had even wanted to put Deng in charge, but was stopped by Mao and the Shanghai group. Without the insertion of Lu Junyi into the discussion, Deng would have been identified with Song Jiang, but with so much attention given to Song Jiang making Lu the number two official, the identification of Song Jiang with Zhou was explicit. In the context of the *Water Margin* campaign, Zhou and Deng were treated as traitors. Most writers for the Shanghai group stressed that the enemy within the revolutionary ranks was much more dangerous than the enemy without. Officials such as Qao Jiu need not be feared, because their corruption and brutality were so obvious, but leaders such as Song Jiang subtly subverted the revolution before others became aware of it.

The theme of a weakening Mao and an increasingly powerful Deng Xiaoping dominated the campaign more and more. While Chao Gai had been alive, Song Jiang did not act openly. He played a dual game. He ostensibly showed respect to Chao Gai but secretly infiltrated his associates and covertly sabotaged the movement. In reality, he made Chao Gai "a commander without an army."[107] Disregarding Chao Gai's preeminent position, Song Jiang "went ahead arbitrarily to give assignments and make decisions . . . all . . . by himself . . . He purposely left out Chao Gai, cultivated his own prestige, and paved the way for his usurpation of the leadership."[108] In time, Chao Gai was reduced to a figurehead, while Song Jiang wielded the real power. Song then filled the administration with his own men and made the policy decisions.

The *Water Margin* campaign also denounced Zhou Enlai and Deng Xiaoping's efforts to curtail the political power of the Shanghai group by criticizing Song Jiang's acts of vengeance against Chao Gai's closest supporters. Although some of Chao Gai's supporters had been ambivalent or even friends of Song Jiang in the actual story, in the campaign they were depicted as representing the interests of the masses and of being suppressed by Song Jiang. At the beginning of the revolution, for example, the Yuan brothers, in meetings of the rebels, were seated among the first ten officials. But in a short time, the "deserters and renegades" whom Song Jiang had brought into the movement were seated ahead of the brothers in the hierarchy. Song Jiang kept Chao Gai uninformed about his reassignment of positions. This scenario resembled the experience of the Shanghai group at the Fourth National People's Congress where, with the exception of Zhang Chunqiao, they received few important positions, while rehabilitated party members gained prominence in the reconstituted government.

Anticipating what might happen to them when Mao died, the Shanghai group, through the *Water Margin* campaign, prophesied their impending demise unless action were taken against the current leadership. When Chao Gai had died, "revolutionary generals, like the Yuan brothers, who adhered to Chao Gai's revolutionary line, were suppressed and their military powers curbed in every possible way."[109] Although Chao Gai had expressed opposition to Song Jiang as his heir, his directives were ignored. Consequently, as soon as Chao Gai died, Song Jiang made him into an idol in order to fool the population while enthroning himself and his "reactionary" associates. He and his associates then demoted and executed those who had upheld Chao Gai's revolutionary policies. The Shanghai group's description of their own demise proved prophetic. There was a desperate quality to their *Water Margin* campaign, most likely for fear of their own survival. This feeling of desperation was revealed in a note that Zhang Chunqiao wrote in February 1975, "In recent years, it sometimes occurred to me that I might get beheaded at any time."[110]

In addition to their desire for vengeance and power, Song Jiang and his associates were charged with obstructing the revolutionary movement with their antirevolutionary ideology. Although their uprising had eliminated corrupt officials, it had not succeeded, because it "did not touch the economic base and the superstructure of the feudal rule."[111] In this context, the phrase "capitulation to the emperor" could be interpreted as Zhou Enlai and Deng Xiaoping's unwillingness to change the prevailing economic and political system. Although Song Jiang agreed with Chao Gai and his associates on the need to purge corrupt officials, he did not agree that it was necessary to carry the revolution through to the end. He abandoned it halfway. The campaign charged that Song Jiang had regarded all revolutionary activity of the masses as "totally devoid of respect for law and heaven and simply unthinkable."[112] He refused to violate the laws and institutions of the state and devised ways to uphold and use them to suppress the insurgents, a description of first Zhou's and then Deng's actions after the Cultural Revolution.

By contrast, Chao Gai's associates, the analogues to the Shanghai group, were described as even more dedicated to revolution than their leader, that is, than Mao himself. Although the *Water Margin* campaign portrayed the Shanghai group in alliance with Mao against the reactionaries, it thus implicitly criticized Mao in the portrayal of Chao Gai. One writer denounced Chao Gai for reluctance to attack his friend Song Jiang, that is, Zhou Enlai: "In carrying out the two-line struggle against Song Jiang, Chao Gai failed to acquit himself well and with determination because he was bound by a sense of loyalty to his friends."[113] Little attention was given to Chao Gai's revolutionary feats, whereas his followers were depicted as revolutionary zealots in the manner of the radical intellectuals in the Cultural Revolution, who not only opposed existing laws and institutions but used violent means to destroy them.[114] They were committed to carrying out the struggle against the capitulationists to the bitter end. Again the Shanghai group, like the liberal intellectuals in the early 1960s, criticized Mao before his death publicly, albeit indirectly.

Since Chao Gai's associates had believed corruption, bureaucratism, and elitism were not just the aberrations of certain "reactionary individuals" but were inherent in the system itself, it was necessary to overthrow the system that produced them. To purge corrupt officials merely helped to stabilize the existing system because it lessened the resistance of the peasants and weakened their revolutionary will. Thus, the *Water Margin* campaign advocated more radical actions than either the previous dictatorship of the proletariat campaign or Mao had advocated. Whereas the prior campaign had recommended the gradual change of the economic system along with an ideological struggle against the leadership, this one advocated the complete overthrow of the existing political system. Anarchism was implicit in its symbolic summons to overthrow the bureaucratic leadership: "Without the seizure of power, it is not possible to touch fundamentally the economic base and the superstructure of feudal rule."[115] The campaign legitimized once again the slogan of the Cultural Revolution that "Rebellion is justified." Because revolution could not rely on the evolution of economic forces, the leadership must be purged in order to change the system. Here again, Mao may have wanted to dispense with some of the "capitalist roaders" in the party, particularly Deng Xiaoping, but not with the bureaucratic leadership itself. His statements in this period preached unity and denounced factionalism.

Unlike the anti-Confucian and dictatorship of the proletariat campaigns, there was only slight representation of the bureaucratic position in the *Water Margin* campaign. Some writers were very academic, as if purposely contriving to divert the discussion toward historical rather than current questions. Along with criticisms of the uprising as an aborted peasant rebellion, there were erudite discussions on whether peasant rebellions should or should not be considered part of the class struggle and therefore a motive force of history. As Peng Zhen had been charged with diverting the attack on Hai Rui into an academic discussion in the Cultural Revolution, so Deng Xiaoping was later charged with using the same device in the *Water Margin* campaign. Although the bureaucratic leaders were able to dull the attack, they were less able than previously to divert it to their own purposes. The reason for the Shanghai group's virtual monopoly of the media on ideological issues by the fall of 1975 is unclear. It could be that Deng's proposals, formulated in the summer of 1975, for a return to more conventional educational and scientific practices and increased material incentives had prompted Mao to throw his support to the Shanghai group's attack on Deng in the *Water Margin* campaign.

However, the bureaucratic leaders appear to have confined the campaign to the cultural and educational realms. They did not allow it to spill over into the economic and political spheres. Some factories and communes in Shanghai and a few other areas discussed *Water Margin*, but this campaign generally did not have the widespread mass participation of the anti-Confucian and dictatorship of the proletariat campaigns. Thus, whereas the bureaucratic leaders had less leverage on ideological issues, they had more in the economic realm and even in the media discussion of nonideological issues.

The success of the bureaucratic leaders in limiting the campaign to the cultural realm was reflected in the November 1975 issue of *Red Flag*. Alongside articles on *Water Margin* were several on the need for agricultural mechanization, stability, and unity. Whereas the *Water Margin* articles stressed that criticism of the tale and study of the dictatorship of the proletariat would help the economy, other articles made little mention of *Water Margin*. Instead of ideology, they emphasized that "mechanization not only provides the only way to develop a large-scale socialist agriculture, but also serves as an important link in . . . achieving modernization of agriculture, industry, national defense, and science and technology."[116] Production would increase, not because of the overthrow of capitulationists, as in the *Water Margin* interpretation, but because of attention to economic development. And whereas a Shanghai group spokesman described *Water Margin* as the preoccupation of the nation, the widespread coverage given to agricultural mechanization in that fall issue, at the height of the campaign, made virtually no reference to *Water Margin*.

Despite Mao's quotations, the *Water Margin* campaign also went in a direction that apparently evoked his displeasure. Jiang Qing had requested that a recording of a speech of hers criticizing Song Jiang for making a figurehead of Chao Gai be played at a conference on agriculture in Dazhai in September-October 1975. When Hua Guofeng, then head of public security, reported this to Mao, he replied: "Shit! Barking up the wrong tree." He ordered Hua, "Don't publish the talk, don't play the recording, or print the text."[117]

Some of the writers on economic development indirectly criticized the Shanghai group, though not with the same venom that the Shanghai group injected into the campaign against the bureaucratic leaders. These writers pointed out that a small handful of people were impeding economic development by trying "to create confusion, sow seeds of discord, and spread rumors in order to fish in troubled waters." But the recommended treatment of these sowers of discord, unlike the crusading zeal advocated toward capitulationists in the *Water Margin* campaign, was to be mild, as Mao recommended at various times: "Cure the sickness to save the patient."[118] Farm mechanization and increased output needed stability, unity, and discipline. The revolutionary fervor hailed in the *Water Margin* campaign would only undermine the current efforts to create those conditions and oppose factionalism. Press attention was also given to the fortieth anniversary of the Long March. Joint editorials in the army and party newspapers paid respect to the martyrs of the Long March and, by extension, to the veterans still alive—Zhou Enlai, Deng Xiaoping, and many of the rehabilitées. This acknowledgment, along with the wide coverage given to agricultural mechanization and economic development, appeared as a concerted effort to relegate the *Water Margin* campaign and its sponsors to minor status.

When Zhou Enlai died in January 1976, press coverage of agricultural development and the Long March suddenly vanished. Deng Xiaoping was now attacked not symbolically but directly as "an unrepentent capitalist-roader." The *Water Margin* continued to be criticized, but the analogue of Song Jiang shifted from Zhou or Deng to Hua Guofeng, who was made acting premier on February 3. Dismayed that Mao had chosen Hua over one of their members but unable to attack him openly, the Shanghai group now identified Hua with Song Jiang. At the end of February Liang Xiao described Song Jiang as having nothing to do with the military destruction of the enemy.[119] The connection with Hua was clear, because unlike Zhou and Deng, Hua had not participated in the Long March or in the guerrilla and civil wars.

Another Shanghai group spokesman reinterpreted the Song Jiang–Lu Junyi relationship in the post-Zhou Enlai era so that it was more applicable to the Deng–Hua than to the Zhou–Deng relationship. Song Jiang, here an analogue to Deng, wanted to hand over his post to Lu Junyi, now an analogue to Hua, because he had already occupied "the number one position," and his position was "insecure." But this transfer of power was just "a trick" to keep power away from the revolutionaries.[120] As before, *Water Margin* was called a negative teaching example, but this time not because it taught one to discern capitulationists so much as because it taught that "conceding one's post" to someone else was done to maintain the status quo. The lesson to be drawn was that there was collusion between Hua Guofeng and Deng Xiaoping's followers against the Shanghai group and revolutionary change. The *Water Margin* campaign wound down and stopped abruptly with the purge of the Shanghai group by Hua Guofeng, the bureaucratic leaders, and the military in October 1976, a month after Mao's death.

The anti-Confucian, dictatorship of the proletariat, and *Water Margin* campaigns raise the question of whether campaigns waged with allusive articles and editorials and accompanied by forums and discussions in universities, factories, and communes could be transformed into actual power. Could they create public opinion for or against certain policies or for or against certain individuals to the point where public opinion would influence the policy makers? One of their objectives, the denial of the premiership to Deng Xiaoping, was achieved, but that denial had more to do with Mao's opposition than with the campaigns themselves. The other objectives of the campaigns—the rejection of pragmatic economic policies and the repudiation of the bureaucratic leadership—were not achieved. Although the views of the bureaucratic leaders were not represented in the media during the direct attack made on Deng by the Shanghai group in early 1976, this did not mean that their approach was not followed in important economic and political decisions. Zhou Rongxin, the minister of education, and a few of Deng's associates were purged at the time Deng was attacked, but most of the rest of the bureaucratic leadership continued in office virtually unscathed.

Still, the Shanghai group's domination of the media was sufficient to set the general ideological tone and prevent the opposing political side from defending its views in a sustained way. It also hindered the bureaucratic leaders' efforts to return to more conventional educational and economic practices. The impact of the campaigns was therefore a negative one. They created the impression of popular indignation against certain policies and people, but they did not create popular support for certain policies or people. They created the impression of general opposition to the dismantling of Cultural Revolution programs, which may have slowed their dissolution, but did not stop it. At the same time, the campaigns did not build up public support for the continuation of Cultural Revolution policies or for the Shanghai leadership itself. That the Shanghai group was purged with ostensible public delight indicates not only the unpopularity of their programs and the rejection of their leadership but also their ineffectuality in influencing public opinion. No matter how zealous and persistent their efforts, the Shanghai group could not build up a strong, unified public opinion in support of their cause, because they were forced to wage their campaigns with obscure analogies. And the bureaucratic leaders were able to inject their own analogies into the media. Furthermore, the Shanghai group's political patron, Mao, gave them only sporadic support at a time when his goals diverged from theirs. Most important, like their qingyi predecessors, the Shanghai group's ideological exhortations could not be translated into political power because, without a strong organizational base, they were no match for the political, economic, and military forces arrayed against them.

Public opinion was apparently confused rather than aroused by the variety of messages conveyed by the media. In the first two campaigns, the public was assaulted by a bifurcated and at times multifaceted ideological offensive. In the third campaign, it received a message on ideological issues that conflicted with the one it received

THE SHANGHAI GROUP

on economic issues. Confronted with an onslaught of contradictory messages in the official press, the public either ignored them or made their own interpretations. Thus, before the fall of the Shanghai group, China's population was already presented with officially sanctioned, alternative views which could prove a greater obstacle to the reimposition of the party's overall ideological control than any other legacy of the Cultural Revolution.

7

THE SCIENTISTS
AND
DENG XIAOPING

T he Shanghai group stopped playing by the traditional rules and stripped away their historical, ideological, and literary camouflage in early 1976. They were emboldened by Zhou Enlai's death in January and, most important, by Deng Xiaoping's efforts in 1975 to dispense with Cultural Revolution educational reforms in the universities and reconstitute and strengthen China's scientific and technological elite. They believed that this was an area, like that of material incentives, where Mao, despite his current concern with economic development, did not want to retreat from Cultural Revolution programs.

Between spring and fall 1975, there had been renewed efforts to reestablish achievement-oriented education in the universities and Western-oriented methods in the research institutes. These efforts were under Deng's auspices, for ever since the Great Leap Forward he had opposed campaigns to remold the thoughts of intellectuals. In 1959, he had said, "It would be sheer illusion to think that they can be transformed properly by creating such tension every day."[1]

THE SCIENTISTS

Furthermore, he had supported education that stressed expertise and defended conventional educational practices. When Mao in 1964 called for shortened courses, Deng demanded they remain as they were. When the radical professors were attacking Lu Ping, the president of Beijing University, and his associates in the spring of 1966, Deng complained that "excessive struggle" harmed intellectual life.[2]

Reestablishment of a Scientific Elite

Soon after he was rehabilitated in 1973, Deng Xiaoping led an effort by bureaucratic leaders to reenergize science. Following standard practice, the bureaucratic leaders convened conferences among intellectuals and rehabilitated officials. The outcome of these efforts was three major documents on science, technology, industry, and trade, called the Three Documents, which not only called for an elite class of scientists and professionals but also counterattacked the Shanghai group and the Cultural Revolution by calling for reforms in industry, education, and science.

As in 1971–1972, the documents reflected input from scientists and experts. Specialists concerned with a policy area under discussion were used as a source of expertise and as mobilizers of support. Nevertheless, these documents were drawn up under the initiative of the bureaucratic leaders, primarily Deng. At this point, the political interest of the bureaucratic leaders coincided with the professional and scholarly community's desire for more authority and autonomy in academic endeavors. Both groups opposed the Shanghai group and Cultural Revolution programs and sought to introduce practices that would achieve scientific and economic modernization.

The Shanghai group managed to get copies of the Three Documents, which they reprinted in large numbers with appended criticisms in early 1976, without authorization from the Central Committee. Although selective and incomplete, the published excerpts revealed the general dismay of the bureaucratic leaders at the state of China's scientific and economic development. The first document, "Some Problems on Speeding Up Industrial Development," was the result of a number of conferences on industry and transportation held in 1975. In the course of its drafting, opinions were solicited from experts in industry and from provincial party committees.

Then the document was submitted to the Politburo for discussion and went through several revisions and corrections. "Some Problems" presented a bleak picture of the economy, with industries in many areas partially paralyzed, production stagnating, and iron and steel output drastically reduced.

These conditions were implicitly blamed on the Shanghai group, whose followers were inexperienced and labeled anyone who disagreed with them "restorationists" and "revisionists." Not only did they demoralize workers and disrupt production, but their "indiscriminate opposition to enterprise management and rules and systems will inevitably result in an anarchist state."[3] Some of them willfully ignored the plans of the central authorities by discontinuing coordinated relations between various enterprises and spending funds without regard to limitations. Those who were "supporting them behind the scenes" must be struggled against "in a manner of blow for blow and fighting every inch of the way."[4] At the very least, this was a call for stepped-up opposition to the Shanghai group.

An even more explicit picture of the "anarchy" induced by the Shanghai group was seen in the remedies that "Some Problems" proposed: rational economic organization, financial accountability, strong central lines of management, fulfillment of quotas, maintenance of prescribed quality, work discipline, strict work attendance, and statistical reporting that reflected realities. Although both extremes of wage differentiation and egalitarianism were condemned, the document called for more material incentives. On the one hand, it recommended raising the wages of low-paid workers in order to reduce the gaps in society; on the other hand, it recommended further differentiation as a means to increase labor productivity. It stated that "Equal distribution without regard to intensity of labor performed and to different degrees of ability and contribution will be detrimental to mobilization of the socialist initiative of the broad masses." Furthermore, every year or so it would be necessary to raise the wages and benefits of a portion of the workers on the basis of "their attitudes toward work, technical and professional abilities, and contributions made in labor and work."[5]

These reforms were to be made in conjunction with the modernization of science and technology and the full utilization of China's intellectuals. The economic approach of the early 1960s, with its emphasis on agriculture as a foundation of the economy, was restated. Agricultural production was to be increased by modernizing agricultural machinery, chemical fertilizers, power, and transport. However, the major concern was with iron, steel, and raw material output, which was characterized as the "weak link" in the economy. The document recommended that the most advanced equipment be brought from abroad to develop these areas. To adapt this equipment to China's needs, "full play" must be given to experts and research units in the ministries, Chinese Academy of Sciences, universities, factories, and mines.[6] These experts could no longer be treated as unproductive and must be allowed to act as "the main leadership" in these endeavors.[7] Furthermore, China could no longer maintain a closed-door attitude toward the outside world. In fact, one purpose of Mao's diplomacy, the document asserted, was to bring in and learn about foreign technology that was urgently needed. The importation of complete sets of modern equipment would be paid for by deferred and installment payments as well as by "export as much as possible," particularly items that brought a high rate of exchange, such as coal and oil.[8] Accordingly, the importation of coal-mining and oil-drilling equipment would be repaid with the oil and coal produced.

Deng Xiaoping's comments of August 18, 1975, on "Some Problems" stressed that China's science and technology had gone as far as they could with China's existing knowledge. He pointed out that, "with our geological prospecting techniques, we can only find poor mines," whereas foreigners had technology that could find rich deposits. His view of foreign imports involved more than foreign machinery. He explained that "Agricultural modernization does not mean mechanization alone; it includes the development of science and technology." Concerned that "Some intellectuals have not put to use the skills they have learned," Deng sought to increase their number in proportion to the labor force. Another major concern was to reimpose discipline on industrial enterprises. He pointed out that "the present problem is that no one takes responsibility." He also insisted on the imposition of "rules and regulations," describing Mao's attitude toward regulations as "consistently endorsing revision, not abolition."[9]

The second document, "The Outline Report on the Chinese Academy of Sciences," was a more detailed, elaborate discussion of scientific and technical manpower. It was written in reaction to the Shanghai group's virtual dismantling of the scientific establishment in the Cultural Revolution. The few institutes of the academy that still functioned were wholly concentrated on applied science and engineering. They were primarily concerned, as Deng Xiaoping pointed out in his comments on "Some Problems," in utilizing existing knowledge rather than creating new knowledge. Highly trained scientists were engaged in manual labor or forced to work on narrow, practical problems instead of helping China raise its overall scientific and technological level.

The bureaucratic leaders, with Mao's approval, called in late 1974 for the rebuilding of the Chinese Academy of Sciences. Several of Deng Xiaoping's associates went to the academy in July 1975 to investigate conditions there and formulate a new science policy. They were led by two recently rehabilitated party officials closely associated with Deng, Hu Yaobang, former head of the China Youth League, and Hu Qiaomu, party ideologist. They spent nearly three weeks examining relevant documents and talking with people in and out of the academy. Hu Yaobang drew up a draft that he sent to Hu Qiaomu for revision. Both men then worked together with Deng, Hua Guofeng, and other officials, as well as with various scientists and experts. After several drafts, written over a period of two months, they produced the "Outline," dated September 26, 1975.

With a view similar to the one enunciated by Zhou Peiyuan in 1972, the "Outline" asserted that production and applied science could not replace laboratory experiments and research work on theoretical science. The research institutes of the academy and the institutes of higher education had the responsibility to carry on such work, but they had been unable to do so because their staffs were engaged in manual labor and no new personnel had come in for years. In addition to an increase in the number of scientists and their return to research, it was important to change the atmosphere of the academic community. Distinctions must be made between academic and political problems. Academic debates could no longer be handled, as in the past, by "administrative orders, nor must we support one faction and suppress another."[10] No longer should an academic question be judged by whether it was supported by the majority or the minority, the young or the old, or the proponents of a certain political view. Academic work was to be depoliticized, and academic issues were to be settled by means of scholarly discussion and scientific practice. Experts with professional skills rather than cadres with political skills were to exert leadership in academic matters. The "Outline" urged an increase in the quality and quantity of academic

THE SCIENTISTS

journals and the acquisition of advanced foreign science and technology in order to enhance scientific discussion and research in China.

On hearing a summary of the "Outline," Deng Xiaoping expressed disgust at the decline in scientific research and the ill treatment of China's scientists and professors caused by the Shanghai group. He complained that in the past few years, knowledgeable scholars, instead of working on their research projects, were forced to "see films" and engage in "factional battles." A small number continued their research, but they had to do it secretly, "like criminals." Deng cited the case of an expert in semiconductors who was forced to work on another subject and did research in his specialty in his spare time. Deng lamented, "There are a great number of such people who cannot put what they have learned to use."[11] He urged that experts who continued their work in spite of persecution and slander be protected, assisted, and given improved living conditions. Finally, he asked, why should those "who have no professional knowledge . . . and are factionalists be retained? Why should those who have a high level and knowledge among scientific researchers not be promoted to institute directors?"[12] He insisted, "We should support even those . . . [with] big faults, provided they do something good for the People's Republic of China."[13] His 1961 remark that it did not matter whether a cat was black or white as long as it caught mice, for which he had been condemned in the Cultural Revolution, was paraphrased in his comment about a well-known mathematician: "What does it matter if one is a little white and expert?"[14] He jeered, "Even people who are 'white and expert' are better than those who occupy the toilet without discharging, who stir up factionalism and pull our legs [hold us back]."[15]

The third document, "On the General Program for All Work of the Whole People and Whole Country," denounced the Shanghai group for disrupting the economy. Its final draft, dated October 7, 1975, rejected a major premise of the Shanghai group, that ideological and class struggle would increase economic production: "Only those who take to such fairy tales as turning a rock into gold will believe in the idea that a successful revolution will naturally be followed by successful production and that there is no need to exert efforts at production."[16] Even if one has "mastered the characteristics and laws of class struggle . . . this does not mean that we have grasped the characteristics and laws of the production struggle and scientific experiment."[17] The "General Program" compared the Shanghai group's disregard of economic issues with the views of Mao's old political rival from the 1930s, Wang Ming. Turning to Mao's past remarks for support, the document cited his criticism of Wang Ming: "The idea that economic construction is unjustified in the environment of revolutionary war is extremely erroneous ... Only by unfolding the work on the economic front and developing the economy of the Red areas can we provide the revolutionary war with a solid material base."[18]

Although not as visible or as noisy as the Shanghai group, Deng Xiaoping and his associates also sought to disseminate their views in the public arena. The Shanghai group charged that Deng spread his views by organizing writing groups to influence public opinion, give lectures, compose letters to the Central Committee, and spread rumors. In other words, he used the same tactics as they used. Deng also asked Hu Qiaomu to establish another journal, called the *Ideological Front*, to compete for ideological leadership with the *Red Flag*, which was under the dominant control of the Shanghai group. Such a journal was needed, Deng remarked, because "Mao's directives have not been reflected in [existing] publications."[19] Although it was announced on October 6, 1975, that a new national journal concerned with "practical" questions facing China would appear in April 1976, it never came out. Most likely, it was a casualty of the imminent campaign against Deng himself.

The bureaucratic leaders' difficulty in gaining control of the major ideological-intellectual journals was shown by the fate of *Historical Research*. In April 1973, Mao had directed that academic journals resume publication. However, the publication of *Historical Research* was stalled for over a year because the Shanghai group withheld the instructions. When the journal finally appeared in December 1974, the editorial board, which was to come from the Philosophy and Social Sciences Department of the Chinese Academy of Sciences, had been displaced by followers of the Shanghai group. In October 1975, the Shanghai group was forced to return the editorial responsibility to the Philosophy and Social Sciences Department. Yet it continued to put pressure on the new editorial board. There was a constant tug of war for control, which was reflected in the contradictory views presented in *Historical Research*, although again the Shanghai group's position predominated.

In addition to drafting documents, mobilizing the party bureaucracy, and convening conferences, Deng Xiaoping asked his associates to investigate specific problem areas. He directed the minister of education, Zhou Rongxin, to investigate and draft a report on higher education. Based on his findings, Zhou began to criticize the academic level at the universities as being no higher than that which existed in middle schools before the Cultural Revolution. He warned that the method of "learning by doing" would not meet China's skilled manpower needs. He demanded that academic standards be raised and that professionals and professors be given more authority in their fields and in the classrooms. He even debated publicly with Zhang Chunqiao on this issue. Some of Deng's associates also used the time-honored Confucian practice of memorializing the ruler. Liu Bing, vice-chairman of the Qinghua University Party Committee, and some colleagues wrote Mao two letters, on April 13 and September 3, 1975, in which they criticized the low academic level of university education. They asked for a de-emphasis of Cultural Revolution educational practices, such as manual labor and enrollment only after a period of work. These talks and letters were in the traditional pattern of authoritative representatives making private appeals to the ruler in an effort to convince him to adopt or change a policy.

The Shanghai Group's Retaliation

In a comment on "Some Problems," Deng Xiaoping revealed that the bureaucratic leaders planned to act on the views expressed in the Three Documents in November-December 1975. The summons to do battle with the Shanghai group, implicit in the documents, most likely provoked that group to move against Deng before he moved against them. In November 1975 they launched a campaign against his basic proposals on education. Moreover, Zhou Rongxin and Liu Bing's pleas for a more academic educational system, instead of convincing Mao to change his policies, aroused him—and certainly the Shanghai group—to defend the Cultural Revolution's politicized educational programs.

Liu Bing's letters to Mao were brought to the attention of Qinghua students in November 1975, and soon afterward large posters went up at Beijing and Qinghua Universities attacking Liu Bing and Zhou Rongxin. Universities, particularly in Shanghai and Liaoning, quickly followed suit. Zhou and Liu Bing paid a high price for their failure to persuade the ruler. They were purged from office, and Zhou was persecuted to death. The national media continued to praise the politicalization of higher education. Without any of the subtlety and indirection of the previous dictatorship of the proletariat and *Water Margin* campaigns, this drive then moved into a denunciation of the Three Documents as "three poisonous weeds," and of Deng himself as "the unrepentant capitalist roader."

The Shanghai group's anti-Deng campaign hindered the bureaucratic leaders in implementing the proposals set forth in the Three Documents. It demonstrated how a group of ideologues, with the permission of the political leader, could disrupt and even block the policies of the state and economic apparatus. There were disruptions in some industrial areas and some armed clashes, supposedly instigated by the Shanghai group's followers, but on the whole their methods were ideological. The group was able to pass off their views in the media as those of the regime's. They doctored pictures to show members of their group standing close to Mao by airbrushing out the bureaucratic leaders. They placed a constant stream of articles, written by their writing groups, in the major party journals and newspapers.

Some lines of their attack on Deng Xiaoping and the Three Documents were so exaggerated as to defy credibility. For example, as in the Cultural Revolution, they charged the party leaders with being "capitalist roaders." The lead article in the March 1976 *Red Flag* talked of "an unrepentant capitalist roader in authority," an obvious effort to separate Deng from his associates in the bureaucracy. But by May 1976, the writing groups were talking not about one or even a few leaders, but about a large portion of the leadership. Although acknowledging that these leaders had contributed before 1949 to the democratic revolution, they charged that in the socialist stage of the revolution they had become "capitalist roaders at the highest level of power." The Shanghai group offered no evidence to prove that the old party leaders were "capitalist roaders," but their questioning of the revolutionary or even the socialist nature of Deng Xiaoping and the bureaucracy's view of economic modernization had more validity. The *People's Daily* pointed out that Deng "talks only about 'boosting' while saying not a word about production relations and revolution in the superstructure."[20] Deng and his associates were accused of regarding things rather than people as the principal force in development and viewing production as dependent on science, technology, tools, managers, experts, and regulations rather than on the mobilization of the masses. Although Deng projected himself as concerned with the masses, he "actually used cheap promises to induce the masses to take into consideration only immediate material interests instead of basic long-term interests."[21]

The Shanghai group's charge that the Three Documents smacked of Soviet revisionism and Liu Shaoqi's programs, while not wholly accurate, had some relation to reality. Deng Xiaoping's desire to reimpose "direct and extensive control of enterprises by the ministry concerned" was supposedly copied from the "Rules and Regulations of the Soviet Magnitogorsk Iron and Steel Combine." The shift from the lower-level, decentralized control of an enterprise that had occurred during the Cultural Revolution back to direct supervision by a ministry meant that a few people at the top would impose a vertical line of authority. Local party committees, and even the Central Committee, would not have a voice in the development of the enterprise. As a result, the ministries would treat enterprises under them as "their own private property," and the ministries would become "separate fiefdoms." These moves toward tighter centralization would result in "undermining rational overall planning of the national economy."[22] Furthermore, the use of material incentives would lead not to, but away from, communism: "Enthusiasm 'stimulated' in this way can never be socialist enthusiasm but bourgeois individualist 'enthusiasm.' "[23]

As the bureaucratic leaders charged the Shanghai group with economic irrationality, so did the Shanghai group level the same charge against them. Their arguments stemmed from the belief, which they themselves did not practice, that it was necessary to have the participation of the local areas and the masses in the industrial process in order fully to transform China. Both groups cited the same quotations of Mao to legitimize their arguments. Where Deng Xiaoping used Mao's call in 1956 for "central and local initiative" to support his plea for centralization, the Shanghai group used that call to support their plea for local initiative. They argued that if Deng "were allowed to have his way . . . the initiative of the localities and masses would be dampened."[24] Moreover, Deng's regulations for workers would tie them to their machines and eliminate their participation in enterprise management.

Deng Xiaoping's overriding stress on scientific and technological development, particularly as learned from the West, was treated as even more detrimental to the continuance of the revolution than his economic proposals. This emphasis, the Shanghai group charged, would lead to sharper social inequalities. Just as a centralized industry would be controlled by a small number of bureaucrats, so a Western-oriented scientific and technological development would be controlled by an elite of Westernized intellectuals. Deng's demands for experts rather than officials to direct science and technology and his proposals to separate scientific research from production would remove workers and peasants from participation in technological change. The Shanghai group claimed that mass participation in scientific agricultural experiments and research in factories and fields had improved productivity, but Deng and his associates treated science as the concern of only a small number of professionals: "It matters little whether the broad masses learn a bit more or less. To them, therefore, the work of popularizing natural science is a matter of no consequence." But if China were truly to modernize, the Shanghai group insisted, "the broad masses need to grasp . . . all kinds of advanced techniques."[25] Moreover, they pointed out, the technological accomplishments in Chinese history were the creation of the masses in villages and in small urban factories as well as of the elite in the cities.

Although inevitably each faction's position polarized in the campaign, Deng Xiaoping did recommend mass participation in technological change in the Three Documents, and the Shanghai group did not discount altogether the work of experts, as long as it had practical application. At the same time, the Shanghai group addressed a crucial issue for China's development: whether a few hundred, or even a few thousand, highly trained Westernized scientists could transform Chinese science and technology without the understanding and participation of the masses in scientific and technological change.

In addition to these arguments from the Cultural Revolution, the Shanghai group countered the bureaucratic leaders with arguments that resonated with the nineteenth century attack of Confucian conservatives against the Westernizers. Although they dispensed with the traditional indirect methods of dissent, the Shanghai group in this campaign used some of the same arguments as their predecessors. They would never have consciously identified with the conservatives, but the nineteenth century debate over similar issues may have unconsciously colored their arguments.

THE SCIENTISTS

Like the conservatives and a contingent of their qingyi predecessors who became militantly anti-Western when confronted with the West, the Shanghai group conveyed a sense that the world—their world—was falling apart and that the only way it could be saved was to resist foreign technology and return to fundamental Chinese values. They equated Deng Xiaoping with such nineteenth century Westernizers as Zeng Guofan, Li Hongzhang, and Yuan Shikai. Like them, Deng allegedly suffered from a "slavish comprador" mentality. His plan to pay for the newest, most advanced foreign technology and equipment with the minerals and oil produced with that equipment would be "selling out China's natural resources and state sovereignty." Like the Westernizers, Deng would permit "the imperialists to plunder China's natural resources."[26] As a result of such a policy, the group asserted with Leninist phraseology, China would gradually become a raw materials supply base, commodity market, and investment ground for imperialists.

In addition to comparing Deng Xiaoping to nineteenth century Westernizers, the Shanghai group compared him more appropriately with the Soviet revisionists who also mortgaged Soviet natural resources to bring in foreign capital and know-how and used part of the output to pay the foreigners for their investment. Ironically, a similar debate was going on in the Soviet Union in the 1970s between those representing the Solzhenitsyn position and those representing the technocratic position, in which both sides repeated some of the same arguments used in nineteenth century Russia by the Slavophiles and Westernizers. Both Russia and China used nineteenth century arguments to fight twentieth century conflicts.

In this debate, the Shanghai group also stated the traditional Chinese view of China's uniqueness in the world. To import foreign technology, copy foreign designs, and pattern equipment on foreign models, they claimed, would not solve China's particular problems. One of their writing groups quoted Mao, "We cannot just take the beaten track traversed by other countries in the world in the development of technology." Yet Deng Xiaoping and his associates, the writing group continued, "want us to believe there is a road to be traversed, 'regardless of different political systems.' "[27] The Shanghai group did not reject foreign technology altogether but feared that it would downgrade indigenous science and technology, further depriving the masses of meaningful participation in industrialization and modernization. Moreover, they rejected vociferously the way in which Deng intended to pay for it. They reiterated Mao's argument that China should rely mainly on its own efforts while making external assistance subsidiary. Contrary to Deng's proposal of giving priority to foreign technology for transforming China, they sought to limit contact with the West to the selective buying of technology in order to preserve the distinctiveness of China's form of socialism. Like the nineteenth century conservatives, the Shanghai group warned that if China took the Western scientific and technological path, it would lose its own way.

To erase the image that the bureaucratic leaders projected of them as revolutionary utopians, the Shanghai group asserted that Deng Xiaoping and his associates were actually the utopians in the Chinese context. The group's arguments again represented a strain that had its roots in nineteenth century Chinese history: the view that foreign entanglement, science and technology, and a Westernized bureaucracy would not transform China; they would only transform a small elite and leave the rest of the country unaffected. Overcentralization would not work in a large, agricultural country like China, nor would a simple transfer of technology fulfill China's particular needs.

The bureaucratic leaders were not unappreciative of these arguments. They often cautioned that China must not merely imitate the West. Like their nineteenth century Westernized predecessors, they sought to combine Western methods with their own culture. The writer Lu Xun became a symbol of this view. As if to change the radical image of Lu Xun conveyed by the Shanghai group, the bureaucratic leaders depicted him as assimilating selective aspects of Western culture. Lu Xun, a writer noted, was "most familiar with both Chinese and foreign things," and his creative writings were "not only different from those of foreign countries but also different from the Chinese classical style of writing." Yet his works had "the Chinese flavor and spirit."[28] Lu Xun was now made to represent the use of Western and Chinese culture to produce something new, but still Chinese.

Mao's Position

Again, as in previous campaigns of the 1970s, there was a divergence between Mao's position and that of the Shanghai group. Mao appears to have generally accepted some of the ideas of the Three Documents, while at the same time becoming increasingly disenchanted with their prime sponsor, Deng Xiaoping. Whereas the Shanghai group vociferously denounced the Three Documents, comparing them to Khrushchev's secret report to the Twentieth Party Congress denouncing Stalin and to Lin Biao's 1971 criticism of Mao, Mao's view on them was ambivalent. On the one hand, his statements and actions signified approval of the emphasis on economic development, order, stability, science, and technology. On the other hand, they indicated disapproval of the disinterest in class struggle and the acceptance of economic and intellectual inequalities. This ambivalence reflected his own contradictory goals at the time: to accelerate economic development and train scientists and engineers to achieve a modernized society by the end of the century, while at the same time moving toward a more egalitarian society; and to achieve unity and stability, while continuing class struggle. Deng became a scapegoat for the failure to carry out these contradictory visions.

Although Mao made no public comments on the Three Documents, he did read them. In Deng's remarks on the documents, he invariably asked that they be shown to Mao. There is evidence that Mao even made some revisions. For example, a statement about Mao's Three Directives as "the key link" was deleted from a mid-September draft of "Some Problems." Thus Mao suggested changes but did not reject the documents in toto, as did the Shanghai group.

Mao's approach to scientific modernization may have been inconsistent and relatively passive, but it was not negative. His interest in the early 1970s in stimulating economic development apparently led him to approve the rebuilding of the Chinese Academy of Sciences. When Deng Xiaoping instructed his associates to show Mao the "Outline Report" on the academy, he said of Mao, "He is very concerned about this problem."[29] Mao wanted scientists to have more favorable conditions in which to pursue their work. Certainly Zhou Enlai and his associates could not have embarked on the importation of Western technology in the early 1970s without Mao's consent. Still, there are no statements in this period comparable to those in 1956 on the need to learn the science and technology of capitalist countries.

Mao was more assertive in expressing the need for stability and unity. He was concerned not only with the disruption of the economic system at this time but also with the disruption of the political system. A statement of his in late 1974, perhaps at the Plenum before the Fourth National People's Congress, stressed unity: the "Great Proletarian Cultural Revolution has gone through eight years. Now let us have stability. The whole party and the whole army must unite."[30] This quotation was not published at the time, which was another indication of the Shanghai group's ability to interfere with communications, even from their supposed political patron.

Mao also repeatedly criticized the Shanghai group's factionalism and some of their practices at party meetings and in private conversations. In a letter to Jiang Qing on November 12, 1974, he wrote: "You have offended too many people. Be sure to unite with the majority. These instructions are of utmost importance."[31] In a talk with party officials in July 1975, Mao blamed the Shanghai group's sway in the cultural arena for having produced a lack of variety and richness in China's creative life. After Wang Hongwen visited Mao a second time in December 1975 to complain about the bureaucratic leaders, Wang was forced to write a self-criticism in which he disclosed that Mao had advised him again, "You should not form the Shanghai faction."[32]

Still, it was also Mao's decision to deny Deng Xiaoping the premiership when Zhou Enlai died and to allow a campaign against him and the proposed educational changes. Although Mao became increasingly less active in 1975–1976, all important decisions were still passed to him for approval. Such a high-level attack could not have been carried out without his permission. It was not until June 1976 that he was apparently too ill to function.

Since the Shanghai group was aware that Deng Xiaoping was preparing to move against them, they probably did their best to turn Mao against Deng. Although Mao's relationship with Jiang Qing had reportedly cooled after the Cultural Revolution, his failing health gave the Shanghai group more exclusive access to him, particularly after Zhou Enlai's hospitalization in 1974. It is likely that they found Mao receptive. Mao had approved Deng's rehabilitation and return as vice-premier in 1973, but he did not regard him as a friend, as he did other rehabilitated leaders, such as Chen Yi, with whom he exchanged poetry until Chen's death in 1972. There had been an estrangement between Mao and Deng dating from at least the Great Leap Forward. At a meeting on October 4, 1966, Mao complained that Deng "never came to consult me: from 1959 to the present, he has never consulted me over anything at all . . . I don't like being treated as a dead ancestor."[33] There were indications that Mao connected the slackening of revolutionary spirit after the Cultural Revolution to Deng. The *People's Daily* on January 1, 1976, quoted Mao, "Unity and stability to not mean writing off class struggle; class struggle is the main theme and the rest are merely details," which was an indirect criticism of the lumping together of the Three Directives. On February 24, the *People's Daily* quoted Mao as directly referring to Deng: "He does not understand Marxism-Leninism; he represented the capitalist class. He said he will never 'reverse verdicts'; this cannot be trusted. What does this mean, 'Three Directives as a link?' The class struggle is the key link, everything else hinges on it. This man does not comprehend class struggle."

The attacks on Deng Xiaoping and his programs climaxed with demonstrations in Tiananmen Square in early April 1976 to honor Zhou Enlai. After Zhou's death in January 1976, the Shanghai group had made him virtually a nonperson through their control of the media. In April, the Qingming annual occasion to commemorate the dead provided the occasion for a partly orchestrated, partly spontaneous demonstration by workers and intellectuals to pay tribute to Zhou Enlai and indirectly to support policies that Deng as well as Zhou had espoused. At the same time, it implicitly attacked the Shanghai group and even Mao. Among the poems recited for the occasion were a number that used the Legalist analogy not to praise but to assail Mao, as in:

China is no longer the China of yore;
And the people are no longer wrapped in utter ignorance,
Gone for good is Qin Shi Huang's feudal society.[34]

The demonstration was brutally suppressed by the police and public security forces. Deng was blamed for the demonstration and was dismissed from all his posts. Hua Guofeng was appointed first vice-chairman of the party and premier, replacing Deng as the successor to Mao.

At this time a new Maoist quotation expanded the criticism beyond Deng Xiaoping to the party hierarchy: "You are making the socialist revolution and yet don't know where the bourgeoisie is. It is right in the Communist Party—those in power taking the capitalist road."[35] The explanation later given that this statement was directed against a few party officials and not against the veteran party leaders as a whole was not clear from the words themselves. Nevertheless, given Mao's concern at this point with political unity and his opposition to factionalism, the explanation that the statement was directed against a handful, particularly Deng, rather than at the bureaucratic leadership, is plausible. The fact that only Deng and a few of his close associates, such as Hu Yaobang, lost their positions at this time, while the rest of the bureaucratic leaders remained, indicates that the attack on Deng and his educational changes may have had Mao's consent, but that the attack on the leadership as a whole did not.

The bureaucratic leaders' continued exercise of real authority was a reflection of their own power and support in the military, as well as of Mao's wishes. It further signified the ineffectualness of the Shanghai group's effort to seize power through the media and campaigns. Despite the vociferousness and incessant nature of the group's media attacks, no major bureaucratic, provincial, or military leader associated himself with the campaign against Deng Xiaoping. In fact, the campaign never got going on a mass level, the very area in which the Shanghai group claimed to have support. Although copies of the Three Documents and of the Shanghai group's criticisms were distributed to the masses, the group complained that, "The resistance is tremendous."[36] They were able to arouse little response except in pockets in the universities. Even the wall posters denouncing Deng were few in number.

Ironically, the Shanghai group's attack on the Three Documents and on Deng Xiaoping contributed to the group's eventual overthrow. In the process of blaspheming the documents, they gave publicity to the bureaucratic leaders' proposals which they had blocked from media coverage. Such suggestions as more material incentives and a return to more regularized, conventional procedures elicited a positive response from a population that had worked without wage increases and been subjected to continual turmoil for ten years. Whereas these proposals had originated with the bureaucratic leadership, the Shanghai group identified them primarily with Deng, which only enhanced his popularity. With the fall of the Shanghai group and their followers in October 1976, just a month after Mao's death, Deng was characterized allegorically with the traditional maxim, "To know how noble and pure the pine is, one has to wait for the thaw." This saying had been used traditionally to describe an official of great integrity who was removed unjustly. Mao's poem

"Reply to Guo Moruo," written in 1963 to predict his eventual triumph over his enemies, was paraphrased in 1977 to extol Deng's triumph over his enemies:

The few mayflies that plotted to topple the majestic green
    pine tree
Have now been swept into the garbage pile of history.[37]

With his enemies quashed and the thaw underway, Deng Xiaoping returned to power in July 1977 to lead the way in implementing the Three Documents. He could now articulate their principles clearly in the media and carry them out with less obstruction. In a speech of March 1978, he granted scientists a degree of professional independence. As the documents signified, he and his colleagues were prepared to concede some authority to intellectuals in order to obtain their assistance in China's scientific and economic modernization. Admitting that political leaders did not understand many aspects of science, Deng recommended that the directors and deputy directors of the research institutes under the Chinese Academy of Sciences be given a free hand in scientific and technical matters. He urged the party to listen to these experts in evaluating scientific personnel and scientific research.

Despite their recognition of the importance of scientists to China's modernization, Deng Xiaoping and the bureaucratic leaders continued to act in the traditional role of political patrons to the intellectuals. They set the direction, priorities, and framework within which the scientists were to apply their knowledge and expertise. As in the past, the alliance between the bureaucratic leaders and the scientists had an inherent tension. The bureaucratic leaders' authority was based on their political control; the scientists' authority on their expertise. If the scientists found that their work led them in directions other than the ones set by the party, they could threaten the party's control. In the past, this threat has broken the alliance. Today, though a broad consensus now exists between China's political leaders and its scientists, the question is whether a Communist Party leadership, no matter how flexible, can accommodate a group of experts whose work at times might diverge from the party's political demands.

8

THE CONSEQUENCES
OF ADVICE
AND DISSENT

After the fall of the Shanghai group, the rehabilitated bureaucratic leaders led by Deng Xiaoping encouraged intellectuals to speak out, much in the fashion of the Hundred Flowers and the early 1960s. As in the past, their call for criticism arose from factional rivalry as well as from a desire to win the intellectuals' cooperation in China's modernization. The *People's Daily* admitted on January 4, 1979, that Lin Biao and the Shanghai group's "reactionary fallacies still influence some of our comrades."[1]

In order to counter the resistance to economic modernization from those who had come to power during the Cultural Revolution, the bureaucratic leaders printed the writings of intellectuals who had criticized Mao's use of mass mobilization and ideological movements at the expense of economic development. Likewise, to reestablish legal and orderly procedures of government after fifteen years of disruption, they rehabilitated intellectuals as well as party officials who had been arbitrarily persecuted. They needed them not only to help modernize China but also to rectify the irregular, arbitrary practices of the previous two decades. The persecution, injury, and in some cases death of large numbers of intellectuals were described as "a disaster without precedent in 5000 years of Chinese culture."[2]

This disaster was blamed on Lin Biao and the Shanghai group, or what is now called the "Gang of Four." The bureaucratic leaders sought to channel the hostilities produced in the Cultural Revolution and its aftermath onto these two targets. Yet as in the past, the unleashing of criticism may build up a momentum of its own that goes beyond what its political backers intended. It may hit at other targets, among them even the party itself. The rehabilitation of intellectual dissidents whose ideas, as formerly, overlap but do not coincide with the party's has the potential for a similar challenge to the regime and even to the political system.

The villains of the past twenty-five years have been transformed into heroes and the heroes into villains. Supposed "bourgeois-revisionist" ideas have become "correct," and "revolutionary" ideas have become "incorrect." These dramatic transformations not only directly reject Lin Biao, the Shanghai group, and even Mao, but inadvertently undermine the party. In addition to the liberal intellectuals and their political patrons purged in the Cultural Revolution, the regime has officially rehabilitated most of the victims of pre-Cultural Revolution campaigns. These were intellectuals who had been purged for unorthodox ideas not by the Shanghai group but by the party itself. The posthumous rehabilitation of Peng Dehuai and the restaging of plays such as Wu Han's *The Dismissal of Hai Rui* and Tian Han's *Xie Yaohuan*, which allegorically defend Peng, is a form of repudiation, not only of Mao, but indirectly of the party, because the party acquiesced in Mao's purge of Peng. Despite Mao's criticism of the party in his later years and the current stress on collective leadership, the party is still regarded as Mao's creation.

Potentially more threatening to party control is the reprinting of the essays of Deng Tuo, Wu Han, and Liao Mosha, whose expression of humanistic and liberal values may prove as inimical to the regime's policies of economic rationality and efficiency as the radicalism of the Shanghai group. The liberals' criticism of the ideological path to modernization and their encouragement of study and professionalism bolster the regime's current approach. But their essays also advocate a degree of pluralism and intellectual participation in political decision-making that the regime has not sanctioned.

Deng Tuo's counsel to China's leaders to "seek advice from all sides" and to draw on "a wide range of knowledge" from nonscientific as well as scientific intellectuals in policy making, was not practiced by the party before the Cultural Revolution, and may in the future prove as threatening to party control as it was to Mao's control, despite Deng Xiaoping's expressed intentions.[3] The genre of these writers, the zawen, is now praised for "criticizing shortcomings and extending justice." Zawen "can still play the deserved positive role."[4] Yet this genre—whether in Shanghai in the 1930s, in Yanan in the 1940s, or in the People's Republic in the 1950s and early 1960s—invariably has been used to criticize the shortcomings of the party leadership.

The liberal intellectuals are now extolled because they "adhered to the principle of seeking truth from fact" and "spoke out at the risk of their own personal safety."[5] On the basis of their example, scholars are urged to write about officials in Chinese history who, despite strong opposition, had the courage to defend the law, criticize social injustice, and show concern for the people's suffering. Such deprecated historical figures as Hai Rui and Li Xiucheng are praised because they were courageous in speaking the truth and bold in pointing out the shortcomings of the regime at the time. Yet there is no guarantee that emulation of the courage to criticize authority represented by these historic figures and by the liberal intellectuals can be limited to specified targets and not directed at any party officials who do not live up to their standards.

The three young men who in 1974, under the collective name of Li Yi Zhe, wrote a wall poster condemning China's legal system as unjust and its system of government as dictatorial were freed from prison in February 1979, an occasion marked by great fanfare and a mass rally. The regime then officially published their underground protest as a demonstration of its commitment to respect law and democracy. Here again, although the poster ostensibly attributes the violence of the Cultural Revolution to Lin Biao and the Shanghai group's destruction of legal and democratic rights, it also condemns the lack of such rights before the Cultural Revolution. Its denunciation of China's rulers as a privileged elite who governed without legal or democratic procedures and who condemned innocent people as counter-revolutionaries for personal political purposes could be attributed as well to the party as to Lin Biao and the Shanghai group, for the poster implies that these faults are inherent in one-

CONSEQUENCES OF ADVICE AND DISSENT

party rule. For the first time in the People's Republic, Western concepts of law were being published and discussed positively with the party's approval. Yet these concepts implicitly undermined the party's own credibility.

Similarly, the rehabilitated former mayor of Beijing, Peng Zhen, put in charge of devising the new legal code in 1978–1979, used the very same slogan he used prior to the Cultural Revolution to characterize the new laws: "Everyone is equal before the law." Now, as then, he signifies that all people, party as well as nonparty, senior as well as humble, must obey and be punished according to the law. As the *People's Daily* noted on June 13, 1979, "Truth cannot be controlled by the high-ranking bigwigs."[6] Yet concern for impartial justice and criticism of past illegal, arbitrary treatment may make the population sensitive to the fact that party leaders, including the present ones, have always given precedence to the demands of politics over the rule of law.

In addition to the rehabilitation of early victims of the Cultural Revolution, the return of intellectuals who were purged before the Cultural Revolution is also potentially threatening to party authority. From the 1930s until their banishment in the mid-1950s, such May Fourth writers as Hu Feng, Ding Ling, and Ai Qing had criticized party leaders whenever they appeared to deviate from fundamental Marxist ideals and had demanded an autonomous area of creative activity over which the party exercised little control. Certainly their repeated criticisms and refusals to conform despite severe punishment might make them figures of emulation in a period that prizes courage. Younger writers, purged as rightists for dissent during the Hundred Flowers, have since their rehabilitation publicly criticized the evils not just of the Shanghai group but of the party itself. It was not the Shanghai group which purged them, but the party bureaucracy, the regime that is in power today.

The literary works of the 1920s and 1930s, condemned in the Cultural Revolution, are now being republished and extolled in a culture that has been virtually barren for over twenty years. Their gloomy, satiric views of society are acclaimed as being more realistic than the model revolutionary works of the Cultural Revolution. Literary exposés of the Cultural Revolution may guard against such movements in the future, but the regime cannot guarantee that an individual writer will depict the dark side of life only during the Cultural Revolution, not before or after. Lu Xun is once again being re-evaluated.

CHINA'S INTELLECTUALS

The Shanghai group is charged with having distorted his life and his works to such an extent that they were unrecognizable. His stories, which could not be found in the bookstores during the Cultural Revolution even though he was then a hero, are now being sold—and they question everything, including political authority.

The regime has reevaluated two archvillains of the party since the late 1920s, the Western-educated intellectuals Chen Duxiu and Hu Shi, who were leaders of the May Fourth movement and of China's opening to the West. Chen's efforts at introducing Western culture before he became a Trotskyite are now regarded positively. But examination of his whole life would show that he was also treated ruthlessly by the party. Although Hu Shi is still called a reactionary in the political sense, his academic achievements are praised because he sought to apply Western methods and concepts to Chinese history and literature, an approach that the regime now condones. But here again, an in-depth study of Hu's life and works would bring to light his condemnation of the Chinese Communist Party and of Communism as inapplicable to Chinese needs. Similarly, although Qu Quibai is now acknowledged to have introduced Marxist literary theory into China and is extolled as one of China's major revolutionary leaders, a close look at his life would show that the party had arbitrarily purged him from the leadership in the late 1920s.

Western writers, particularly nineteenth century European ones—including Shakespeare, Hugo, Gogol, Turgenev, Heine, Balzac, Ibsen, Tolstoy, Chekhov, Dickens, Flaubert, and Pushkin—are being reprinted. Young writers are especially urged to study Western writing techniques, structure, and character portrayal. But the contents of these Western works express criticism and, in some cases, rebellion against the status quo, which the party may find inimical to its present effort to reestablish authority and discipline.

Not only Western culture but also traditional Chinese culture is being revived in an effort to correct the distorted, ahistorical approach of the radical intellectuals. Historians such as Jian Bozan, who were reviled because they questioned the revolutionary nature of peasant uprisings, are now commended because they spoke the truth about Chinese history. The sharpest switch is in the re-evaluation of Confucianism, undertaken to correct the Shanghai group's simplistic treatment of two thousand years of Chinese history as a conflict between the decaying elements of Confucianism and the rising forces of Legalism. Yet despite the demand for more scholarly, objective analysis of Chinese history, the use of history for political purposes continues. The current stress on technological-economic change rather than class struggle as the motive force of history coincides with the regime's present emphasis on scientific and economic development.

Similarly, since the Shanghai group associated Zhou Enlai with a negative appraisal of Confucius, Confucius has been treated positively in the period of glorification of Zhou after Mao's death. As Qin Shi Huang's achievements were used earlier to praise Mao, now Shi Huang's shortcomings, such as his dictatorial nature and his standing above the law, are used to shrink Mao down to life size. In this period of consolidation, when the regime is trying to reconcile differences, Confucius is praised because his values, such as *ren*, or benevolence and cooperation, were a progressive force in Chinese history, putting the emphasis on "the commonality of man and not on man's social differences."[7] Confucian values purportedly helped lead the fight for human rights in Chinese history. Ironically, although this interpretation of Confucianism stems from Feng Youlan's work, Feng himself was first censured by the present regime for his assistance to the Shanghai group in the anti-Confucius campaign and was only gradually rehabilitated.

Confucianism is also affirmed because its concern for teaching and learning coincides with the regime's emphasis on education and research. Confucius' instruction "to learn broadly and inquire dilligently" is said to be in accord with the present regime's respect for objective facts and its opposition to subjective bias.[8] His commitment to "education without any differentiation of classes" is now in line with the regime's effort to return the skilled elite to the classrooms and research institutes.[9] Confucius, like the present regime, taught students of all classes and enlivened the community's cultural life, in contrast to the Shanghai group, which excluded children of officials and intellectuals and suppressed intellectual vitality. Here again, the resurgence of interest in Confucius may correct the distortion of history wrought by the Shanghai group and reinvigorate intellectual activity, but it may also lead to an appreciation of the Confucian doctrine that a government does not rule through orders but by virtuous acts and attention to ideological education, a doctrine that could lead back to the Maoist emphasis on ideological indoctrination or to the humanist values of the Confucian moral code.

The tale *Water Margin* has also been retrieved from the Shanghai group's "garbage pile of history." Although its author, because of the times in which he lived, admittedly believed in loyalty to the emperor, it is now pointed out that he depicted characters who opposed oppressive rulers. The rehabilitation of *Water Margin* accepts a traditional culture that preached rebellion against incompetent and unjust officials, a legacy that could prove as disruptive to the current regime as it was to the traditional regimes.

Whereas the nineteenth century reformers like Li Hongzhang and Zeng Guofan were condemned in the Cultural Revolution and in the early 1970s for betraying China's national interests, they now are praised because "their advocacy of modern industry and modern technology from Western capitalist countries was beneficial to the development of social productivity and Chinese capitalism."[10] Yet the conservatives who opposed the reformers in the nineteenth century, the "die-hards," while obviously analogous to the Shanghai group, could also be analogous to those in the present regime who oppose adoption of Western science and technology, particularly the use of Western experts in China's development. The historian Li Kan prophesied that "the use of aliens to transform China is historically inevitable. No matter whether die-hards like it or not, the 'transformation' is bound to come, even though they can delay its historical progression ... It symbolizes growth and progress, not stagnation and retrogression."[11] The current homage to Western science resonates with the May Fourth movements' exaltation of science, technology, and Western learning as the answer to China's problems and the key to its modernization. As these expectations were not fulfilled in the early twentieth century, it is unlikely that they will be fulfilled now. China's recent past has shown that there is no one solution to its problems. An already cynical population may become even more so when it finds that science and technology do not quickly bring the results it has been led to expect.

Marxism too is being reinterpreted in more traditional terms. Whereas the radical intellectuals and the Shanghai group stressed revolutionary consciousness as the precondition for economic development, Hu Qiaomu, president of the newly established Chinese Academy of Social Sciences, pointed out in July 1978 that the laws of economic development not only are independent of but also determine human will and consciousness. Accordingly, the Marxist theorist Yang Xianzhen, who in the early 1960s stressed that man and society could not be shaped at will irrespective of economic development, has been rehabilitated and made an adviser to the Party School. Yang is another case of an individual who was purged, not by the Shanghai group, but by the very leadership in power today.

The slogan "Do away with bourgeois rights" which was extolled by the Shanghai group is also called a misrepresentation of Marxism because it negates material incentives, disregards profits, and fosters egalitarianism, thus damaging production. As explained by the *People's Daily* on April 9, 1978, "in the historical period of socialism where social products are not in enormous abundance and the people's political consciousness is not yet greatly enhanced, moral encouragement alone is not enough, and the material interests of the masses must be taken into consideration . . . Marxism affirms material rewards."[12] In line with this policy, the economist Sun Yefang and his associates, who were criticized by the party before the Cultural Revolution for suggesting profits as a determinant of investment, have been rehabilitated, and a number are at work on economic planning.

These sudden, radical switches in the interpretation of Marxism, plus the contradictory messages of the dictatorship of the proletariat campaign, apparently have created utter confusion in ideology. The regime admits that the population is bewildered by Marxism. It attributes the confusion to the Shanghai group who, "peddling their revisionist fallacies as though they were correct principles . . . confused the people and made them uncertain as to which course they should follow."[13] The regime also admits, according to the *People's Daily* of May 5, 1979, that "At the moment there is a tiny, incipient trend of skepticism toward socialism." The regime ascribes this trend to the Cultural Revolution, but does not acknowledge that it might have contributed to the skepticism by its own shifting interpretations of Marxism. While insisting on the necessity to doubt blind faith as represented by the Shanghai group, the regime warns, "There must be no vacillation over the principle of socialism."[14] Despite its emphasis on pragmatic methods and its acknowledged lack of interest in ideology, the regime intends to uphold Marxist ideology. As the *People's Daily* asserted on April 19, 1979, "To promote what is proletarian and liquidate what is bourgeois is still a long-term task on the ideological front; we must in no way relax our political and ideological education of the masses."[15]

These rehabilitations and reinterpretations may help the drive to achieve modernization by the end of the century, but the question now is how far, beyond ridding itself of the "pernicious" influence of Lin Biao and the Shanghai group, the regime will go to allay the suspicions of the intellectuals. In the past, when the forces let loose by a relaxation undermined the party's authority, those forces were quickly suppressed. As seen in the Hundred Flowers, a movement that started as a criticism of political practices became a demand for democratic rights, which led to a questioning of party rule and of communism itself. Again in the early 1960s, criticism of the Great Leap Forward became an attack on the party leader and a call for a more open society. Participants in both movements were brutally silenced. As before, the current relaxation rests not on institutional and legal guarantees that can protect the intellectuals if they express an unpopular idea or seek to preserve their autonomy. Rather, the tolerance of criticism arises out of political disagreements and pressing economic needs. Thus, if the intellectuals, as in the past, go beyond the limits of independence that the party has granted them, this relative liberalization could be rescinded as quickly as it has been released.

It is true that in 1978–1979 the unofficial forms of protest, such as underground journals and Democracy Wall in Beijing, where individuals put up posters expressing political criticism, were allowed to function relatively freely. These unofficial protests were tolerated because they coincided with Deng Xiaoping's movement against officials who had been closely associated with Mao and the Shanghai group. But when the criticisms also began to be directed against Deng and the party's policies, they were suppressed in late 1979. Will official protest suffer a similar fate? Is it possible for a group of intellectuals to go beyond merely articulating the interests of their political backers and sway public opinion and policy makers in their own right? The failure of the liberal intellectuals in the early 1960s to achieve more scholarly input into policies and the failure of the radical intellectuals to continue the Cultural Revolution suggest that such groups cannot survive on their own. In the past they gained access to the media for a short time, but their views, rather than evoking support, provoked a reaction.

The intellectuals' expression of dissident views, even when camouflaged in scholarly articles, theatrical productions, and ideological debates, has not been sustained without the support of either the political-economic-military apparatus or a leader of Mao's prestige. Since the ability of intellectuals to be heard publicly is dependent on factional struggle and the tolerance of their political patrons, their opportunity to influence policy and to suggest programs of their own is inevitably short-lived, because of the shifting struggle and the diverging interests of their patrons. Furthermore, the opposing political faction is in a position to dissipate or counter their efforts. Since each side uses the intellectuals to avoid an open conflict and to strengthen its position by means of ideological persuasion, the arguments of the intellectuals postpone conflicts but do not resolve them. As one side seeks to dominate the other, ideological conflicts inexorably culminate in power struggles by the chief protagonists as well as by their surrogates.

Yet history never truly repeats itself. There are some new factors in the situation today. Mao, who in his later years had an animus against intellectuals as well as the power to suppress them, is gone. The cost of continued suppression in terms of talent and impairment is accelerating. Increasing modernization brings increasing functional differentiation and specialization. As a network of scientists and engineers who are indispensable to China's modernization emerges, these specialists may be given increasing autonomy in their research centers. Allowing scientists to direct their own work would remove certain areas of activity from party authority, and this in turn could weaken the party's control over scientific and professional endeavors. As in the Soviet Union, scientific autonomy may lead in China to a quasi-independent elite that can influence political decisions in its area of competence, but this does not mean that scientists will exert general political influence.

Moreover, a degree of independence and a voice in one's area of expertise does not necessarily extend to nonscientific intellectuals. The signals in this area are contradictory. The old Philosophy and Social Sciences Department, from which the criticism of the old regime emanated on both the liberal and the radical sides, has now been dislodged from the Chinese Academy of Sciences to form its own unit, the Chinese Academy of Social Sciences. The new academy is led by officials close to Deng Xiaoping and by pre-1966 cultural officials. Jiang Qing's old enemy Zhou Yang has become a vice-president, as well as chairman of the All-China Federation of Literature and Art, and is once again making authoritative statements on cultural and intellectual life. Although Tian Han died from harsh treatment in the Cultural Revolution, Jiang Qing's other erstwhile enemies from the 1930s, Xia Yan and Yang Hansheng, have been appointed advisers to the central Propaganda Department and Ministry of Culture.

The establishment of a separate academy for the social sciences is based on the premise that China's modernization is dependent on modernization of the social sciences as well as the sciences. The new academy is designed to energize China's intellectual life, which has stagnated for over twenty years, and to bring academic thinking into line with that of the rest of the world, from which it has been isolated since even before the Cultural Revolution. As one journal defined the academy's goal: "If we introduce only advanced technology and advanced equipment without corresponding changes in industrial relations, the superstructure, and styles of thought and work, the development of new productive forces will be handicapped. This explains the need for increased research not only in the natural sciences but also in the social sciences."[16]

Another purpose of the Academy of Social Sciences is to correct the distortions that the Shanghai group created in the social sciences and the humanities for its own political purposes. The regime has acknowledged that some intellectuals are reluctant to resume their work because intellectual differences in the past were treated as political deviations. Accordingly, there is an effort to separate the social sciences from a specific political view of history and society. The Marxist theoretician Zhang Wen stated that, "Academic and political problems in the sphere of the social sciences are intimately connected, but the two, in the final analysis, are not one and the same thing."[17] Hu Qiaomu in March 1979 expressed hope that sociologists would try to provide some answers to China's social problems. In this endeavor, he advised, it is not necessary to look at these problems from a Marxist approach or to resolve them with a Marxist conclusion. Marxism provides the basic framework, method, and theory for studying society, but it should not supersede those branches of science that specifically deal with various aspects of social phenomena. The social sciences and culture, as well as the sciences, need free discussion in which to develop. Zhou Yang declared with respect to the social sciences that, "Without a lively democratic atmosphere, they will not develop soundly. We must support and encourage free discussion and must specifically protect and encourage all differing art styles and academic viewpoints. It can be said that without a personal style there is no true art, and without independent views there is no true scholarship."[18]

CONSEQUENCES OF ADVICE AND DISSENT

Yet, the extent to which the regime will allow the social sciences to be independent of the political line and Marxist ideology is still a question. Diversity is stressed more in the sciences than in the social sciences. A diversity in the arts and social sciences is allowed primarily in terms of style and methodology, whereas in the sciences it is in viewpoint as well. Science is regarded as devoid of class characteristics and outside of the social structure, but the social sciences are still thought to be shaped by class and economic structure. In his characteristic contradictory fashion, Zhou Yang in September 1979 asserted that there can be no distinct separation between the social sciences and politics: "Some comrades have a naive and mistaken idea in wanting to mark off a clear division between politics and academia ... The relationship between the two is extremely complex, unstable, and in constant flux." The normal relationship between politics and culture or academia is one of "coordination and not one of exclusion."[19] Zhou made the relatively uncommon admission that "Some bold and startling works produced in the future may not have been designed by our plan, but then, how many great and startling works in the history of civilization were produced according to a plan? Scarcely any of them." Acknowledging the value of autonomy, Zhou nevertheless served notice that the party will not give up its control: "Despite this, in our socialist society, a plan is a necessity, a must."[20]

Although party leaders repeatedly urge a hundred flowers to bloom and a hundred schools to contend, there is still no institutional or legal way for intellectuals to separate themselves from the party's overall determination of what flowers will bloom and which schools will contend. And although the separation of the Academy of Social Sciences from the Academy of Sciences may enhance the social sciences and the humanities, this very separation might make it easier to isolate the scientific from the nonscientific intellectuals when the regime once again feels the need to tighten controls over intellectuals and academic inquiry.

Nevertheless, even before Mao's death the People's Republic experienced fleeting moments of debate and a degree of intellectual and ideological pluralism. In the most repressive periods, intellectual groups proposed policies and values that differed from the prevailing ones. These intellectual groups were never powerful, but at the times when their views overlapped with the leadership's, they were stimuli for change. As in traditional times, the alliance with political patrons gave the intellectuals an opportunity to ask questions, initiate discussions, make suggestions, and galvanize popular support that entered into policy decisions. The tension in this alliance, and the fact that it arose from political rivalries, made the intellectuals' impact short-lived, and at times fatal to them personally. Yet the views of the liberal intellectuals, forcefully rejected in the Cultural Revolution, were coopted and resurrected after the fall of the Shanghai group. The views of the radical intellectuals, curbed in 1964–1965, were implemented in the Cultural Revolution. And the scientific concern with theoretical science in the early 1970s, subsequently repressed, has become a major focus of China's present modernization. Thus these expressions of dissidence had a delayed effect. They were ended abruptly because they arose from political conflict rather than from an institutionalized system, but this very political factionalism, as in traditional times, explains their appearance and reappearance.

The political in-fighting of the past two decades, waged through obscure and contradictory messages in the public media, by its very nature tended to confuse rather than enlighten those who did not understand the code. Ironically, the public debates, carried on by means of literary symbolism and historical allusions for the purpose of preventing direct confrontation, undermined the very consensus they were meant to ensure. They inadvertently opened the public to a choice of views, which at times led individuals to seek answers of their own. Even when in the Cultural Revolution ideological battles burst through their intellectual camouflage into open conflict, a small number of intellectuals continued, until they were silenced, to defend humane values and depict a version of reality that diverged from the official version. The result has been a loss in the party's monolithic ideological control, much as it lost its "infallibility" in the Cultural Revolution.

The swings of the pendulum between different interpretations of beliefs that are basic to Chinese society, such as Confucianism, Legalism, Marxism, and Maoist thought, may have set in motion a process of myth deflation and critical judgment that has gone so far it will be increasingly difficult to stop. Sometimes, as in the case of the radical intellectuals, the challenge has not been liberalizing, but its effect is still to undermine the imposition of one doctrinal truth. The public opinion to which the various intellectual groups addressed themselves has been exposed for a number of years to a variety of

CONSEQUENCES OF ADVICE AND DISSENT

conflicting symbols, models, and values. If and when the leadership once again regards alternative views as a threat to its authority, it will be more difficult to impose a monolithic view of reality than in the past. If these alternatives survive long enough and gain sufficient strength, a monolithic ideology could prove virtually impossible.

The continued expression of alternative views may ultimately unravel the traditional pattern of relationships between dissident intellectuals and the regime. The new pattern may not emerge in the Western style of dissent as a consistent, institutionalized expression of loyal opposition, but it may differ from what has hitherto existed. The traditional pattern itself, in conjunction with China's increasing exposure to Western ideas, has given rise to the alternatives. By intermittently allowing informal groups of intellectuals to express dissident views publicly and officially, the leadership has helped create the opportunity for the People's Republic to weave a new pattern of relationships between intellectuals and the regime. Inadvertently, it has also undermined the very ideological consensus that Chinese governments have always thought necessary in order to rule.

NOTES

Abbreviations

CB   *Current Background* (U.S. Consulate General, Hong Kong)
FBIS   Foreign Broadcast Information Service
GMRB   *Guangming Ribao (Guangming Daily)*
IASP   International Arts and Sciences Press, White Plains, N.Y.
JPRS   *Joint Publication Research Service*
NCNA   New China News Agency
RMRB   *Renmin Ribao (People's Daily)*
SCMM   *Survey of the China Mainland Magazines*
SCMMS   *Supplement to the Survey of the China Mainland Magazines*
SCMP   *Survey of the China Mainland Press*
SCMPS   *Supplement to the Survey of the China Mainland Press*
SPRCM   *Survey of the People's Republic of China Magazines*
SPRCP   *Survey of the People's Republic of China Press*
ZGQN   *Zhongguo Qingnian (China Youth)*
ZGQNB   *Zhongguo Qingnian Bao (China Youth Press)*

1. DISSIDENT INTELLECTUALS AND THE REGIME

1. Frederic Wakeman, "The Price of Autonomy: Intellectuals in Ming and Ch'ing Politics," *Daedalus*, no. 2, Spring 1972.

2. David Nivison, "Ho Shen and His Accusers," in David Nivison and Arthur Wright, eds., *Confucianism in Action* (Stanford: Stanford University Press, 1959), p. 221.

3. Translated in William T. deBary, "Chinese Despotism and the Confucian Ideal," in John K. Fairbank. ed., *Chinese Thought and Institutions* (Chicago: University of Chicago Press, 1957), p. 197.

4. Charles Hucker, "The Tunglin Movement in the Late Ming Period," in Fairbank, *Chinese Thought*, p. 61. See also Wakeman, "The Price of Autonomy."

5. Translated in John E. Schrecker, "The Reform Movement of 1898 and the Ch'ing-i Reform as Opposition," in Paul A. Cohen and John E. Schrecker, eds., *Reform in Nineteenth-Century China* (Cambridge: Harvard University Pres, 1976), p. 302.

6. James Polachek, "Literati Groups and Literati Politics in Early Nineteenth Century" (Ph.D. diss., University of California, Berkeley, 1976), pt. 2.

7. Mao Zedong, Speech at Tenth Plenary Session of the Eighth Central

Committee, Sept. 24, 1962, in IASP, *Chinese Laws and Government* 1, no. 4 Winter 1968-1969): 92.

8. Andrew Nathan, "Liang Ch'i-ch'ao's New Style of Writing and Late Ch'ing Propaganda" (paper delivered at Association of Asian Studies, Mar. 25-27, 1977).

9. Lucian Pye, "Communications and Chinese Political Culture," *Asian Survey* 28, no. 3 (March 1978): 221-246.

10. James Polachek, "Institutional Background of Ch'ing-i Rhetoric in Late Ch'ing" (paper delivered at Association of Asian Studies, Mar. 25-27, 1977).

11. Pye, "Communications."

12. Vera Schwarcz, "Renaissance to Revolution: The May Fourth Movement" (Ph.D. Diss., Stanford University, 1977).

13. See Merle Goldman, *Literary Dissent in Communist China* (Cambridge: Harvard University Press, 1967).

14. Pye, "Communications."

2. THE LIBERAL INTELLECTUALS

1. Chen Yi, Speech to Beijing Institute of Higher Studies, *GMRB*, Sept. 3, 1961, p. 2.

2. Zhou Enlai, "On Literature and Art," Speech of June 19, 1961, *Wenyi Bao* (*Literary Gazette*), February 1979, *Beijing Review*, Mar. 30, 1979, p. 9.

3. Ibid., pp. 13-15.

4. Stuart Schram, ed., *Chairman Mao Talks to the People: Talks and Letters, 1956-1971* (New York: Pantheon Books, 1974), p. 169.

5. Mao Zedong, Speech at Enlarged Work Conference of the Central Committee (Peking: Foreign Languages Press, 1978), p. 31.

6. Ibid., p. 10.

7. "Let 100 Flowers Blossom and 100 Schools of Thought Contend in Academic Research," reprinted in *Peking Review*, Mar. 24, 1961, p. 6.

8. *GMRB*, Nov. 5, 1961, p. 2.

9. Liu Jiqi and Zhou Bo, "Concerning Free Discussion of Academic Problems," *Hongqi*, no. 15/16, Aug. 10, 1961, *SCMM*, no. 276, p. 10.

10. NCNA, Enlarged Session of Committee of the Department of Philosophy and Social Sciences under the Chinese Academy of Sciences, *GMRB*, Jan. 12, 1961, *SCMP*, no. 2457, p. 2.

11. "Pleading to Fight a Bloody Battle with Liu-Deng-Tao to the End," Liaison Station, April 1967, *SCMM*, no. 651, p. 21.

12. "Liu Shaoqi Violently Attacks the Three Banners," *SCMMS*, no. 25, p. 28.

13. Liaison Center of the Chinese University of Science and Technology, Red Guard Congress, June 10, 1967, "Counter-revolutionary, Revisionist Peng Zhen's Towering Crimes of Opposing the Party, Socialism, and the Thought of Mao Zedong," *SCMM*, no. 639, p. 8.

14. Wu Donghui, "Destroy the Black Backstage Manager of 'The Three-Family Village,' " GMRB, June 18, 1967, SCMP, no. 3977, p. 14.

15. Roderick MacFarquhar, The Origins of the Cultural Revolution (New York: Oxford University Press, 1974), p. 193; Mao's speech of February 27, 1957, "On Correct Handling of Contradictions among the People," and Mao's talk of March 12, 1957 before the Propaganda Department.

16. Ma Nancun (Deng Tuo), Yanshan Yehua (Evening Talks at Yanshan) (Beijing: Beijing Publishing, 1962), V, 105–107.

17. "Is Wisdom Reliable?," ibid., IV, 17–19.

18. Timothy Cheek, "Deng Tuo and Alternative Marxism," (M.A. thesis, University of Virginia, 1980).

19. Deng Tuo, "Study More, Criticize Less," Yanshan Yehua, IV, 84.

20. Wu Nanxing, Notes from the Three-Family Village, "A Special Treatment of Amnesia," Qianxian (Frontline), no. 14, 1962, CB, no. 792, p. 4.

21. Deng Tuo, "The Royal Way; the Tyrant's Way," Yanshan Yehua, IV, 13–16.

22. Deng Tuo, "Treasuring Labor Power," ibid., I, 58.

23. Deng Tuo, "The Stake in One Egg," ibid., I, 77.

24. Deng Tuo, "In Defense of Li Sancai," ibid., III, 150.

25. Deng Tuo, "Is Wisdom Reliable?," ibid., IV, 17–19.

26. Deng Tuo, "The Case of Chen Jiang and Wang Geng," Beijing Wanbao (Beijing Evening News), Jan. 22, 1961.

27. Deng Tuo, "A Concern for All Things," Yanshan Yehua, II, 60–62.

28. Deng Tuo, "Sing the Praise of Lake Taihu," GMRB, Sept, 7, 1960.

29. Deng Tuo, "About Li Shan and His Paintings," GMRB, Feb. 14, 1961.

30. Deng Tuo, "Ancient Cartoons," Yanshan Yehua, III, 51–53.

31. Deng Tuo, "The Art of Making Friends," Yanshan Yehua, I, 33–34.

32. Deng Tuo, "Who Discovered America?" Yanshan Yehua, II, 3.

33. Wu Nanxing, Notes from a Three-Family Village, "Great Empty Talk," Qianxian, no. 21, 1961; CB, no. 792, p. 2.

34. Frederick C. Teiwes, Politics and Purges in China (White Plains, N.Y.: M. E. Sharpe, 1979), p. 478; Gao Zhi, "A Big Frame-up That Shook the Whole Nation," GMRB, Dec. 29, 1978, p. 3, FBIS, Jan. 17, 1979, E13.

35. Liu Mianzhi (Wu Han), "Hai Rui Scolds the Emperor," GMRB, June 16, 1959, p. 8.

36. Wu Han, "On Hai Rui," RMRB, Sept. 17, 1959.

37. Wu Han, Hai Rui Baguan (The Dismissal of Hai Rui from Office), (Beijing Publishing, 1961), pp. 7–8.

38. Clive Ansley, The Heresy of Wu Han (Toronto: University of Toronto Press, 1971), p. 76.

39. Wang Zhengping et al., "Comrade Wu Han's Antiparty, Antisocialist, Anti-Marxist Political Thinking and Academic Viewpoints," in IASP, Chinese Studies in History 3, no. 11 (Fall 1969): 64, 67, 70, 63.

40. GMRB correspondent, "Talk Freely about and Evaluate Personalities," GMRB, Sept. 15, 1961, SCMP, no. 2457, p. 12.

41. Bai Ye, "Listening to Divergent Opinion Is Essential in Fostering Democratic Work Style," *ZGQN*, Apr. 16, 1962, *SCMM*, no. 312, pp. 1, 5, and 3.

42. Sha Ying, "Ready to Listen to Different Opinions," *RMRB*, May 23, 1961, *SCMP*, no. 2513, p. 6.

43. Wu Jiemin, "On Whipping and Spurring," *Hongqi* (*Red Flag*), June 16, 1962, *SCMM*, no. 321, p. 38.

44. *Beijing Wenyi* (*Beijing Literature*), Sept. 1962, *CB*, no. 792, p. 57.

45. Gong Weidong, "What Poison Has Zhou Yang Spread in the Northeast?" *RMRB*, Aug. 7, 1966, *SCMP*, no. 3763, p. 18.

46. *Wenyi Bao*, no. 3, 1961, pp. 2, 3, 6.

47. Zheng Jijiao, "Get to the Bottom of Zhou Yang's Antiparty, Antisocialist Crimes," *RMRB*, Aug. 6, 1966, *CB*, no. 802, p. 50.

48. *RMRB*, May 13, 1962.

49. Gong Weidong, "What Poison Has Zhou Yang Spread in the Northeast?" pp. 21, 20.

50. Tian Han, "Xie Yaohuan," *Juben* (*Theater Script*), July/August 1961.

51. Tian Han, "The Problem of Choosing Themes," *Wenyi Bao*, no. 7, 1961, Union Research Service, 25, no. 2, p. 23.

52. Li Chao, "The Resurrection of 'Xie Yaohuan,'" *RMRB*, Sept. 17, 1979, p. 3.

53. Qi Xiangchun, "Recriticism of Meng Chao's New Adaptation, 'Li Huiniang,'" *RMRB*, Mar. 1, 1965, *SCMP*, no. 3425, p. 8.

54. Ibid., p. 10.

55. "Legacies Must Be Critically Accepted and the Old Must Make Way for the New in Traditional Drama," *Beijing Ribao*, Sept. 17, 1963, *SCMPS*, no. 122, p. 11.

56. Wu Han, "Do Fairy Plays Spread Superstition?" *ZGQN*, Aug. 1, 1961, *SCMM*, no. 278, p. 24.

57. Xia Yan, "Raise Our Country's Cinematics to a Newer Level," *Hongqi*, Oct. 1, 1961, *SCMM*, no. 284, pp. 8, 9, 15.

58. Jay Leyda, *Dianying: Electric Shadows* (Cambridge: M.I.T. Press, 1972), p. 261, reports that the film was made with great care and was well received.

59. Zhou Yang, "The Path of Our Country's Socialist Literature and Art in China," *RMRB*, Sept. 4, 1960, pp. 5–7.

60. Kang Zhuo, "On Short Stories in Recent Years," *Wenxue Pinglun* (*Literary Criticism*), no. 5 (1962), p. 26.

61. Kang Zhuo, Excerpts of speech at Dalian conference, *Guangzhou Yangcheng Wanbao* (*Guangzhou Evening News*), July 7, 1966, *SCMP*, no. 2750, pp. 4, 3.

62. Shao Quanlin, *Xingxiong* (*Heroes*), (Shanghai, 1948), pp. 2, 3.

63. *Wenyi Bao*, no. 8/9 (1964), p. 15.

64. "Point and Look at South Guangdong," *Zhikan Nanyue*, no. 3, Oct. 1, 1967, *SCMP*, no. 4063, p. 3.

65. *Wenyi Bao*, no. 8/9 (1964), p. 18.

66. Ibid., pp. 17–18, 18.

67. Zhao Shuli, "Duanlian, duanlian" (*Tempering*), *Renmin Wenxue* (*People's Literature*), Sept. 1958, pp. 8–16.

68. Mao Dun, "A General Review of Short Stories Published in 1960," *Wenyi Bao*, no. 4, 1961, CB, no. 663, p. 4.

69. Mao Zedong, "Talk at an Enlarged Central Work Conference," in Schram, *Chairman Mao Talks*, p. 168.

70. "A Collection of Zhou Yang's Counter-revolutionary Revisionist Speeches," *SCMM*, no. 648, pp. 11, 5.

71. Feng Youlan, *New Compendium of History of Chinese Philosophy* (Beijing, 1962), I, 133.

72. Feng Youlan, "Criticism and Self-Criticism in Discussion about Confucianism," *Zhexue Yanjiu* (*Philosophical Research*), no. 6, 1963, in IASP, *Chinese Studies in History and Philosophy* 1, no. 4 (Summer 1968): 84.

73. IASP, *Chinese Studies in Philosophy*, Fall–Winter 1972–1973, p. 18.

74. Liu Jie, "Mo Zi's Love for All Without Distinction and His Utilitarianism," *Xuexi Yanjiu* (*Academic Research*), no. 1, 1963, SCMP, no. 3128, p. 6.

75. Jian Bozan, "Some Questions Found in Present-Day Research," *Jianghai Xuekan*, May 4, 1962, excerpted in *Wenhui Bao*, Mar. 28, 1966, SCMPS, no. 151, pp. 4, 5.

76. RMRB, June 2, 1964, p. 6.

77. Feng Youlan, "Criticism and Self-Criticism," pp. 86–87.

78. Wu Han, "More on Morality [A Reply to Comrade Xu Qixian]," GMRB, Aug. 19, 1963, p. 2, written in reply to Xu Qixian, "Some Problems on Class Character and the Inheritability of Morality [a discussion with Comrade Wu Han]," GMRB, Aug. 15, 1963, p. 5.

79. Wang Xuhua, "A Question of Critical Inheritance of the Morality of the Ruling Classes," GMRB, Apr. 6, 1964, pp. 2–3.

80. Zhou Gucheng, "A Critique of Some Problems of Artistic Creativity," *Xin Jianshe* (*New Construction*), June 1963, excerpted in Zhou Gucheng, "A Brief Discussion of the Problems of the Spirit of the Age," GMRB, Sept. 24, 1963, p. 3.

81. Gong Wensheng, "Sun Yefang's Theory Is a Revisionist Fallacy," RMRB, Aug. 8, 1966, SCMP, no. 3766, p. 17.

3. RESPONSE OF THE RADICAL INTELLECTUALS

1. RMRB, Oct. 13, 1958. See also Parris Chang, *Radicals and Radical Ideology in China's Cultural Revolution* (New York: Columbia University Press, 1973), p. 81.

2. See Lars Ragvald, "Yao Wen-yuan as a Literary Critic and Theorist" (University of Sweden).

3. "Chronology of Events in the Struggle Between the Two Lines on the Cultural Front since the Founding of the People's Republic of China Seven-

teen Years Ago," *Wenhua Geming Tongxun* (*Cultural Revolution Bulletin*), no. 11, May 1967, *CB*, no. 842, p. 5.

4. *Shanghai Wenxue* (*Shanghai Literature*), no. 5, 1962, p. 3.

5. Ibid., p. 4.

6. Guan Feng and Lin Youshi, "The Use of the Class Viewpoint and Historicism in Historical Research," *Lishi Yanjiu*, Dec. 15, 1963, *SCMM*, no. 409, p. 15.

7. Schram, *Chairman Mao Talks*, p. 216.

8. Guan Feng, "On the Problem of Struggle Between Materialism and Idealism," *GMRB*, June 6, 1958, in IASP, *Chinese Studies in History and Philosophy* 2, no. 4 (Summer 1969): 32.

9. Guan Feng and Lin Youshi, "Some Problems of Class Analysis in the Study of the History of Philosophy," *Zhexue Yanjiu* (*Philosophical Research*), no. 6, 1963, in IASP, *Chinese Studies in History and Philosophy* 1, no. 4 (Summer 1968): 47, 46.

10. Ibid., p. 48.

11. Ibid., p. 55.

12. Ibid., pp. 34, 66, 34.

13. Qi Benyu and Lin Jie, "Comrade Jian Bozan's Outlook on History Should Be Criticized," *Hongqi*, Mar. 24, 1966, pp. 19–30, *JPRS*, no. 35, 137, pp. 31, 39.

14. Qi Benyu, "Comment on Li Xiucheng's Autobiography," *Lishi Yanjiu* (*Historical Research*), reprinted as "How Should We Look at the Surrender of Li Xiucheng?" *RMRB* and *GMRB*, Aug. 23, 1963; also in Beijing: Da Gong Bao *JPRS*, no. 26, 631, pp. 13–14, 15.

15. Chang, *Radicals and Radical Ideology*, p. 93.

16. Yao Wenyuan, "A Brief Discussion of the Problems of the Spirit of the Age," *GMRB*, Sept. 24, 1963, p. 3.

17. Zhou Gucheng, "Unified Whole and Separate Reflections," *GMRB*, Nov. 7, 1963, p. 2.

18. Yao Wenyuan, "On Mr. Zhou Gucheng's Views on Contradictions," *GMRB*, May 10, 1964, p. 2.

19. Li Kan, "In Refutation of the New 'Venerate Confucius' Doctrine," *GMRB*, Aug. 17–18, 1963, *SCMP*, no. 3070, p. 4.

20. Xu Qixian, "Some Problems on Class Character," *GMRB*, Aug. 15, 1963, p. 5.

21. Zhou Yang, "A Fighting Task Confronting Workers in Philosophy and Social Sciences," Oct. 26, 1963, *CB*, no. 726, p. 4.

22. Ibid., p. 15.

23. Ibid., pp. 23, 24, 25.

24. See Roxane Witke, *Comrade Chiang Ch'ing* (Boston: Little, Brown, 1977).

25. Ibid., pp. 240–241.

26. Jiang Qing, "Do New Services for the People," *Dong Fang Hong* (*The East Is Red*), June 3, 1967, *SCMPS*, no. 192, p. 7.

27. "A Great Strategic Measure," editorial, *Hongqi*, no. 9, 1967, *SCMM*, no. 581, p. 1.

28. "Chairman Mao's Important Instructions on Literature and Art since the Publication of 'Talks at the Yanan Forum on Literature and Art' (1942-1967)," *Wenyi Hongqi* (*Red Flag of Literature and Art*), May 30, 1967, *SCMP*, no. 4000, p. 23.

29. Editorial, *Jiefang Ribao*, Dec. 25, 1963, p. 3.

30. Chen Guangyan, "The Old Drama and the Actual Life of Socialism," *Beijing Ribao*, Jan. 23, 1964, *SCMPS*, no. 124, p. 32.

31. Ke Jingshi, Speech, *RMRB*, Dec. 29, 1963, *SCMP*, no. 3144, p. 10.

32. A quote from Chen Huangmei in "Chronology of Events," p. 12.

33. NCNA, Feb. 5, 1964, *SCMP*, no. 3157, p. 16.

34. This interpretation of the struggle over opera reform has benefited from discussions with Steven Goldstein, professor of political science at Smith, and from his unpublished paper on the subject.

35. "Create More and Better Dramas for the Broad Masses," *RMRB*, Apr. 1, 1964, *SCMP*, no. 3205, p. 11.

36. Peng Zhen, Speech at the Beijing Opera Festival, July 1, 1964, *SCMM*, no. 433, pp. 13, 12.

37. Jiang Qing, "On the Revolution of the Beijing Opera" (Beijing: Foreign Language Press, 1968), pp. 3, 5, 4.

38. "Chen Yi's Soul Viewed from the Point of Literature and Art," *SCMPS*, no. 218, pp. 24, 27.

39. "Liu Shaoqi's Counterrevolutionary Revisionist Utterances on Culture and Art," *Hongse Xuanchuan Bing* (*Red Propaganda Soldier*), May 10, 1967, *SCMPS*, no. 205, p. 37.

40. "Welcoming the Festival of Beijing Opera on Contemporary Themes," *GMRB*, June 6, 1964, p. 1.

41. NCNA, June 6, 1964, *SCMP*, no. 3235, p. 21.

42. "Firm Direction of Musical Drama in Order to Assume a New Socialist Appearance," *GMRB*, June 2, 1964, p. 1.

43. See Peter Moody, *Opposition and Dissent in Contemporary China* (Stanford: Hoover Institution Press, 1977), p. 279.

44. Tiewes, *Politics and Purges*, p. 399.

45. *RMRB*, June 3, 1959, p. 7. See also Moody, *Opposition and Dissent*, p. 279.

46. Tao Zhu, Speech of Sept. 28, 1961, Guangzhou, *Guangya Basanyi*, April-May 1968, *SCMP*, no. 4200, pp. 11, 14.

47. "Tao Zhu Is the Khrushchev of Central-South China," *CB*, no. 824, p. 31.

48. "Tao Zhu's Report to Higher Intellectuals," *Guangya Basanyi*, April-May 1968, *SCMP*, no. 4200, pp. 12, 13.

49. Tao Zhu, "Views on Bringing Prosperity to Creative Work," *CB*, no. 824, pp. 23, 25.

50. Tao Zhu, "Revolutionary Modern Drama Must Be Successfully Produced," *Yangcheng Wanbao*, July 3, 1965, *SCMP*, no. 3511, p. 14.

51. "Excerpts from the Closing Ceremony of the Festival of Drama and Opera of the Central-South," *Yangcheng Wanbao*, Aug. 20, 1965, *SCMP*, no. 3536, pp. 10, 14, 15.

4. THE PARTY RECTIFICATION OF 1964–1965

1. Mao Zedong, "Comment on Comrade Ke Qingshi's Report," *Long Live Mao Zedong Thought*, in *CB*, no. 901, p. 41.
2. Mao Zedong, "Instruction of the Central Committee on Strengthening of Learning from Each Other and Overcoming Conservatism, Arrogance, and Complacency," *Long Live Mao Zedong Thought*, in *CB*, no. 892, p. 15.
3. *Chinese Literature*, no. 5, 1966, pp. 13–14. See also Jeremy Ingalls, unpub. ms. on Mao's poetry; Stuart Schram, "Mao as a Poet," *Problems of Communism*, September–October 1964, pp. 38–44.
4. Schram, *Chairman Mao Talks*, p. 204.
5. Ibid., p. 207.
6. "The Tempestuous Combat on the Literary and Art Front," *Shoudu Hongweibing (Capital Red Guards)*, July 7, 1967, *CB*, no. 842, p. 17.
7. Ibid., p. 15.
8. *Red Flag* on Zhou Yang's "Two-Faced" Dealings, FBIS, no. 4 (Jan. 6, 1967), p. ccc12.
9. "Hail the Victory of the Mao Zedong Line on Literature and Art," NCNA, May 27, 1967, *SCMP*, no. 3950, p. 13.
10. "Instructions Concerning Literature and Art," *Long Live Mao Zedong Thought*, in *CB*, no. 891, p. 41.
11. Schram, *Chairman Mao Talks*, p. 243.
12. Ai Hengwu and Lin Qingshan, "One Divides into Two and Two Combines into One," *GMRB*, May 29, 1964, p. 5.
13. Wang Zhong and Guo Peiheng, "Discussing with Comrade Yang Xianzhen 'Two into One,'" *RMRB*, July 17, 1964, p. 5.
14. Xiao Shu, "Antidialectical Substance of the 'Uniting Two into One,'" *RMRB*, Aug. 14, 1964, *SCMP*, no. 3296, p. 5.
15. Cong Wei, "Yang Xianzhen and the 'Identity of Thinking and Existence,'" *GMRB*, Dec. 11, 1964, *SCMP*, no. 3380, p. 5.
16. Ai Siqi, "In Refutation of Yang Xianzhen's Composite Economic Base Theory," *RMRB*, Nov. 1, 1964, *SCMP*, no. 3337, p. 13.
17. Ai Siqi, "Surreptitious Substitution of the Theory of the Reconciliation of Contradictions and Class for Revolutionary Dialectics Must Not be Permitted," *RMRB*, May 20, 1965, *SCMP*, no. 3475, p. 7.
18. Ibid., p. 9.
19. See e.g. Guan Feng, "On the Problem of Struggle Between Materialism and Idealism," *GMRB*, June 6, 1958, p. 5.
20. Mao Zedong, "Where Do Correct Ideas Come From?" *Four Essays on Philosophy* (Beijing: Foreign Language Press, 1966), pp. 134–135.
21. Cheng Xing, "Expose Comrade Yang Xianzhen's Substitution of the

Metaphysical Mechanical Theory for Dialectical Materialism," *GMRB*, Dec. 25, 1964, *SCMP*, no. 3392, p. 4.

22. Li Lunzu, "Is There Any Class Character in Truth?" *Qianxian*, no. 10, 1965; reprinted in *RMRB*, May 28, 1965, *SCMP*, no. 3482, p. 12.

23. Lu Yucun and Shen Guohui, "Refuting Comrade Yang Xianzhen's Fallacious Argument Against Revolutionary Activity," *Wenhui Bao*, Mar. 15, 1965, *SCMPS*, no. 137, p. 1.

24. Ibid., p. 2.

25. Ibid., p. 7.

26. Zhou Liangxiao, "Understanding the Antifeudal Nature of Peasant Wars," *RMRB*, June 2, 1964, p. 6.

27. Yao Wenyuan, "A Theory Which Causes Socialist Literature and Art to Degenerate," *GMRB*, Dec. 20, 1964, *SCMP*, no. 3374, p. 9.

28. Ibid., p. 4.

29. *Lei Feng, Chairman Mao's Good Fighter* (Beijing: Foreign Language Press, 1968), p. 25.

30. Su Nanyuan, "*The Lin Family Shop* Is a Picture for Prettifying the Bourgeoisie," *RMRB*, May 29, 1965, *CB*, no. 766, p. 9.

31. Gao Kejin, "Is the Treatment of Love in *Three-Family Lane* and *Bitter Struggle* Unimpeachable?" *ZGQNB*, Dec. 12, 1964, *JPRS*, no. 28, 061, p. 23.

32. *GMRB*, Oct. 4, 1963.

33. Ya Hanzhang, "Follow the Party Line in Developing Musical Drama," *GMRB*, June 2, 1964, p. 2.

34. Fan Xing (Liao Mosha), "My 'Ghosts Are Harmless' Theory Is Wrong," *RMRB*, Feb. 18, 1965, *SCMP*, no. 3411, p. 6.

35. Mao Zedong, "On Khrushchev's Phoney Communism and His Lessons to the World" (Beijing: Foreign Language Press).

36. Feng Ding, *Commonplace Truth*, p. 3, quoted in *ZGQN*, Oct. 16, 1964, *SCMM*, no. 446, p. 8.

37. Feng Ding, *The Historical Task of the Working Class*, p. 67, quoted in "The Working Class Must Carry Through the Revolution to the End," *Gongren Ribao (The Workers' Daily)*, Jan. 28, 1965, *SCMP*, no. 3400, p. 8.

38. Feng Ding, *The Communist View of Life* (1958 ed.), p. 59, quoted in "Which Comes First, the Revolution or the Interests of the Individual?" *ZGQNB*, Dec. 22, 1964, *SCMP*, no. 3383, p. 10.

39. *Gongren Ribao*, Apr. 5, 1964, *SCMP*, no. 3219, p. 13.

40. *Nanfang Ribao*, Sept. 24, 1963, *SCMP*, no. 3184, p. 20.

41. *Nanfang Ribao*, Dec. 5, 1963, *SCMP*, no. 3145, p. 17.

42. *Nanfang Ribao*, Nov. 14, 1963, p. 2.

43. Feng Ding, "Which Comes First, the Revolution or the Interests of the Individual?" *SCMP*, no. 3383, p. 10.

44. Zhang Qixun, "A Critique of Feng Ding's 'Communist Philosophy of Life,'" *ZGQN*, no. 20, Oct. 1964, pp. 5-9, *JPRS*, no. 27414, p. 47.

45. Mao Zedong, "Talk at the National Conference on Propaganda Work of the CCP," *CB*, no. 740, p. 10.

46. Schram, *Chairman Mao Talks*, p. 249.

47. Luo Siding, "The Historic View of Zhou Gucheng," *GMRB*, Nov. 19, 1964, p. 3.

48. Cong Wei, "Yang Xianzhen and 'Identity of Thinking and Existence,'" *GMRB*, Dec. 11, 1964, *SCMP*, no. 3380, p. 5.

49. Jin Weimin and Lin Yunchu, "Some Queries on the Spirit of the Times," *RMRB*, Aug. 2, 1964, *CB*, no. 747, p. 25.

50. Ibid., p. 27.

51. Liaison Center, Chinese University of Science and Technology, "Counter-revolutionary Revisionist Peng Zhen's Towering Crimes of Opposing the Party, Socialism, and the Thought of Mao Zedong," June 10, 1967, *SCMM*, no. 640, p. 8.

52. "The Tempestuous Combat on the Literary and Art Front," *Shoudu Hongweibing*, June 7, 1967, *CB*, no. 842, p. 27.

53. Schram, *Chairman Mao Talks*, p. 208.

54. Tian Heshui, "When One Cannot Be Both Red and Expert," *ZGQNB*, Dec. 26, 1964, *CB*, no. 757, p. 6.

55. "Redness and Expertness Is What the Era Demands of Our Youth," editorial, *ZGQNB*, July 24, 1965, *SCMP*, no. 3517, p. 5.

5. THE CULTURAL REVOLUTION

1. "The Tempestuous Combat," *CB*, no. 842, p. 30.

2. "Counter-revolutionary Revisionist Peng Zhen's Towering Crimes," *SCMM*, no. 639, p. 23.

3. "Excerpts of Sinister Works of Tao Zhu, Lin Mohan, Qi Yanming, Tian Han, and Yang Hansheng at Black Meeting," Guangzhou, *Xiju Zhanbao* (*Drama Combat Bulletin*), June 24, 1967, *SCMPS*, no. 203, p. 39.

4. "Counter-revolutionary Revisionist Peng Zhen's Towering Crimes," p. 23.

5. Yao Wenyuan, "On the New Historical Play *Dismissal of Hai Rui*," in Jurgen Domes, James T. Myers, and Erik Von Groeling, eds., *Cultural Revolution in China, Documents and Analysis* (Brussels, 1974), p. 87.

6. *RMRB*, Nov. 30, 1965.

7. Chen Shengxin et al., "Self-exposure of a Big, Antiparty Plot," *Yangcheng Wanbao*, June 3, 1966, *SCMP*, no. 3721, p. 13.

8. "Preparation, Release, and Collapse of the Counter-revolutionary 'February Outline Report,'" *Jinggangshan*, May 27, 1967, *SCMPS*, no. 195, p. 21.

9. "Carrying Out Antiparty Activity under the Pretext of Holding a Symposium," *RMRB*, May 12, 1966, *SCMP*, no. 3704, p. 2.

10. "Smash Deng Tuo's Conspiracy of Inciting Youth to Oppose the Party in the Cultural Revolution," Notes of participants in Dec. 13, 1965 symposium, *ZGQNB*, May 14, 1966, *SCMP*, no. 3709, p. 7.

11. Ibid., p. 9.

12. Fan Yiben, "Look How Vicious Anticommunist, Antipeople

Counter-revolutionaries Are!" *ZGQNB*, May 21, 1966, *SCMP*, no. 3712, p. 8.

13. Xiang Yangshen (Deng Tuo), "The Question Is One of Moral Inheritance," *Beijing Wanbao*, Dec. 12, 1965.

14. You Bai, "*Dismissal of Hai Rui* Should in the Main Be Affirmed," *Wenhui Bao*, Dec. 17, 1965, *SCMPS*, no. 148, p. 17.

15. Yu Luoke, "It Is High Time to Combat Mechanical Materialism," *Wenhui Bao*, Feb. 13, 1966, *SCMPS*, no. 149, p. 34.

16. Zhu Xi, "How to Evaluate the *Dismissal of Hai Rui*" *GMRB*, Dec. 22, 1965, in IASP, *Chinese Studies in History and Philosophy*, Fall 1968, p. 59.

17. Wu Han, "Self-criticism on *Dismissal of Hai Rui*," *RMRB*, Dec. 30, 1965, *CB*, no. 783, pp. 31, 48.

18. Gao Zhi, "A Big Frame-up that Shook the Whole Nation," *GMRB*, Dec. 29, 1978, FBIS, Jan. 17, 1979, E17.

19. He Qifang, "There Are Bourgeois Ideas in Comrade Xia Yan's Works," *RMRB*, Apr. 1, 1966, *CB*, no. 786, p. 37.

20. Asahi, May 19, 1967, reprint from Red Guard paper, FBIS, May 23, 1967, p. ccc27.

21. Ibid.

22. "Minutes of the Forum on Literature and Art in the Armed Forces," convened by Jiang Qing, Feb. 2–20, 1966, *SCMP*, no. 3956, p. 11.

23. Schram, *Chairman Mao Talks*, p. 87.

24. Ibid., p. 235.

25. *Hongqi*, Sept. 1969, p. 10.

26. "Renegade Qu Qiubai," *Denounce Qu Combat Bulletin*, May 6, 1967, *SCMPS*, no. 238, p. 34.

27. Yao Xu, "Pull Down the Black Flag of Zhou Yang's Capitulationist Line of Literature and Art of the 1930s," NCNA, Aug. 23, 1966, *SCMP*, no. 3771, p. 2.

28. Frederic Wakeman, "Historiography in China Today," *China Quarterly*, December 1978, p. 899.

29. "In Memory of Lu Xun, Our Forerunner in the Cultural Revolution," editorial, *Hongqi*, no. 14, 1966, *SCMM*, no. 550, p. 6.

30. Lu Xun, "Literature of a Revolutionary Period," *Lu Xun Quanji* (*Complete Works of Lu Xun*), (Beijing, 1963), III, 313.

31. "Preparation, Release, and Collapse," p. 26.

32. Wu Donghui, "Destroy the Black Backstage Manager of 'Three-Family Village,'" *GMRB*, June 18, 1967, *SCMP*, no. 3977, p. 16.

33. "Preparation, Release, and Collapse," p. 27.

34. "The Tempestuous Combat," p. 29.

35. Mao Zedong, "Supreme Instructions," *CB*, no. 897, p. 18.

36. "Never Forget Class Struggle," editorial, *Liberation Army Daily*, May 4, 1966, *Beijing Review*, May 13, 1966, pp. 41, 40.

37. "Raise High the Red Banner of the Thought of Mao Zedong," *Liberation Army Daily*, June 6, 1966, reprinted in *RMRB*, July 15, 1966, *Peking Review*, July 15, 1966, p. 15.

38. Guo Moruo, "Learn from the Masses of Workers, Peasants, and Soldiers and Serve Them," *GMRB*, Apr. 28, 1966, *SCMP*, no. 3691, p. 7.

39. Mao Zedong, "Bombard the Headquarters—My Big-Character Poster," NCNA-English, Beijing, Aug. 4, 1967, *SCMP*, no. 3997, p. 13.

40. "Develop National Science and Culture in the Anti-imperialist Revolutionary Struggle," *RMRB*, July 23, 1966, *CB*, no. 799, p. 12.

41. "Premier Zhou's Important Speech (excerpts)," *Zaofan* (*Rebellion*), Feb. 25, 1967, *SCMPS*, no. 181, p. 17.

42. "Having the Daring to Blaze the Path Untrodden by Those Before Us," *Jiefang Ribao*, Oct. 17, 1966, reprinted in *GMRB*, Oct. 23, 1966, *SCMP*, no. 3819, p. 12.

43. "Shanghai Workers Speed Technological Revolution," NCNA, FBIS, no. 191 (Sept. 30, 1968), p. c4.

44. "Riddle of Not Speaking at Meetings Unraveled," *Beijing Ribao*, Sept. 22, 1968, *SCMM*, no. 660, p. 13.

45. Schram, *Chairman Mao Talks*, p. 237.

46. Hong Yung Lee, *The Politics of the Chinese Cultural Revolution* (Berkeley: University of California Press, 1978), pp. 213-225.

47. Wang Li, Jia Yixue, and Li Xin, "The Dictatorship of the Proletariat and the Great Proletariat Cultural Revolution," *Hongqi*, no. 15, 1966, *Peking Review*, Dec. 23, 1966, p. 20.

48. Ibid.

49. "What Does This 'Speech' Demonstrate?" in *Tao Zhu Is the Krushchev of Central-South China* (Wuhan Revolutionary Rebel Headquarters), Jan. 14, 1967, *CB*, no. 824, pp. 40, 44.

50. Ibid., pp. 40, 45.

51. Yao Wenyuan, "Comment on Tao Zhu's Two Books," NCNA, Sept. 7, 1967, in Domes et al., *Cultural Revolution*, p. 301.

52. Tao Zhu, "To My Wife," *Chinese Literature*, no. 8 (1979), p. 119.

53. John Bryan Starr, "Revolution in Retrospect: The Paris Commune Through Chinese Eyes," *China Quarterly*, January–March 1972, p. 115.

54. Schram, *Chairman Mao Talks*, p. 277.

55. Ibid., p. 234.

56. Qi Benyu, "Patriotism or National Betrayal? A Commentary on the Reactionary Film *Inside Story of the Ch'ing Court*," *Hongqi*, no. 5, Mar. 1967, *SCMM*, no. 571, pp. 6, 8, 12, 11.

57. "On Eradicating Anarchism," NCNA, May 11, 1967, *SCMP*, no. 3939, p. 1.

58. *GMRB*, May 8, 1967, *SCMP*, no. 3947, p. 28.

59. Domes et al., *Cultural Revolution*, pp. 311, 308, 311, 313.

60. Yao Wenyuan, "Comments on Tao Zhu's Two Books," in Domes et al., *Cultural Revolution*, p. 301.

61. Mao Zedong, "Supreme Instructions," 1967, *CB*, no. 897, p. 32.

62. "Shanghai Paper Denounces Ultraleft Elements," editorial, *Jiefang Ribao*, Sept. 12, 1967, FBIS, no. 180, Sept. 15, 1967, p. ddd12.

63. Guangzhou Red Guards, "Whither China?" in Klaus Mehnert, *Peking*

and the New Left at Home and Abroad (Berkeley: University of California Press, 1969), p. 85.

64. "Comrade Jiang Qing Talks on Hunan Provincial Proletarian Revolutionaries' Great Alliance Committee," Guangzhou, *Bawu* (*Eight-Five*), Feb. 1968, *SCMP*, no. 4136, p. 13.

65. "Comrade Yao Wenyuan Talks on Hunan Provincial Proletarian Revolutionaries' Great Alliance Committee," Guangzhou, *Bawu*, Feb. 1968, *SCMP*, no. 4136, p. 15.

66. Yao Wenyuan, "The Working Class Must Exercise Leadership in Everything," *Peking Review*, Aug. 30, 1968, p. 4.

67. Schram, *Chairman Mao Talks*, p. 265.

6. IDEOLOGICAL DIVERGENCE OF THE SHANGHAI GROUP

1. Lowell Dittmer, "Bases of Power in Chinese Politics: A Theory of Analysis of the Fall of the Gang of Four," *World Politics*, October 1978, p. 52.

2. Luo Siding used other pseudonyms as well, such as Gang Li and Shi Lun.

3. Chu Lan, meaning "first wave," also wrote under such pseudonyms as Zhang Tien and Xiao Lun. There were also other writing groups, such as Tang Xiaowen.

4. Schram, *Chairman Mao Talks*, p. 286.

5. Ibid., p. 298.

6. "Mao Zedong's Private Letter to Jiang Qing," *Issues and Studies* 9, no. 4 (January 1973): 96.

7. Li Feng, "Insist on the Integration of Theory with Practice and Strengthen Scientific and Technical Research," *RMRB*, Nov. 19, 1972, *SCMP*, no. 5267, p. 208.

8. "Strengthen Teaching of Basic Knowledge and Fundamental Theories," *RMRB*, Oct. 15, 1972, *SCMP*, no. 5244, p. 4.

9. Lu Ke, "Importance Must Be Attached to Scientific Experiment," *RMRB*, Aug. 17, 1972, *SCMP*, no. 5204, p. 18.

10. Jin Feng, "Scientific Experiment Is a Great Revolutionary Movement," *RMRB*, Oct. 7, 1972, *SCMP*, no. 5239, p. 165.

11. Zhou Peiyuan, "Some Views on Educational Revolution in the Science Faculties of Universities," *GMRB*, Oct. 6, 1972, *SCMP*, no. 5238, pp. 119–120, 121.

12. Party Committee of the Shanghai Machine Tools Plant, "Organize Theoretical Teaching According to the Characteristics of Working Students," *Hongqi*, no. 9, Sept. 1, 1972, *SCMM*, nos. 737–738, p. 57.

13. Revelations published since Mao's death have led me to revise my earlier emphasis on the bureaucratic leaders' predominance in this campaign. See Merle Goldman, "The Anti-Confucian Campaign of 1973–1974," *China Quarterly*, September 1975.

14. *Miscellany of Mao Zedong Thought (1949–1968)*, pt. 2, JPRS, no. 61269-2, p. 334.

15. China Information Service, *Report on Mainland China*, no. 26 (June 26, 1972), p. 6.

16. Luo Siding, "Learn the Thoroughgoing Revolutionary Spirit with Which Lu Xun Criticized the Confucian Shop," RMRB, Sept. 25, 1971, FBIS, Sept. 29, 1971, pp. B2, B5.

17. Although Mao's friend Guo Moruo had written a number of articles on this subject and one just prior to the campaign about the ideological struggle during the transition from slaveholding to feudalism, "The Problem of Periodization in China's Ancient History," *Hongqi*, no. 7, 1972, he did not take an active role in the campaign itself.

18. Yang Rongguo, "The Struggle Between the Two Lines in the Ideological Sphere During the Periods of the Spring and Autumn Annals and the Warring States," *Hongqi*, Dec. 1, 1972, SCMM, nos. 743–744, p. 62.

19. Li Yi Zhe, "Concerning Socialist Democracy and Legal System," *Issues and Studies*, January 1976, p. 135.

20. Yang Rongguo, "Confucius: The Thinker Who Stubbornly Defends the System of Slavery," RMRB, Aug. 7, 1973, SCMP, no. 5436, pp. 110, 114.

21. Luo Siding, "The Struggle for and Against Restoration in the Course of the Founding of the Qin," *Hongqi*, Nov. 1, 1973, SPRCM, no. 763–764, p. 38.

22. Ibid., pp. 42, 43, 44.

23. Ibid., p. 44.

24. Jing Bing, "To Subdue Oneself and Return to Propriety," RMRB, Feb. 22, 1974, SPRCP, no. 5579, p. 9.

25. Zhe Zhun, "The Confucian Doctrine of the Mean Is the Philosophy for Opposing Social Reform," RMRB, Jan. 12, 1974, p. 2.

26. Liu Wenyi, Shaanxi Normal University, "Confucius: An Educator of the Reactionary Slave-owning Class," GMRB, Jan. 6, 1974, SPRCP, no. 5556, p. 40.

27. Yuan Chuicai, Qinghua University, "Firmly Occupy the Educational Front," RMRB, Jan. 16, 1974, SPRCP, no. 5545, p. 53.

28. Liang Xiao, "On Shang Yang," *Hongqi*, no. 6, 1974, FBIS, June 17, 1974, p. E2.

29. Luo Siding, "The Development of the Polemic Between Confucianism and Legalism as Seen from the Reforms Made by Wang Anshi," *Hongqi*, no. 2, 1974, FBIS, Feb. 7, 1974, p. B2.

30. Luo Siding, "The Struggle for and Against Restoration," p. 40.

31. Shi Ding, "Analysis of 'Book Burning and Burying Scholars Alive,'" RMRB, Sept. 28, 1973, p. 2.

32. Liang Xiao, "Study 'On Salt and Iron': The Big Polemic Between the Confucian and Legalist Schools in the Middle Western Han Dynasty," *Hongqi*, no. 5, 1974, FBIS, May 21, 1974, pp. E2, E4.

33. Ibid., pp. E7, E6.

34. Luo Siding, "On the Struggle Between Patriotism and National Betrayal During the Northern Song Period," *Hongqi*, no. 11, 1974, FBIS, Nov. 20, 1974, pp. E4, E2, E2–3.

35. Ibid., p. E5.

36. Ibid., p. E6.

37. Liang Xiao, "On Shang Yang," p. E6.

38. "The Legalist Line Promoted the Development of Scientific Technology in Our Country's History: Qinghua University Studies the Legalists' Role in History," *GMRB*, July 21, 1974, p. 2.

39. Ibid.

40. Mass criticism group of Wuhan University, "The Struggle Between the Two Lines of Appointing People in the Course of Founding the Qin Dynasty," *GMRB*, July 11, 1974, p. 2.

41. Luo Siding, "The Struggle Between Restoration and Counter-restoration in the Establishment of the Qin Dynasty: The Social Basis of Polemics Between Confucian-Legalist Schools," *Hongqi*, February 1974, FBIS, Feb. 17, 1974, p. B2.

42. Yang Rongguo, "The Struggle of Materialism in Opposition to the Idealist Theory of Apriorism During the Western Han and Eastern Han Dynasties," FBIS, Feb. 6, 1974, p. B5.

43. No. 4 Workshop of Shanghai Watch Plant, "Uphold National Unification, Oppose Splits," FBIS, July 16, 1974, p. G7.

44. Chu Lan, "Juvenile Songs Should Have a Clear-Cut Style," *RMRB*, Dec. 1, 1973, *SPRCP*, no. 5519, p. 95.

45. Chu Lan, "Importance Should Be Attached to This Discussion," *RMRB*, Jan. 14, 1974, *SPRCP*, no. 5551, p. 46.

46. Chu Lan, "Grab Hold of the Essence and Make a Penetrating Criticism," *RMRB*, Feb. 8, 1974, *SPRCP*, no. 5569, p. 2.

47. "A Vicious Motive, Despicable Tricks," a commentator article, NCNA, Jan. 30, 1974, *SPRCP*, no. 5549, pp. 186–187.

48. Chu Lan, "It Is Necessary to Pay Attention to Class Struggle in the Sphere of Culture and Art," *RMRB*, Dec. 15, 1973, *SPRCP*, no. 5526, p. 39.

49. Chu Lan, "Commenting on the Shanxi Opera *Three Visits to Taofeng*," *RMRB*, Feb. 28, 1974, p. 2, FBIS, Mar. 1, 1974, p. B2.

50. Ibid., p. B7.

51. Chu Lan, "Typify Contradictions and Struggle in Everyday Life," *RMRB*, Oct. 14, 1974, FBIS, Oct. 17, 1974, p. E9.

52. Han Fei, "Solitary Indignation," *RMRB*, July 24, 1974, p. 2.

53. Liang Lingyi, "The Chief Experiment of pre-Qin Legalist Thinking: A Comment on 'Han Fei Zi,'" *Hongqi*, no. 9, 1974, FBIS, Sept. 19, 1974, p. E6.

54. Shi Dajing, "Struggle Between Restoration and Antirestoration in the Period of Warring States: A Review of Han Fei Zi," *GMRB*, Sept. 7, 1974, p. 2, FBIS, Sept. 20, 1974, p. E8.

55. "Important Measures for Persevering in Progress and Guarding Against Restoration," *RMRB*, Dec. 15, 1974, *SPRCP*, no. 5763, p. 52.

56. Ibid., p. 53.

57. Luo Siding, "On Class Struggle During the Qin-Han Period," *GMRB*, Aug. 6, 1974, p. 2, originally published in *Hongqi*, no. 8, 1974, *SPRCM*, no. 787–788, p. 18.

58. Tang Xiaowen, "Causes of the Downfall of the Qin Dynasty," *GMRB*, Sept. 1, 1974, SPRCP, no. 5708, p. 103.

59. Luo Siding, "On Class Struggle During the Qin-Han Period," p. 26.

60. Zhai Qing, "On Politics and Daoism during the Early Western Han Dynasty," *Study and Criticism*, no. 11, Nov. 20, 1974, *SPRCM*, no. 801, p. 12.

61. Yang Chunqiu and Zhou Zushan, "On Han Xin," *GMRB*, Nov. 22, 1974, *SPRCP*, no. 5747, p. 152.

62. Excerpts from prosecutor's statement, Dec. 29, 1980, *Beijing Review*, Jan. 12, 1981, p. 24.

63. Qu Jiang, "We Must Have the Revolutionary Spirit of Daring to Go Against the Tide," *RMRB*, Nov. 7, 1973, *SPRCP*, no. 5502, p. 2.

64. "On Zhi Hong," *Hongqi*, Aug. 1, 1978, pp. 90–100, *JPRS*, no. 71961, p. 146.

65. Kenneth Lieberthal, *Central Documents and Politburo Politics in China* (Ann Arbor: University of Michigan Center for Chinese Studies, 1978).

66. Franz Schurmann, *Ideology and Organization* (Berkeley: University of California Press, 1968), p. 58.

67. *Xuexi yu Pipan* (*Study and Criticism*), no. 4 (December 1973), pp. 94–95.

68. Li Yi Zhe, "Concerning Socialist Democracy and Legal System," *Issues and Studies*, January 1976, p. 128.

69. Ibid., p. 119.

70. Ibid., p. 146.

71. Ibid., p. 117.

72. Ibid., p. 119.

73. Ibid., p. 140.

74. *Chinese Law and Government* 10, no. 3 (Fall 1977): 12.

75. Schram, *Chairman Mao Talks*, p. 238.

76. The conventional Marxist term is "bourgeois right," but China's media in 1975–1976 used the term "bourgeois rights" in its English translation.

77. Liang Xiao, "It Is Necessary to Enforce the Dictatorship of the Proletariat over the Bourgeoisie," *RMRB*, Feb. 10, 1975, p. 1, FBIS, Feb. 11, 1975, pp. E5, E3.

78. Zhou Si, "This Historical Mission of the Dictatorship of the Proletariat: Study of 'A Great Unprecedented Action,'" *Hongqi*, February 1975, FBIS, Feb. 10, 1975, pp. E7, E6.

79. Jing Hua, "Restrict the Bourgeois Rights and Consolidate the Dictatorship of the Proletariat," *RMRB*, Feb. 28, 1975, *SPRCP*, no. 5810, p. 138.

80. Yao Wenyuan, "On the Social Base of the Lin Biao Antiparty Clique," *Peking Review*, no. 10 (Mar. 7, 1975), pp. 7, 6.

81. Ibid., p. 8.

82. Ibid., p. 9.

83. *Hongqi*, April 1975, reprinted in *RMRB*, Apr. 3, 1975, p. 1, FBIS, Apr. 3, 1975, p. E3.

84. Nan Yu, "The Masses of People Must Be Relied upon to Consolidate the Proletarian Dictatorship," *RMRB*, Mar. 16, 1975, p. 2.

85. Liang Xiao, "Criticize Following the Beaten Path and Sticking to the Old; Persevere in Continued Revolution," *Hongqi*, no. 3, 1975, *SPRCM*, no. 814-815, pp. 44-45.

86. Mao Zedong, "Introductory Note to a Serious Lesson," quoted in Zhou Si, "This Historical Mission," FBIS, Feb. 10, 1975, p. E6.

87. Yan Qun, "Forever Preserve the Proletarian Revolutionary Spirit," *Hongqi*, no. 3, 1975, *SPRCM*, no. 814-815, pp. 54, 55.

88. Qi Xian, "The Dictatorship of the Proletariat Must Restrict the Bourgeois Rights," *GMRB*, Feb. 18, 1975, *SPRCP*, no. 5819, pp. 119, 120.

89. "Marx, Engels, and Lenin on the Dictatorship of the Proletariat," *RMRB*, Feb. 22, 1975, *SPRCP*, no. 5803, pp. 40, 46-47.

90. Zhang Chunqiao, "On Exercising All-round Dictatorship over the Bourgeoisie," *Hongqi*, Apr. 1, 1975, *SPRCM*, nos. 819-820, pp. 9, 10.

91. Ibid., p. 9.

92. Ibid., p. 10.

93. Mao Zedong, "The Situation and Our Policy after the Victory in the War of Resistance Against Japan" *Selected Works* (Beijing: Foreign Language Press, 1961), IV, 11-26.

94. Zhang Chunqiao, "On Exercising All-round Dictatorship," p. 7.

95. Mass criticism groups of Beijing University and Qinghua University, "The Dictatorship of the Proletariat and the Renegade Lin Biao," *Hongqi*, May 1, 1975, *SPRCM*, nos. 823-824, p. 26.

96. "Study Well and Have a Good Grasp by Integrating Theory with Practice," *Hongqi*, April 1975, *RMRB*, Apr. 3, 1975, p. 1, FBIS, Apr. 3, 1975, p. E4.

97. "The Whole Story about the Farce of Opposing Empiricism Staged by the Gang of Four," NCNA, Mar. 2, 1977, FBIS, Mar. 7, 1977, p. E19.

98. Ji Yan, "Ideological Weapon for Restricting Bourgeois Rights," *Hongqi*, April 1975, FBIS, Apr. 9, 1975, p. E6.

99. Yue Hai, "Deepen the Study of Theory; Promote Stability and Unity," *Hongqi*, June 1975, *SPRCM*, nos. 827-828, p. 2.

100. Schram, *Chairman Mao Talks*, p. 135.

101. Liu Zhenxiang and Nian Jinghua, "*Water Margin* Is Teaching Material Using a Negative Example to Advertise Capitalism," *GMRB*, Aug. 23, 1975, p. 2.

102. Liang Xiao, "Lu Xun Has Effectively Criticized *Water Margin*—'A Study of the Evolution of Rascals,'" *GMRB*, Aug. 30, 1975, p. 2.

103. Zhu Fangming, "Comment on *Water Margin*," *RMRB*, Aug. 31, 1975, p. 2.

104. "Promote Comments on *Water Margin*," editorial, *RMRB*, Sept. 4, 1975, FBIS, Sept. 4, 1975, p. E12. Mao's statement was made on Sept. 12, 1971. Schram, *Chairman Mao Talks*, p. 290.

105. Bo Qing, "Commenting on the Capitulationist Song Jiang," *GMRB*, Sept. 17, 1975, *SPRCP*, no. 5943, p. 139.

106. Gu Fang, "*Water Margin* Is a Black Specimen Publicizing and Extolling 'Combining Two into One,' " *GMRB*, Dec. 9, 1975, *SPRCP*, no. 6022, p. 11.

107. An Qun, "Comment on Song Jiang, the Capitulationist," *Hongqi*, Oct. 1, 1975, *SPRCM*, nos. 844-845, p. 50.

108. Preface to *Water Margin* (Beijing: People's Literature Publishing House, September 1975), FBIS, Nov. 4, 1975, p. E4.

109. Zhen Dagang, "On the Three Yuan Brothers," *Study and Criticism*, no. 9, Sept. 9, 1975, *SPRCM*, no. 842, p. 8.

110. Li Lie, "The Mournful Cry of the Gravestones," *RMRB*, Feb. 22, 1977, *SPRCP*, no. 6296, p. 135.

111. Mass criticism groups of Beijing University and Qinghua University, "A Textbook by Negative Example Advertising Capitulationism: A Criticism of *Water Margin*," *Hongqi*, no. 9, 1975, FBIS, Sept. 9, 1975, p. E4.

112. Mass criticism groups of Beijing University and Qinghua University, "A Textbook by Negative Example," p. E1.

113. Du Xuncheng, "On Chao Gai," *Study and Criticism*, no. 9, 1975.

114. Yuan Liang, "Song Jiang and 'Laws and Institutions,' " *GMRB*, Nov. 9, 1975, *SPRCP*, no. 5982, p. 40.

115. Zhe Bian, "Historical Materialism Brooks No Distinction," *GMRB*, Sept. 25, 1975, *SPRCP*, no. 5955, p. 83.

116. Tan Feng, "Quicken the Pace of Farm Mechanization," *Hongqi*, Nov. 1, 1975, *SPRCM*, nos. 848-849, p. 25.

117. Criticism group of Literature Institute of the Chinese Academy of Sciences, "The Reactionary Essence of the Theory of 'Making Chao Gai a Figurehead' Advanced by the Gang of Four," *RMRB*, Feb. 26, 1977, FBIS, Mar. 2, 1977, p. E17.

118. Ba Shan, "Develop the Excellent Situation of Stability and Unity," *Hongqi*, no. 10, Oct. 1, 1975, *SPRCM*, nos. 844-845, pp. 82, 83.

119. Gao Lu (Liang Xiao), "The Moment Song Jiang Came to Liangshan," *GMRB*, Feb. 28, 1976.

120. Ren Xiuling and Zhao Shentian, "What Is Song Jiang's 'Abdication' for?" *RMRB*, July 20, 1976, *SPRCP*, no. 6148, p. 1.

7. THE SCIENTISTS AND DENG XIAOPING

1. "Collection of Reactionary Utterances of Liu and Deng," Beijing Railroad Red Guard Congress, April 1967, *SCMPS*, no. 208, p. 13.

2. Ibid., p. 14.

3. "Some Problems in Speeding Up Industrial Development," *Issues and Studies*, July 1977, p. 97.

4. Ibid., pp. 94, 96.

5. Ibid., p. 108.

6. Ibid., p. 106.

7. Ibid., p. 107.

8. Ibid., p. 108.

9. "Deng Xiaoping's Talks on Problems Concerning the Development of Industry," *SPRCM*, no 926, pp. 30, 29.

10. "Several Questions on the Work in Science and Technology" (summary report from the Academy of Sciences), *SPRCM*, no. 926, p. 36.

11. Deng Xiaoping's Interpolated Remarks, Sept. 26, 1975, ibid., p. 39.

12. Ibid., p. 40.

13. Ibid., p. 41.

14. Ibid., p. 39.

15. Ibid., p. 41.

16. "On the General Program for All Work of the Whole Party and the Whole Country," trans. from *Ban Gu* in Hong Kong, no. 103, Apr. 1, 1977, *SPRCM*, no. 921, p. 31.

17. Ibid., p. 32.

18. Ibid., p. 29.

19. Hong Xuan, "On Deng Xiaoping's Counter-revolutionary Offensive in Public Opinion," *Study and Criticism*, no. 6, 1976, FBIS, July 26, 1976, p. E7.

20. "The Working Class Is the Main Force in Repulsing the Right Deviationist Wind to Reverse Previous Verdicts: The Shanghai Clock and Watch Parts Factory CCP Committee Leads the Masses in Deepening the Criticism of Unrepentant Capitalist Roaders Within the Party," *RMRB*, Feb. 27, 1976, p. 1, FBIS, Mar. 2, 1976, p. E12.

21. Wu Weiyou, "The Capitalist Roaders Are Still Taking the Same Road," *RMRB*, Mar. 5, 1976, FBIS, Mar. 10, 197, p. E5.

22. Gao Lu and Zheng Ge, "Comment on Deng Xiaoping's Comprador-Bourgeois Economic Concepts," *Hongqi*, no. 7, 1976, FBIS, July 16, 1976, pp. E4, E5.

23. "Criticism of Selected Passages of 'Certain Questions on Accelerating the Development of Industry," *Study and Criticism*, no. 4, 1976, *SPRCM*, no. 873, p. 8.

24. Gao Lu and Zhang Ge, "Comment," p. E5.

25. Xiang Qun, "Attach Importance to Popularizing Sciences," *Hongqi*, no. 11, 1975, *SPRCM*, nos. 848–849, p. 82.

26. Gao Lu and Zhang Ge, "Comments on Deng Xiaoping's Economic Ideas of Comprador Bourgeoisie," *Peking Review*, Aug. 27, 1976, p. 9.

27. Mass criticism group of Fudan University, "A Counter-revolutionary Revisionist Outline: On the Outline of a Working Report by the Academy of Sciences," *RMRB*, Feb. 19, 1976, p. 1, FBIS, July 21, 1976, p. E4.

28. Hu Xing, "Can We Do Away with Electric Lights and Trains?" *RMRB*, July 3, 1977, *SPRCP*, no. 6382, p. 7.

29. *SPRCM*, no. 926, p. 42.

30. *SPRCM*, no. 921, p. 23.

31. *Issues and Studies*, September 1977, p. 102.

32. Ibid., p. 101.

33. Schram, *Chairman Mao Talks*, pp. 266-267.

34. "The Truth about the Tiananmen Incident," *Hongqi*, no. 12, Dec. 2, 1978, *JPRS*, no. 72804, p. 115.

35. Li Xin, "Leading Cadres Must Consciously Restrict Bourgeois Rights," *Hongqi*, no. 7, 1976, *SPRCM*, no. 881-882, p. 18.

36. Theoretical group of Academy of Sciences, "To Know How Noble and Pure the Pine Is, One Has to Wait for the Thaw," *RMRB*, July 30, 1977, *SPRCP*, no. 6379, p. 92.

37. Ibid., p. 102.

8. THE CONSEQUENCES OF ADVICE AND DISSENT

1. "Comprehensively and Accurately Understand the Party's Policy Toward Intellectuals," *RMRB*, Jan. 4, 1979, *Beijing Review*, Feb. 2, 1979, p. 13.

2. *GMRB*, Dec. 29, 1978, p. 3.

3. Su Shuangbi, "Criticize Yao Wenyuan's 'Comments on the Three-Family Village,'" *Hongqi*, Feb. 2, 1979, pp. 41-48, *JPRS*, no. 073304, p. 78.

4. Ibid., p. 87.

5. *GMRB*, Jan. 28, 1979, p. 3.

6. Xing Fengsi, "Should Everyone Be Equal Before the Truth," *RMRB*, June 13, 1979, FBIS, June 14, 1979, p. L7.

7. Pang Pu, "A Re-evaluation of Confucian Ideology," *Lishi Yanjiu (Historical Research)*, Aug. 15, 1978, pp. 48-57, *GMRB*, Aug. 12, 1978, p. 2, *JPRS*, no. 072387, p. 8.

8. Ibid., p. 9.

9. Ibid., p. 12.

10. Li Kan, "Feudalistic Die-hards in Modern Chinese History," *Lishi Yanjiu*, Nov. 15, 1978, pp. 3-18, *JPRS*, no. 073179, p. 7.

11. Ibid., p. 13.

12. "Integrating Moral Encouragement with Material Reward," editorial, *RMRB*, Apr. 9, 1979, *Peking Review*, Apr. 21, 1978, pp. 6-7.

13. Feng Zhi, "Is It a Crime to Pursue 'Big,' 'Foreign,' and 'Ancient' Things?" *RMRB*, Mar. 11, 1978, p. 3, *JPRS*, no. 071002, p. 2.

14. Editorial, *RMRB*, May 5, 1979, *Beijing Review*, May 18, 1979, p. 10.
15. "Strengthen Ideological and Political Work," editorial, *RMRB*, Apr. 19, 1979, *Beijing Review*, May 11, 1979, p. 14.
16. Huang Yifeng, "Undertake Research Work in the Social Sciences to Serve the Four Modernizations," *Xueshu Yuekan* (*Academic Monthly*), February 1979, pp. 7-10, *JPRS*, no. 073406, p. 4.
17. Zhang Wen, "Social Sciences: A Hundred Schools of Thought Contend," *Beijing Review*, Apr. 6, 1979, p. 12.
18. Zhou Yang, "The Development Plan for Philosophy and Social Sciences," speech at Preparatory Meeting for National Philosophy and Social Sciences Development Plan Conference, Sept. 19, 1978, *Zhexue Yanjiu* (*Philosophical Research*), Oct. 25, 1978, pp. 2-11, *JPRS*, no. 072912, p. 100.
19. Ibid., p. 99.
20. Ibid., p. 87.

INDEX

INDEX

INDEX

272

INDEX

INDEX

INDEX